THE FIRST NIGHT OF
TWELFTH NIGHT

MERCURY BOOKS
NO 18

MERCURY BOOKS

General Editor ALAN HILL

DON VIRGINIO ORSINO, DUCA DI BRACCIANO

THE FIRST NIGHT
OF
TWELFTH NIGHT

LESLIE HOTSON

28845

X-11-008265-5

16.166

822.33

A publication of
THE HEINEMANN GROUP OF PUBLISHERS
15–16 *Queen Street, London W*1
Printed in Great Britain by
The Curwen Press Ltd

TO
BRYHER

ACKNOWLEDGEMENTS

It is no small privilege to be enabled to express my sense of indebtedness and gratitude for the kind help of many persons who have furthered this work in a great variety of ways. In Germany, to Dr. Wilhelm Winkler; in Italy, to the Duke of Gravina (Prince Virginio Orsini), Prince Lelio Orsini, Dott. Sergio Camerani, and Dott. Giustiniano Degli Azzi; in England, to the Duke of Northumberland, Margaret, Countess of Suffolk, and Lord de L'Isle and Dudley, Dr. Philip P. Argenti, Mr. S. Wingfield Digby, Commander C. G. Vyner, Professor E. R. Vincent, Sir Hilary Jenkinson, Mr. R. C. Atkinson, Mr. Roger Ellis, and to the Staffs of the Public Record Office and of the British Museum and the Bodleian Libraries; and in America to the Staff of the Yale University Library. For its final form the book owes much to the suggestions of my friends Mr. Rupert Hart-Davis and Mr. Richard Garnett. The friendly devotion, persistence, and extraordinary skill of Miss Nellie McNeill O'Farrell have been mainstays from first to last; and without the unfailing encouragement of my wife, the work would never have been undertaken and carried through.

L. H.

CONTENTS

ILLUSTRATIONS

DON VIRGINIO ORSINO, DUCA DI BRACCIANO

By permission of the owner of the portrait, Prince Virginio Orsini, 21st Duke of Gravina. (From a photograph reproduced in Dr. Philip P. Argenti's work cited below, page 42.) . . . . FRONTISPIECE

QUEEN ELIZABETH

Accademia di Belle Arti, Siena. (Photograph, Alinari.) This superb portrait presents the added interest of apt political motto and aphorism. The great Queen's 'eyes everywhere' are symbolized by the inscription painted on the globe, TUTTO VEDO IL MONDO (I see all the world). And the sieve in her hand—through which the fine flour falls, while the chaff remains above—bears the legend A TERRA IL BEN   MAL DIMORA IN SELLA (Down goes the good; the bad stays in the saddle): an evil way of the world which the wise and just Queen is ever mindful to correct   FACING PAGE 60

QUEEN ELIZABETH DANCING

Penshurst Place, by permission of the Lord de L'Isle and Dudley. (Photograph, National Portrait Gallery.) There is a similar picture at Rennes, and the style of the clothes appears to be French; it has therefore been suggested that it represents a scene at the French Court. The reasons for accepting that it is in fact of Queen Elizabeth at about the 'dancing time' of Alençon's courtship are however strong. At this period French styles in dress were adopted by the English courtiers. Moreover most of the Queen's viol-players were Italians, as they are depicted here. A prime evidence, finally, is the prominence given in the painting to the woman dwarf. As the unpublished Wardrobe Accounts amply show, in the early 1580s Queen Elizabeth's famous woman dwarf, Thomasina de Paris, was high in favour with her Majesty . . . . . . FACING PAGE 89

SIR WILLIAM KNOLLYS, 1st LORD KNOLLYS, K.G., EARL OF BANBURY

Redlynch Park, by permission of Margaret, Countess of Suffolk. (Photograph, Cyril Howe.) .   . FACING PAGE 99

ILLUSTRATIONS

ON THE TRACK

Is there anywhere a more delightful comedy than *Twelfth Night*? The cheerful gale of popular favour has sent it down the centuries full-sailed, on a sea of music and laughter. Grateful for the riches it lavishes, why should we pause to make it abide our question? Nevertheless we instinctively feel that our delight in the experience cannot compare with what the audience enjoyed on the first night of *Twelfth Night*, when it belonged to the moment, presented with the soul of lively action, framed to the life for the height of pleasure. Imagination longs to recapture something of it. As Quiller-Couch truly said, 'We can immensely increase our delight in Shakespeare, and strengthen our understanding of him, if . . . we keep asking ourselves *how the thing was done*.' He might have added, 'and *when and for whom the thing was done*'. For a jest's prosperity lies in the ear of him that hears it; and a comic dramatist is like a merryman—

> He must observe their mood on whom he jests,
> The quality of persons, and the time.

If only we knew the mood, the quality of persons, and the time of *Twelfth Night*, we might less frequently resemble the enthusiastic Aguecheek, 'always enjoying a joke, never understanding it'.

What chance have we of conjuring up some of the atmosphere of that first night, of catching a glimpse of its moment in time? Long enough ago Dr. Johnson said of Shakespeare, 'Whatever advantages he might once derive from personal allusions . . . have for many years been lost; and every topic of merriment, or motive of sorrow, which the modes of artificial life afforded him, now only obscure the scenes which they once illuminated.' And because we so keenly share Dr. Johnson's regret we cannot help asking, Must every lost thing remain lost? May no corner of the dark curtain of oblivion be lifted? Or is it possible that materials already at hand may be put together to make a guide-post to rediscovery of some part of that lost land?

Let us see what may be done with what we have. To begin with, *Twelfth Night* sounds like a comedy written in the first place for a courtly audience; and authorities agree that its date must be in or about 1601. Also it is unique among Shakespeare's plays in having for title an exact calendar-date. Twelfth Night is on the Feast of the Epiphany or the Three Kings, January Sixth.[1] Crowning the Christmas holidays—Spenser's Faery Queen 'kept her annual feast twelve days'—Twelfth Day is the last, and held as the greatest day of all.

Another significant fact, noted early in the nineteenth century, is that Shakespeare's company, the Lord Chamberlain's Men, were paid for presenting a play—title not recorded—at Court on Twelfth Night, January 6, 1600/1.

---

[1] *The Oxford English Dictionary* unhappily defines *Twelfth-night* as 'The evening before Twelfth-day,' and is followed in the error by the Fowlers in their *Concise Oxford Dictionary*, to the misleading of the unwary. One might equally well define *Wedding-night* as 'The evening before the wedding day'. Twelfth Eve is January 5 (the eleventh day of Christmas), and Twelfth Night is January 6, the night of Twelfth Day. In Queen Elizabeth's Household Accounts, the crowning festival night appears indifferently as 'Twelfth day at night' and 'Twelfth night'.

At the end of the nineteenth century, a German Shake-spearean, Dr. Gregor Sarrazin, got hold of a bright thread, a most promising clue to *Twelfth Night*. He noted that 'in the winter of 1600/1 a certain "Duke Orsino" stirred London's attention. Virginio Orsino, Duke of Bracciano, "the most brilliant nobleman of his day", was at that time ambassador to the English Court, and was entertained by Queen Elizabeth and her dignitaries with magnificent festivities, among others also on Twelfth Night. Perhaps it was by this means,' concluded Dr. Sarrazin, 'that Shakespeare came upon his "Duke Orsino".'

For more than fifty years, then, all these facts have been at hand: (*a*) that Shakespeare called his courtly comedy *Twelfth Night*: that is, *January 6*[th]; (*b*) that his company acted at Court on Twelfth Night, January 6, 1600/1; and (*c*) that Queen Elizabeth entertained a duke named Orsino on this very day, January 6, 1600/1. Yet it was not until 1950 that another Shakespearean, Professor J. W. Draper, put these facts together to the cautiously-worded conclusion that Shakespeare's title, *Twelfth Night*, 'would seem to refer . . . more probably to the occasion of its original performance, the Queen's Twelfth Night entertainment to regale the living Duke Orsino.'[1] On this assumption, the audience addressed would be Queen Elizabeth and her splendid Court, a Court well described as being 'at once gay, decent, and superb', the best-ordered and most impressive in Christendom. But forgetting this fact, Mr. Draper's mind apparently wanders to the

---

[1] *The 'Twelfth Night' of Shakespeare's Audience* (1950), 258–9. In referring to Twelfth Night as 'Twelfth-Night Eve' Professor Draper is apparently confused by the *O.E.D.*

performance of the play at the Middle Temple in 1602, for he represents the audience for which Shakespeare was writing as composed of 'wellborn tyro lawyers and young courtiers.'

In my view, the likeliest way to get ahead is not only to cling tightly to the excellent and reasonable hypothesis Mr. Draper reached, but to treat it as a fact until it proves to be wrong. And how should it be wrong? Why call a play *Twelfth Night* unless it was written to be presented on Twelfth Night? And why bring in a 'Duke Orsino' if not to compliment the Queen's listening guest of honour, the noble Orsino, Duke of Bracciano?

As I was looking through the printed synopses of the great manuscript collections of England with such thoughts in mind, it was with a rare thrill that among the papers of the Duke of Northumberland I came upon the following:

1601/2, Jan. 6. A full narrative or description of the reception and entertainment of the Muscovite ambassador and of an Italian nobleman, the Duke of Brachiana, who were received at the Court of Queen Elizabeth, together with the names of the noblemen in attendance on her Majesty at her dining abroad upon Twelfth-day January 6, 1601–2. (Much damaged at the edges by fire. 6 pp.)[1]

What a find! The editor has misdated the document by a year; for there can be no mistake about the occasion, the rare ceremony when the Queen dined not in the privacy of her withdrawing-room, but in the Great Chamber, in splendour and in state. No question but that this is the 1600/1 Twelfth Day visit at Whitehall of Orsino. And here is a 'full narrative' of his entertainment by the Queen.

---

[1] Historical MSS. Comm., *Third Report*, App., 51*b*.

Would it tell anything about the play presented on that day by Shakespeare and his fellows? I was on pins and needles, writing an appeal to his Grace of Northumberland for permission to see the original in the ducal library. Not only was the favour kindly and promptly granted, but when I presented myself at his great Border castle of Alnwick, that magnificent seat of ancient baronial power, the Duke himself most graciously put the book containing the document into my eager hands.

Fortunately the fire had destroyed very little of the text. The manuscript proved to be in two parts: first, a summary description of Queen Elizabeth's festivities at Whitehall to entertain the Russian ambassador and the Italian duke—who was not, as Sarrazin thought, an ambassador, but a visitor; second, and most important, a copy of *the original memoranda of Lord Chamberlain Hunsdon, Shakespeare's master, of things to be done to prepare the palace and to conduct the ceremonies in state.* Fascinating though these were, my eyes raced through them until they were brought up short by the crucial item:

To Confer with my Lord Admirall and the Master of the Revells for takeing order generally with the players to make choyse of [   ] play that shalbe best furnished with rich apparell, have greate variety and change of Musicke and daunces, and of a Subiect that may be most pleasing to her Maiestie.

Nothing of this kind has ever been known before—a Lord Chamberlain's specific requisition of a play for Queen Elizabeth. And at the foot of the memoranda stands a note, added as a record after the performance: '*In the Hall, which was richly hanged and degrees* [tiers of seats, grandstands] *placed rownd about it, was the play after supper.*' Here is the very time and the exact spot—the room at Whitehall Palace in which the play was presented.

With the order before us, can there be any further doubt that the Twelfth Night play chosen for the Queen was Shakespeare's *Twelfth Night*—the most musical and festive of his high comedies, featuring a Duke Orsino to compliment her Majesty's guest? Could any subject be more pleasing to her Majesty than a romance of a Duke Orsino's hopeless love for a beautiful and unpredictable Lady Olivia who rules her household and chooses her own husband? A play written by the greatest poet for a Queen *that graced his desert, And to his lays open'd her royal ear*, and acted by the most distinguished company in England? For Lord Hunsdon's own men, with Shakespeare and Burbage at their head, were undeniably supreme at Court. In four out of the five preceding seasons they had been preferred above the others as the company to play on the crowning feast of Twelfth Night.

On this Twelfth Day at Whitehall, the great day of the Muscovite ambassador and of the Duke, Orsino, we know that three other troupes besides Shakespeare's performed in various rooms at the palace: the Admiral's Men, Derby's Men, and the Children of the Chapel Royal. We also know the name of the lost play given by the Admiral's Men. It was Dekker's *Phaëthon*, retouched by its author. However good it may have been, one cannot imagine the Queen choosing it for her play in the Hall over the one on 'Duke Orsino'. As for Derby's Men, they were a minor troupe, not in a class with the two leading companies.

The newly set-up Children of the Queen's Chapel— Hamlet's 'little eyases'—however, had Ben Jonson writing for them: a rising young playwright with the resounding success of *Every Man In His Humour* to his credit. And although court comedies were expected to treat of love— a theme he could not handle acceptably—Jonson had long been working up a play for the Children in hope that it would be chosen on Twelfth Night for the Queen, as its title proclaimed: *Cynthia's Revels*.

But the incredible Ben, whose conceit was matched only by his want of tact, made his play a harsh distasteful satire on the follies and what he termed the 'essential pride and ignorance' of the courtiers. Here was a clear case where Ben might apply to himself what he said about Shakespeare—*His wit was in his own power; would the rule of it had been so too*. His biting, unbridled *Cynthia's Revels* was rejected as unsuitable, while Shakespeare's romantic and genial *Twelfth Night* was accepted. This was no fault of Shakespeare's. But the official rebuff was a medicine bitter and salutary for Ben to swallow—a dose of rhubarb to purge his choler against the courtiers.

It seems to me that we have found here the solution to a famous and veteran Shakespearean puzzle—that the allusive remark put into Will Kempe's mouth in the Cambridge *Parnassus* play (1601/2) is a sly glance at this recent experience: 'Shakespeare puts them all down; ay, and Ben Jonson too. O, that Ben Jonson is a pestilent fellow ... but our fellow Shakespeare hath given him a purge that made him beray [i.e., befoul] his credit.' Ben had made himself publicly ridiculous by his angry epilogue to the rejected *Cynthia's Revels* when it was later acted in the City: *By God 'tis good; and if you lik' t, you may*. For the short and the long was, it *wasn't* good.

If they did not present Jonson's tedious satire, we may

ask what then did the Children perform at Court on Twelfth Day? And we find the answer here before us as an item of the Lord Chamberlain's orders: '*The Children of the Chappell to come before the Queene at Dinner with a Caroll.*'[1] Nathaniel Giles, the Master of the Children, obviously interpreted this order broadly, and to the singing added embellishments of masque and incidental music. For the troupe of Children was paid five pounds, for giving on Twelfth Day 'a show with music and special songs'—*not* a play. Dinner came before midday, plays after supper at night; and the lowest fee for a play was ten pounds—twice what the Children received for their performance.[2] If *Cynthia's Revels* had been presented before the Queen, that honour would infallibly have been advertised on the title-page of the published play, 1601. But that has only 'privately acted in the Black-Friers.' It is clear that the Children did not act *Cynthia's Revels* or any other play on Twelfth Day at Court.

Mention of dinner takes us back to scrutinize the all-too-short description of the Queen's great Twelfth Day. It relates that she dined '*in State*'—a rare breaking of her custom of privacy at meals: a seldom pleasure, a captain jewel in the carcanet. Was the appointed purpose of this extraordinary ceremony to honour the Italian Duke?

---

[1] The Chapel carol at dinner was traditional. Elizabeth's grandfather had had the same at his Twelfth Day feast in 1487/8, as Leland writes: 'At the Table in the Medell of the Hall sat the Deane and those of the Kings Chapell, which incontynently after the Kings furst Course sange a Carall.'

[2] In his great edition of Jonson (9. 188), Dr. Percy Simpson has been misled by Sir Edmund Chambers (*Elizabethan Stage*, 3. 364) into thinking that *Cynthia's Revels* was acted on Twelfth Night 1600/1. His first opinion (*Jonson*, 1. 393), that it was rejected, and not acted at Court, is the correct one.

No, for '*her Maiestie dyned in the great chamber*' and '*the Duke of Brachiana dined in the Councell chamber.*' The purpose was evidently political—'*The Muskovy Ambassador . . . was appointed to be ther,*' and it was he who represented his Tsar at the Queen's state dinner in the Great Chamber, but sitting at a separate table: '*Ther was also one [on] the right side of the Chamber under the windowes a boord placed, wher was appointed to dine the Muskovy Embassador.*'

In the midst of our eagerness to learn more of the brilliant Italian nobleman who saw himself shadowed before the Queen in Shakespeare's comedy—Don Virginio Orsino, Duke of Bracciano—we find ourselves encumbered with a Russian. This is annoying. But we remind ourselves that if a Muscovite was one of the two Very Important Persons honoured by Queen Elizabeth on the day of Shakespeare's *Twelfth Night*, we neglect him at our peril—if we seriously mean to 'observe the quality of persons and the time'. Looking about, we find here a paper, accidentally attached to this same description-and-memoranda of Twelfth Day at Whitehall, concerning this Russian. It gives us a word-picture of this ambassador from '*the Great Duke of Muskovye*' Boris Godunov, as he had appeared in the preceding October, presenting his credentials and being received in audience by Elizabeth with all magnificence at her Palace of Richmond. We read that the Aldermen, together with his hosts, the Merchants of the London Muscovy Company, escorted the Russian envoy from the City to the Court gate,

wher he alighted forth of his Coach. His company, being some sixteen, went before him two and two together, being

very greate fatt men, especially he himselfe, a man of tall
Stature very fatte with a great face and a blacke bearde cutt
rownde: of a swarfye Colour his face, and his gate very
maiesticall.

Let us put our minds on this very great fat man, and
consult the chronicles about him and his master, the
Tatar-descended, meanly-born, illiterate, cunning, and
suspicious Tsar Boris Godunov.   It appears that during
his guardianship of Ivan the Terrible's feeble-minded heir
Tsar Fedor, Boris had made himself all-powerful, and
on Fedor's death in 1598 he had seized the throne. He
proved to be so far ahead of his time as to anticipate the
modern Communists in tying the Russian peasants as
serfs to the soil; and his name *Boris* furnished an Eliza-
bethan-born rimester with a convenient pun on *Boreas*:

> The spacious Empire of vast Muscovy,
> Whose Duke, like *Boreas*, in his big-built Hall
> Doth foes at hand affright, far off appal.[1]

Of 'this smooth-face usurping tyrant' the Jacobean
chronicler Edmund Howes records that on assuming the
crown, to which he had waded 'through streames of blood',
Boris 'with all expedition sent his Ambassadors unto such
princes as he knew most imminent and propicious for his
present fortunes'. And the envoy he sent to Elizabeth
of England, the imminent prince who wielded the strongest naval power in the world, was 'very honorablie entertained, feasted, & entreated by the queene, and as kindly
used and dyetted for eight moneths space, at the sole
charges of the company of the Moscouie Merchants'.

A brief search under the word *Muscovy* in the col-

---

[1] Richard Zouche, *The Dove* (1613), sig. C 4ᵛ.

lections of history reveals that the ambassador's name was Grigóri Ivánovich Mikúlin; and that the state dinner to which he was summoned on Twelfth Day was in ratification of a treaty of friendship with Russia: *The league between the Muscovites and the English (by eating bread and salt with the Queen) was confirmed 6 Jan. 1601.*[1] Besides trade, the Queen had special reason for maintaining good relations with Russia at this time. Christian of Denmark, the strongest Scandinavian power, was asserting exclusive control over the Baltic fisheries; and beyond that, her uncomfortable protégé James of Scotland had recently allied himself with Denmark by marriage. Elizabeth's proper move is indicated—cement friendship with Russia, the great power to the east of Denmark.

Messengers from the Kremlin, as we know by experience, are grimly accountable for every memorized word they utter and every least thing that happens to them abroad. Since nothing has altered the Russian character, it seems inevitable that Mikulin must have rendered strict account to his Tsar, including of course his important experiences on Twelfth Day at Whitehall. Good, but where is that report now—if it still exists? Answer, in the archives of the Kremlin, and for accessibility to inquirers from the free world it might as well be at the South Pole. But there is still a possibility. Could it have been published as an historical document at some time before the Iron Curtain clanked down? On looking up the modern authorities on Anglo-Russian relations in Queen Elizabeth's time, we find Inna Lubimenko referring not only to our very great fat man, but also to the

---

[1] H.M.C., *Sixth Report*, App., 244, Marquis of Ripon's MSS.

full publication of his report seventy years ago at St. Petersburg, in the magazine of the Imperial Russian Historical Society.[1] The Kremlin may bury the original and welcome, since we are able to borrow a printed copy of it from the Library of Yale University, and struggle through its sixteenth-century Russian with the aid of a dictionary.

It proves a treasure, for here we have sixty lengthy pages 'To the Lord Tsar and Great Prince of all Russia, Boris Fedorovich', from 'thy serf [*kholóp*] Grishka Mikulin', detailing all his eight months' embassy to Queen Elizabeth: his reception, his audiences, his conferences, his entertainments, the information he picked up; and as a parting impression, his sight of the English Queen's men-of-war riding on the Medway—*the ships great, high, and long*—some mustering crews of a thousand men, and mounting more than sixty guns. His account is preceded by the Tsar's long and meticulous instructions. Boris had given him, for memorizing, a catalogue of detailed replies to be made to every conceivable question he might be asked. Mikulin's report shows that in London he had with oriental scrupulosity repeated these to the letter when the proper button was pushed: all of them glorifying the overwhelming power, the benevolent wisdom, and the peaceful intentions of the Tsar.

But we hasten forward to his relation of Whitehall on Twelfth Day. Here, from behind the great fat swarfy face masked with a round black beard, we witness the passing show of Elizabeth's grand day—the Epiphany celebration at the Chapel, the noble officers, the proces-

[1] *Sbornik Imperatorskago Russkago Istoricheskago Obshchestva*, S. Peterburg, Tom 38 (1883), ed. K. N. Bestuzhev-Riumin, pp. 302–63.

sion of ladies, the wonderful ceremony, healths, and entertainments at the state dinner; what the Queen said when she waxed merry; how before the dinner Mikulin, representing an uneasy tyrant who claimed to be the mightiest emperor in the world, had caught sight of the other guest, the Duke, Orsino, and suspiciously demanded to know who he was, and what he was doing there. A Russian eye-witness account which lays the scene for an original Shakespearean first night: this is indeed a rarity unheard of, and we must return to it for fuller treatment in the sequel.

Prospector's luck of this kind breeds an appetite for more. Conviction grew that every detail I could by any means uncover about these Christmas festivities of 1600/1 would be of value. A precious one or two of them might conceivably illuminate something obscure in Shakespeare's greatest comedy, or perhaps cast a gleam on the mystery of Elizabethan play-production—on *how the thing was done*. And after all, if we were getting light from far-away Moscow, might there not be something else undiscovered closer at hand?

With this hope, I turned once more to the chronicles, to get at the important items of contemporary news. In Camden's *Annals* under 'the beginning of the year 1601', and immediately after mention of the Queen's reception of our Russian ambassador, I read: 'She also honourably entertained Wolfgang William, son of Philip Lodowick, Count Palatine, Duke of Zweibruck and Neuburg, Virginio Ursinus, Duke of Bracciano in Tuscany, and the Rohans, Brethren, as they returned from visiting the King of Scots their kinsman.' Here we have princes from three lands—Germany, Italy, and France—travelling late in

1600 to see that western star, the incomparable Elizabeth. The Italian Duke we have already marked down as cardinally important for Shakespeare's *Twelfth Night*. But what of these others, Wolfgang Wilhelm the Bavarian, and the Rohans of France?

Let us look first at the French princes—the Breton Huguenot brothers Rohan. We find that the elder, Henri, Duc de Rohan and 'heir to the Kingdom of Navarre, if the King [Henri IV of France] and his sister die without issue', was at this time barely twenty-one. His younger brother Benjamin, Monsieur de Soubise, was still a boy. These youths have our sympathy, for at the time of their visit everything French was in bad odour in England. Shakespeare's *Henry V* reflected the people's contempt for the French, and their sentiments were the Queen's. To her mind Henri was 'the Antichrist of ingratitude'. She had lent him tremendous sums and military aid for his wars against the Catholic League. As John Donne commented:

> France, in her lunatic giddiness, did hate
> Ever our men, yea and our God of late;
> Yet she relies upon our Angels [gold] well,
> Which ne'er return: no more than they which fell.

Henri had not only made no effort whatever to repay her, but had turned Catholic himself, and in 1598 had concluded peace with the arch-enemy, Spain. In London streets therefore his name was a signal for spitting, and the *Mounsieurs* were 'French dogs'. Ballads were free with scurrility, and in *Jack Drum's Entertainment*, a play of 1600, the main butt is 'a goatish Frenchman called Mounsieur *John fo de King*'—that is, a lewd pun on Henri's ambassador in England. Between 1589 and 1601 the two

resident French envoys were both 'John for the King':
Jean de la Fin (Sieur de Beauvoir-La Nocle de Buhy), and
Jean de Thuméry (Sieur de Boissise).

No wonder that on his arrival in October the young
French Duke, Rohan, found a repulsively warm welcome
among the Cockneys and a cool reception with the Queen,
particularly when he displeased her by carrying out a plan
of going off to Scotland to visit his kinsman King James.
Beyond the Tweed the climate proved very different.
Here was James dropping everything to entertain his
noble French cousins with endless hawking, hunting, and
banqueting, and even making Henri de Rohan godfather
at the christening of his infant Prince Charles: 'Monsieur
de Rohan . . . bare the Bairne in his arms from the Chamber to the Chapel.' The hilarious Scottish visit lasted two
months—unfortunately for our purpose. During the
Twelve Days of Queen Elizabeth's great Christmas, Rohan was out of England. Not until the middle of January
did he return to contemptuous London, and then he
cooled his heels several days before the offended Queen
took any notice of him with 'honourable entertainment'.

But what we want is Rohan's *souvenirs de voyage*, to
match the Russian Mikulin's. Fortunately they have been
preserved. And though not published until many years
later, his account was not 'corrected' in the light of after-
thoughts, but left just as he had written it in 1600.[1] We
find it a document as unique as it is amazing. For Rohan
manages to write quite a story about his months in England *without once mentioning his hostess Queen Elizabeth*,
the most famous monarch in Europe. Yes, indeed. But

---

[1] *Voyage du Duc de Rohan, Faict en l'an 1600.* . . Amsterdam,
1646.

the young Duke's pique cannot conceal the profound impression made upon his mind at Rochester (on the river to which he gives the Falstaffian name of 'Madwag'), by the sight of Elizabeth's mighty Fleet—heavily-gunned warships in fighting trim, a sea-power unmatchable. Disgusted though he is with the English, he is yet a soldier, at the outset of a great military career, and his eye appraises the English Queen's arsenal on the Medway as 'one of the finest treasuries of war which the great Ocean Sea possesses'.

Bidding Rohan *au revoir*, we turn to the Bavarian Wolfgang Wilhelm, with whom Rohan's fortunes were to be bound up a decade later in the Jülich–Cleves wars. A Bavarian? Every lover of Shakespeare pricks up his ears at the news of a German or Dutch visitor to Elizabethan London. For he knows that a succession of those observant methodical folk, taking endless notes, have preserved priceless information for us. It is astonishing, but a fact, that the only known contemporary sketch of the inside of an Elizabethan playhouse was jotted down in a Dutch traveller's notebook. Queen Elizabeth's noble guest Wolfgang Wilhelm, Lutheran Count Palatine and future Duke, should certainly be looked into.

From his notice in the *Allgemeine deutsche Biographie* I gathered that Wolfgang also was a young man, hardly twenty-two when he arrived in England in the winter of 1600–1601. And two notes among the English historical manuscripts reveal that (unlike Rohan) he *was* at Court in the Christmas holidays. First, on December 14, 'Wolfgang William Count Palatine . . . came to the Courte & was entertained by hir Majestie, dined with the Lord Chamberlaine at his chamber'—so we know that Shake-

speare's master, Lord Hunsdon, regaled the young Pfalz-
graf shortly before Christmas. Second, a farewell message of thanks for hospitality to Sir Robert Cecil from
Margate on January 9 (three days after Twelfth Night)
shows Wolfgang Wilhelm on the eve of sailing for the
Continent.[1]

If he had been honoured by the great English Queen at
her festival, what could or would a Wolfgang Wilhelm
do but send off a dutiful and circumstantial letter about it
to his father, the Duke, at Neuburg in Bavaria? Yes, but
would such a letter still be preserved after three centuries
and a half? I learned on inquiry that the family archives of
Pfalz-Neuburg were now at Munich, in the Bavarian State
Paper Office. In reply to my query by post, the Director,
Dr. Winkler, was kind but regretful. He could discover
no such letter. Moreover an exhaustive dissertation on
Wolfgang Wilhelm, compiled fifty years ago, had made
no mention of any report of that visit to England. I had
given up hope, when a few weeks later came Dr. Winkler's
joyful news that he had found it. Not merely one letter,
but two, and he would send me photostats. His staff had
kindly kept my request in mind, and a fortunate 'reorgani-
zation of the files' had brought to light the long-lost and
unknown papers.[2] Our hearty thanks go to Munich.

Both Wolfgang Wilhelm's letters are addressed to
his father—'*Durchleuchtiger hochgeborner Fürst gnediger
geliebter Herr Vatter*'. The first is a copy, a brief missive
dated from London January 3; but the second, dated at
the Hague January 17, is the young nobleman's lengthy

[1] B.M. MS. Cott. Tit. C. X, f. 100ᵛ; H.M.C., *Cecil Papers*, 14. 159.
[2] Bayer. Hauptstaatsarchiv München, Bestand Pfalz-Neuburg,
Fasz. Lit. Nr. 1151.

and detailed account of his experiences in England between December 17 and his sailing from Margate on January 10: an original draft, full of corrections and interlining. Even Dr. Winkler found it difficult to read, but it amply repays the decipherer of Gothic *Fraktur*.

What does he recount? Well, in the first place how he had happily got over an attack of the mumps (*Bakhengeschwulst*) and a bad cold (*Catharro*). Then, how he was tactfully advised not to follow Rohan in a visit to James of Scotland, as such a gesture would not sit well with *Ihre Königliche Majestät* Elizabeth. Accordingly, by the Queen's encouragement, a few days before Christmas he rode to Oxford, where he was received like a duke, and describes the University's learned and various entertainment of him.

On the morrow he went forward to Woodstock—to see Elizabeth's poem, which she scratched on the window when she was a young woman imprisoned there—where its guardian Ranger, that ancient Knight of the Garter Sir Henry Lee, who was sick abed at the Lodge, did everything imaginable to make him welcome. Returning via Hampton Court, he arrived in London on Christmas Eve. Since he found that 'on Christmas Day by the custom of the country every Englishman stays quietly at home', Wolfgang Wilhelm did likewise; but on the day after Christmas, St. Stephen's, the first of the Twelve Days, he betook himself to the festive Court at Whitehall.

And here is the crest of excitement for us. Wolfgang Wilhelm not only reports the delightful feasting, interminable dancing, and a fascinating long conversation with the affable and gracious Queen, but adds that he was present at the comedy played before her Majesty after supper. It was certainly Shakespeare, Burbage, and their fellows whom he saw, for they were the only players at Court on St. Stephen's Night.[1] The name of their play is not preserved, and he does not describe it; but he does say that while they acted, the well-languaged Elizabeth kept helping Lord Grey interpret the gist of it for his benefit. Whether the translation was into Latin or into German he does not specify. But this is a priceless picture we have never had—Queen Elizabeth not only catching Shakespeare's lines from his mouth, but tossing them on in a foreign tongue![2] I find it hard to forgive Wolfgang Wilhelm for not recording at least the name of the comedy. However, he recorded something else: on the way to Margate, the Queen's officers did not fail to show him the formidable array of Her Majesty's Navy Royal on the Medway. And with proper German thoroughness he went on board the three greatest ships of war, and took 'a diligent view'.

Hunsdon, Mikulin, Rohan, Neuburg—English, Russian, French, German: on counting our rescues from the envious wallet of Time, it was plain that Fortune meant to favour the effort to recollect some of the surroundings, scattered by the ages, of Elizabeth's Twelve Days of high festival at Whitehall. Here were lost actualities revived as though they had happened only yesterday. Munich

---

[1] Chambers, *Eliz. Stage*, 4. 113.

[2] 'alss nun die königin herauss kommen hab Ich diselbe neben anderen herrn in den saal darin getanzet und *comedia* gehalten würd *comitiret*, daselbsten ist anfenglich ein tantz und hernacher die *comoedia* ~~tractiret~~ gehalten worden. Da ~~mich~~ insonde[r]heit die Königin einen herrn *Melard Gre* [Thomas Lord Grey of Wilton] genant d[as]s er mir der *comoedianten propositum* (Vorbringen) verdolmetschen solle bevelch geben, ~~selbsten~~ zue Zeiten auch selbsten verdolmetschet . . .' Wolfgang Wilhelm, fol. 6.

had dug up a young Count who had heard Shakespeare playing and the Queen interpreting for him, on the First Night of Christmas. Alnwick Castle in Northumberland had brought out Shakespeare's master with his detailed orders for entertaining her Majesty's guests on the final Twelfth Day and Night, including the command for a pleasing play with 'great variety and change': for a favourite saying of the Queen's was, *per molto variare Natura è bella*—'by her manifold varying, Nature is fair'. From the distant Kremlin had come the report to Tsar Boris Godunov of what his uncouth envoy saw and heard of the entertainment earlier on that triumphal day.

But what of the Italian Duke, Orsino? No Shakespeare's insight is needed to recognize in this 'most brilliant nobleman of his day' the favoured guest. It was notorious that the Queen delighted to meet accomplished *cavalieri* from the land of Castiglione. Eighteen months before this, the Italian-educated Count of Anhalt had arrived. Lord Nottingham's opinion of him was, 'he is the most properest and the best brought up gentleman that I have ever seen, of that country or of any other. I know her Majesty will like him well, for he hath been brought up in Italy.'[1] Queen Elizabeth justly prided herself on her supreme mastery of the Tuscan tongue: the princely Florentine Orsino, patron of Torquato Tasso, could savour the delicate artistry of her speech.

She liked the Italian manners and customs to the point of protesting on occasion that she herself was, 'as it were, half Italian'—and she loved to be nicknamed 'the Florentine'. Not such a far-fetched notion even in a Queen who

---

[1] H.M.C., *Cecil Papers*, 9. 194.

was certainly *mere English*; for 'the English humour', as the seventeenth-century Henry Belasyse remarked, 'is somewhat like unto that of the Italians, and a middling humour between the too much of the French and the too little of the Spaniard. It neither melts away like a snow-ball, nor stands out dully like a stone.' Unquestionably, as we shall find, Elizabeth had every political reason for making much of Don Virginio Orsino. But also unquestionably she enjoyed the personal challenge of his visit. Was it possible for any woman of sixty-seven to charm and delight a young man of twenty-eight? Let no one answer in scorn or disbelief before Elizabeth of England makes the trial.

Don Virginio's story, as it later unfolded itself, proved absorbing in the extreme; but the present and crucial problem was to trace him at the time of his visit to England. First, we must introduce him briefly. Son of Paolo Giordano Orsino, Duke of Bracciano, and of Isabella de' Medici, and orphaned at the age of thirteen, Virginio Orsino had been brought up at Florence by his uncle Ferdinand I, Grand Duke of Tuscany, along with the Grand Duke's niece Maria de' Medici, who was less than a year younger than her cousin Virginio. It was later whispered that the two had a fondness for each other; but however that may have been, they were 'great states', and in those days of political alliances by marriage, it was inconceivable that they should marry. Ferdinand grew deeply and sincerely attached to his nephew, and treated him as a son. Virginio reciprocated the affection of the prudent and able Medici ruler, and long after he had married and had children of his own he continued to pass most of his life assisting his uncle at the Pitti Palace in the

31

government of Tuscany rather than at his own castle of Bracciano near Rome. Late in 1600 his cousin Maria was married in Florence by proxy to Elizabeth's 'Antichrist of ingratitude', the Catholic-converted and divorced French King Henri IV, and Virginio Orsino escorted the royal bride in state to France, where she saw her husband for the first time in her life, at Lyons. Leaving that city in December, the young Duke pursued his way to England, and to his Twelfth Night at Whitehall.

That then was the situation, in bare outline. How to seek the precious touches of colour to give us a living picture? Virginio's devotion to his uncle, the sovereign of Tuscany, seemed the promising track to follow. If the famous English Queen—always the friend of Florence—had fêted him so magnificently, would he not report his success to the uncle who had been a second father to him? On the strength of this surmise, I wrote to Dr. Sergio Camerani, Director of the Archivio di Stato of Florence. In addition to other kind assistance, at my request Dr. Camerani found me an expert investigator, Dr. G. Degli Azzi, and put him on the trail. Tirelessly ransacking the Medici archive-files, Dr. Degli Azzi located and copied for me many interesting missives from the voyaging Orsino to Grand Duke Ferdinand— '*Serenissimo signore mio Padrone osservandissimo*'. Among them all, there was one, but only one, written from London. But that one was written by Orsino the very day after Twelfth Night; and it presents the tantalizing passage,

I have here received, and am receiving, most particular honours: and having written of them at great length to my wife, I have also bidden her inform your Highness, to whom I shall only say that the greater part of them I owe to you, by the service which I have with you. . . .[1]

'At great length' to his wife, Flavia? The very letter we must have, to complete and crown the Twelfth Night story. If it was not in the Medici archives—and it certainly was not—where then might it be? Dr. Camerani gently pointed out that since the Duchess Flavia was an Orsina, the normal place to look for it would be the archives of the Orsini. Why, of course—but that plain piece of common sense had not occurred to me.

Off went the ultimate appeal, this time to the present 'Duke Orsino': Prince Virginio Orsini, 21st Duke of Gravina, at his Roman palace. In the absence of the Duke abroad (the present Virginio was visiting the U.S.A.), his uncle Prince Lelio Orsini took a kindly interest in the pursuit. Noting the exact date of the critical letter, he most generously paid a visit to the ancestral Orsini archives, which contain at least 100,000 letters, and are now incorporated in Rome's Archivio Storico Capitolino.

The fantastic luck held. For Prince Lelio found not only Don Virginio's original Twelfth Night letter, but a second one which rounds off the tale of his visit to Queen Elizabeth—and to my eternal gratitude sent me photographs of both.[2] Fortune had evidently made up her mind to illuminate Queen Elizabeth's Twelfth Night from every

---

[1] '*Io ho qui receuto e recevo honori particolarissimi: et, havendone scritto assai a lungo alla mia moglie, gli ho ancora comandato di darne parte all' Altezza Vostra, alla quale dirò solo che la maggior parte di essi gli riconosco dalla servitù che ho con Lei . . .*'—Virginio Orsino al Granduca, da Londra, 7/17 gennaro 1600/1. Firenze, Archivio di Stato, Carteggio Mediceo del Principato: filza no. 6368.

[2] Roma. Archivio Storico Capitolino. Archivio Orsini, Corrispondenza di Virginio II, Fasc. 109, nri. 0395, 0394.

side. Lights had sprung up all over Europe—in Alnwick, Moscow, Munich, Florence, Rome.

And what a letter was that first one, 'at great length' to Duchess Flavia, when at last I had it in my hands! Don Virginio himself regarded it as so important that he would have put it into cipher—had he been sure that Vettori, his confidant who had the key, was at Florence accessible to the Duchess. But as Vettori might have gone to Rome, Don Virginio took the risk of sending it 'open'—in clear —which spares us a deal of deciphering.

Don Virginio's five sheets written in the sweet Roman hand—a generous three of them devoted to a full report of the marvellous Twelfth Day at Whitehall—leave no doubt that in spite of Boris Godunov's envoy, he, the Orsino, was Elizabeth's guest of honour. He can be re-conciled to leaving the Russian to dine in the Great Chamber, on learning that it is 'the custom of Muscovy that if he [Mikulin] had not been seen eating in the Queen's presence, his Great Duke would have had him beheaded'. And he promises his Duchess a word-of-mouth account of the Muscovite's ridiculous manners—his *costumi ridicolosi*.

Long after midnight the great day ended in the Hall as the Queen had planned it, with Orsino the Duke stand-ing in chat close to her throne, seeing and hearing the pleasing comedy *with great variety and change of music and dances*. 'The Muscovite ambassador', he notes with satis-faction unconcealed, 'was not present.' But not for-gotten by the quick comedian; for Shakespeare included one or two straight-faced jests at his *costumi ridicolosi* which must have convulsed the Court. Both Don Virginio's unique and vivid narrative and Shakespeare's comedy can however be fully savoured only after a taste of what led up to them.

II

ORSINO

SHAKESPEARE'S *Twelfth Night* and Webster's *The White Devil* stand as extremes of the Elizabethan drama: the one, the happiest and most golden comedy of love, music, and laughter, and the other perhaps the blackest and most nerve-racking tragedy of lust, murder, and horrible death. It seems incredible, but these antipodes of the dramatic sphere share one point in common. Among the persons of the play in each of them figures the shadow of Don Virginio Orsino.

Webster's *White Devil* freely telescopes the horrors of Virginio's childhood. Actually he was not four years old when Paolo Giordano, his jealous father, strangled his mother. And he was almost eleven before this same father, infatuated with the beautiful Vittoria Accorambona—wife to Cardinal Montalto's nephew—had her husband murdered. Two years later, on Montalto's election as Pope Sixtus V, Paolo Giordano married Vittoria—he seems indeed to have married her three times to make sure—and escaped with her out of the Pope's power to the Republic of Venice, only to die within a few months. Vittoria's murder followed close after, accomplished by an Orsini cousin. This clansman killed little Virginio's fair stepmother with the loyal and laudable motive of insuring the boy's inheritance of the great Orsini wealth. The fame of these sensational crimes spread throughout Europe.

Against *The White Devil*'s curtain of blood and death,

Webster sets the innocence and charm of the 'sweet prince' Virginio—called Giovanni in the play—showing a boy filled with romantic dreams of future glory as a generous paladin. Excellent for dramatic contrast, but also true to Virginio's real character. Of his father, Virginio tried to remember only the renown won by the hugely corpulent Paolo Giordano as general of Venetian infantry against the Turk, and the glorious arrow-wound he received at the world-famous sea-fight of Lepanto. But something Virginio could not forget was the crippling legacy which that father had left him: the exquisitely painful malady of podagra or gout.

As he grew up with his cousin Maria de' Medici under the affectionate favour of their prudent and energetic uncle the Grand Duke Ferdinand, Don Virginio fed his spirit on the prowess of his forerunners, illustrious Orsini warriors of mark: most of all, perhaps, on that of his fifteenth-century great-great-grandfather, the *gran Contestabile* Virginio Orsino, *capitane di stima grande*—imagining him putting the Spaniards to rout, restoring his kinsman Pietro de' Medici to the throne of Tuscany, and teaching many most valorous leaders the art of war. When Virginio visited his own Tuscan stronghold of Bracciano on the lake near Rome, this mighty ancestor looked out upon him from an imposing fresco on the wall. And closer to his own time there was his grandfather Geronimo *alias* Girolamo, who, 'leading his own forces into Hungary against the Turkish enemies of Christ, had excellently shown his valour and fortitude.'

Young Virginio had the soul of desire, but neither the genius nor the rude strength needed to become another Alessandro Farnese. Despite the assurances of his flatterers, no amount of study of tactics or diligent cavalry practice could do it. Yet his Orsini blood would not give up the dream, more especially since his elder in the household, the Grand Duke's bastard brother Don Giovanni de' Medici, gained success as a soldier, and since there was in Italy also another Virginio Orsini (di Lamentana), five years his senior, making a name for himself in the Flanders wars, and doing battle with the formidable rebels in the Papal States. While nursing his vision through attacks of gout, Don Virginio advanced well in his princely education, acquiring fluency in French and Spanish, together with all the qualities and attributes of a most complete gentleman of the Italian Renaissance.

At sixteen he was chosen to represent his uncle in receiving and escorting Tomaso Contarini, the Venetian ambassador come to congratulate the Grand Duke on the occasion of his marriage. Here is the observant Venetian's appraisal of the youth, *il signor don Virginio Orsino*:

He is much loved by the Grand Duke. . . . He has every grace, is ingenious, and discourses well on all subjects; apt to apply himself and to succeed in any profession, especially in the military, to which it would seem he is pointing himself; to the which there appears no other obstacle than a delicate constitution and a slender body which seems unfitted to support great fatigue. . . . Yet he delights in riding.[1]

On coming to the throne of Tuscany in 1587, his uncle Ferdinand had addressed himself chiefly to strengthening the country in industry and commerce. To defend the latter against the Turks, he built up a navy of war-galleys.

---

[1] *Relazioni dagli Ambasciatori Veneti al Senato* (ed. A. Segarizzi, 1916), 3. 84; *Relazioni . . .* (ed. E. Albéri), Ser. III, 4. 282.

Army and fortifications were likewise increased, for the great aim of his foreign policy was to free himself from the Spanish domination which weighed heavily on the Italian states. And though Philip could oblige him to contribute a ship to the Spanish Armada against England, Ferdinand was delighted to hear of Elizabeth's stunning blow to the might of Spain in the tremendous defeat of 1588; and the glory of Drake and Howard must have stirred the emulous young Orsino.

At the time of his wedding early in 1589 with the French princess, Christine of Lorraine, the Grand Duke also arranged a match for the sixteen-year-old Don Virginio with Flavia Peretti, the grand-niece of Pope Sixtus V. This accomplished several desirable ends. It not only made peace with the Vatican, formed a united front against Spain, and reconciled the Pope to the son of the man who had murdered his nephew; it also delighted Sixtus to join his humble peasant blood with the ancient-noble Orsini. Despite his enormous expenses in rebuilding Rome and setting up obelisks, the old man played up generously, giving Flavia a dowry of a hundred thousand crowns, worth close to a third of a million pounds today, and appointing Don Virginio 'Prince-attendant to the Papal Throne'. The Pope also congratulated himself on having simultaneously married his Flavia's sister, Orsina, to the chief of the great rival Roman house of Colonna. And to accommodate the perennial dispute of primacy between Orsini and Colonnesi—now linked by these Peretti sisters—Sixtus ruled that as between the chief Orsino and the chief Colonna, the elder in age should have the *pas*; but that in all other respects they were equal, and outranked all the other Roman barons. This was one Papal decree which Don Virginio was not apt to forget.

In April 1589 young Virginio travelled to Rome for his wedding, and was 'received with the greatest marks of love and honour by the Pope and all the Roman barons and nobility . . . the nuptials being celebrated with such state as befitted so great a Prince and a niece of the Pope'.[1] Torquato Tasso, prince of Italian poets, bestirred himself to hymn Don Virginio's marriage in rime. For, as he wrote to a friend, despite 'infirmity of soul and body . . . I wish to seek in every way to avail myself of the favour of this nobleman'. [2] His five sonnets of epithalamium play gracefully on *Flavia* (golden hair), on *Rosa* (the rose, heraldic charge of Orsini and flower of love), and on *Orsa* (the Bear in the Orsini coat of arms)—beginning

De le più fresche rose homai la chioma . . .

Virginio he celebrates as 'the chaste Lover' and 'the valorous Duke . . . of the ancient line illustrious in war, whose fame resounds beyond furthest Oxus and the Moorish Atlas'.[3]

Two years after the marriage Don Virginio evidently asked for another poem to give to his cherished duchess. Replying with the sonnet beginning *La bella donna, che nel fido core*, Tasso wrote to apologize for it: 'If I were so full of love as your Excellency is, or if at least I might make myself *feel* somewhere in my heart, instead of this melancholy which unceasingly molests me!' [4] Young as he was, Don Virginio also knew what sorrow and

---

[1] Cesare Campana, *Dell' Historie del Mondo* (1607), II. x. 409.
[2] *Lettere di Torquato Tasso* (ed. Cesare Guasti, 1864), 4. 198.
[3] *Delle Rime del Sig. Torquato Tasso* (Venice, 1608), 196–8.
[4] *Lettere*, 5. 36.

physical misery were, and he extended his favouring hand in sympathy to the world-renowned but unhappy poet, whose affliction was so famous that in 1594 Shakespeare's rivals, the Admiral's Men, produced a play in London entitled *Tasso's Melancholy*.

Meanwhile life looked bright to him. His duchess had lost no time in presenting him with twins, a boy and a girl. Ten years in the future, and a thousand miles away, Queen Elizabeth's poet Shakespeare would charmingly remind him of this good fortune, with a vivid scene of a beautiful boy and a lovely girl 'both born in an hour. . . . An apple cleft in two is not more twin Than these two creatures.' And as the seasons passed, his first-born twins were supplemented. Flavia, a model of wives, industriously kept adding small Orsini to the honour of her husband's house. Before he was twenty-nine he had six of them.

But his career: he must make himself a true Orsino, a soldier of whom his children might be proud. At last came his chance to show his ancestral crest, the black Bear with the red Rose in her paw, in the forefront of battle. The invading Turks were once more driving deep into Hungary. Emperor Rudolph appealed to Christian princes for strength to oppose them, and Don Virginio set forward with a force of two hundred horse—musketeers and cuirassiers—to emulate his grandfather Geronimo on the bloodstained Hungarian soil. The Pindar of Florence, Gabriello Chiabrera, sped him on his way with a farewell ode beginning *Amabil gioventute, Tesor di nostra vita*, and proclaiming, 'It is no vain memory to shut up in his thoughts—the ancient glory of Medici and Orsini.'[1]

---

[1] *Rime di Gabriello Chiabrera* (Milano, 1807), i. 52-53.

We are told that Virginio campaigned long against the Turks, fighting at the stubborn siege of Giavarino (Raab). Evidently the slim and delicate young nobleman bore himself well, for the Emperor's citation declared that Don Virginio had gained no less fame than his grandfather had done, 'as the wounds received in the front of his body sufficiently witness'. At Prague in 1595 he was presented by a grateful Rudolph with a gift of 'sables, crystal glasses, and plate to the value of five or six thousand crowns'. In the hope, however, of further glorious employment abroad, Don Virginio sought out an English commander returning home, and by him did 'earnestly recommend his service to her Majesty'—the victorious Queen Elizabeth. And there can be no doubt that he sent similar messages by the succession of English nobles and gentlemen who visited the splendid Tuscan Court in the Palazzo Pitti.

The impression which he and his youthful Medici uncle, the bastard Don Giovanni, made in 1598 on the worldly-wise French Cardinal d'Ossat deserves attention. 'These are two young noblemen of very great worth and valour,' d'Ossat reported, 'and I do not know if there be in Italy two others who surpass them.'[1] Don Virginio's thirst for honour and glory in war reminds us of his contemporary, the Earl of Essex. But the Orsino's was the gentler soul, not self-devoured by the fierce and ruinous pride of 'a nature not to be ruled'.

His appetite whetted by a beginning so propitious, Don Virginio's next military enterprise must have appealed to him as an adventure both heroic and Homeric. What a

---

[1] *Letres du Cardinal d'Ossat* (ed. Amelot de la Houssaie, 1698), I. 564.

trumpet to the soul—to ride a swift war-galley, its oars beating rhythm on the wine-dark sea, and to seize an island of the enemy's by storm. As conceived, the plan was to proceed east into the Ægean with a flotilla and capture Chios from the Turk. And the Grand Duke appointed Don Virginio supreme commander of the expedition. Setting out from Leghorn with his galleys in 1599, he must have hoped for a triumph like the Earl of Essex's at Cadiz.[1]

The attack proved a fiasco, alas, a bloody and costly reverse which the Florentines would gladly forget. Don Virginio had no experience in this kind of war, and the skilled commanders under him quarrelled over tactics. The advantage of surprise was lost, the landing forces were killed or captured by the Turks. Though Don Virginio stood in with his galleys in the rough roadstead so long as almost to lose them too, at length he had to draw off in despair. The sum of his good luck was a bullet-wound to carry home and show to the bitter and sorrowing Tuscans. Despite the misery of failure, his courage and honour remained untarnished. The English sea-dogs remembered the bold but bungled effort of Florentine naval power, and Shakespeare did not omit to glance briefly in his comedy at 'a sea-fight 'gainst the Count his galleys', with the observation, 'Belike you slew great number of his people?'

By this time—1599—Ferdinand felt himself strong enough, now that Spanish Philip was succeeded by a weak son, to plan an important political move against

---

[1] For the full story, with admirable documentation, see Philip P. Argenti, *The Expedition of the Florentines to Chios, 1599* (London, 1934).

Spain in the shape of a marriage alliance. Even Don Virginio's marriage of ten years earlier had been political. The Venetian ambassador reported that the union between Pope Sixtus and the Grand Duke in the marriage of Flavia Peretti to Don Virginio was hated by Spain and Savoy, 'who did not omit any sort of evil means to unsettle it'. Unfortunately for the Grand Duke and Don Virginio, Pope Sixtus died a year after the wedding; and the next supreme pontiff of any importance, Ippolito Aldobrandini, elected in 1592 as Clement VIII, was, as we shall see, a very different character.

The common talk about Don Virginio and his political marriage was picked up in Italy by an English traveller and translator, Robert Tofte.[1] He observes,

Twas thought by the common people that the foresaid Duke [Orsino] would have poisoned his wife as soon as Sixtus Quintus died, or at least have cast her off by reason of her beggarly parentage. For most certain it is that their old grandmother Camilla, before her brother Sixtus [Felice Peretti] came to be Cardinal, was very poor, and no better than a common herbwife. And these two grand ladies' [i.e., Flavia's and her ?halfsister Orsina's] mothers, no better than common laundresses when they [the ladies] were born. Yet Fortune favouring this poor friar Sixtus Quintus and advancing him to be Pope, they were brought up like great states, and married to two of the greatest Princes that live at this day in Rome. And this was the cause that these two nobles would [as it was thought] make small account of their wives when once the Pope their kinsman should die. But it is proved now far otherwise; for both these

---

[1] Tofte is chiefly famous for his report of gaining 'small joy' as an unwilling witness of a London performance of *Love's Labour's Lost*. His priceless bit of Italian gossip I found by hunting out his manuscript *Discourse of the five last Popes of Rome* (1598) in Lambeth Palace Library.

sisters have so good a grace and carrying in all their actions, and so virtuously and honourably carried themselves towards their husbands, as they now love them better than ever they did before.[1]

The low-born Peretti girls' success in maintaining their great estate and increasing their husbands' love by sheer good character, to the confusion of the cynics, makes very pleasant reading—and adds a grace to Don Virginio's Twelfth Night letter to his Flavia, *Signora Consorte amatissima*.

From the story of Pope Clement's trip of 1597 to Viterbo, with a visit to Bracciano on the way back, we get a lively glimpse of that mighty ancestral castle of Don Virginio's which so powerfully seized the attention of Sir Walter Scott in 1832, and also an instructive symptom of the palpable coolness between an Aldobrandini Pope and a Medici–Orsini prince. Ill-informed diplomatic agents thought that Don Virginio would be at home to receive His Holiness; but having had sufficient notice of the itinerary, when the Pope arrived the Orsino was already far away to the north-east—a blameless foot-pilgrim, trudging the six-score mountainous miles to the shrine of Loreto. Yet aside from the absence of its master—for which Don Virginio afterwards gracefully apologized by letter—the Pope could have found no fault with Bracciano's royal reception of him. Here is a passage translated from the surviving relation of the Papal journey:

Passing by way of La Tolfa, riding by rocky declivities, and crossing the Mignone [*Mugnone*] which threads these mountains with its waters clear and most cold, we entered the fair

---

[1] Lambeth Palace Library, MS. 1112, f. 47.

and delectable country of Monte Verano [*Monterano*], famed for the best vineyards, green with thick and very rich grain.

Proceeding a little farther, we met some seventy well-mounted musketeers of the Duke of Bracciano, and afterwards another cavalcade escorting the ambassador of Tuscany, who was come to Bracciano to receive the Pope, since at that very time Don Virginio, the duke of that place, was gone pilgrimaging on foot with but two or three, in fulfilment of a vow, to Madonna Santissima di Loreto.

At sight of Bracciano, which was by night, the castle with a handsome *gazzarra* of guns great and small saluted the Prince; while the soldiers, beating drums in the outskirts of the town, bowed to the Pope and the cardinals as they passed, and then with a fine volley made all the neighbouring vales resound. Meantime the highest points showed blazing with fires and beacons, which made of dark night well-nigh the brightest daylight.

Our Master was lodged in that very ancient stronghold, where one sees the effigies of the greatest heroes known to fame of the most noble family of the Orsini. The accommodation, besides the largeness of the rooms and the noble hangings, was marvellous for the apartments and good attendance —many Roman gentlemen being there—, for the quantity and choiceness of the viands, and for the quiet. And, since the longest stage of the whole journey had been made that day, after supper everyone went to rest.

At break of the morrow's dawn, with sound of drum and trumpet and with artillery great and small, the captain of the castle saluted the coming day. His Holiness arose, at a suitable hour said Mass, and then, escorted by the musketeers and horse of Bracciano to the frontier of the domain, set forward towards Rome.[1]

Very human elements in the bad relations between the Grand Duke and this new Pope culminated in a

---

[1] Bibl. Vat. Cod. Ottobon. lat. 2694, as printed by J. A. F. Orbaan, 'Un viaggio di Clemente VIII nel Viterbese' in *Archivi della R. Società romana di storia patria*, XXXVI (1913), 143–4.

dramatic scene in which Don Virginio was a protagonist, and which did much to produce his visit to England. Since the ancestral Aldobrandini family had been driven out of Tuscany by the Medici for stirring up republican rebellion, the new Pope and his all-powerful nephew-Cardinal, Pietro Aldobrandini, had old scores to settle with the Medici. Secondly, though both the Pope and the Grand Duke chafed under the hard hand of Spain, and therefore cultivated the French King Henri IV and persuaded him to change his religion, it was the Pope who engineered Henri's peace with Spain in 1598. This detached Henri from Elizabeth and struck a blow at England; and also (which pleased an Aldobrandino) at England's friend, Ferdinand de' Medici. And this Pope even shared Philip II's dream of conquering that stiff-necked island of the heretic Queen's for the Catholic Church. The French, who were only across the Channel from Albion, knew better. Shortly after the English had sacked Cadiz in 1596, Cardinal d'Ossat reported an illuminating conversation with the Pope.

I told him [*writes d'Ossat*] that it would be easier for the Turk to conquer the remainder of Hungary, and all of Austria, and several other countries after those, than it would be for the Spaniards to invade England; that the Crown of England had more men-of-war on the ocean than any other power in the world; that the Spaniards had suffered great loss of such vessels, as well as of men and munitions and of all supplies for war at sea; that the English Channel was commonly so storm-tossed that if one couldn't make port very soon, one must get out of there or perish; that England abounded in men valiant by sea and by land, enemies of the Spanish.

The Pope answered me that all this was true; but that England had been conquered in the past, and she might well be at the present; that she was little united in herself, because of diversity of religions, and ruled by an old woman with no husband and no certain successor; that this woman ought by now to be at the bottom of her finances, having made many expenditures; that besides he had observed that women who had reigned long, and loved the amorous sport in their youth and in the vigour of their prime, afterwards in their old age became despised by the very ones to whom they had given themselves.[1]

Such a picture might remind one of Catherine the Great of Russia, but it bears no resemblance whatever to Elizabeth of England. Old Sixtus had shown far less ignorance of his foe. Though lowly born, his was no gross or grovelling mind. From the enemy's point of view he applauded Elizabeth's admirable policy, her courage, her masterly rule. For him she was ever the 'great brain' —*Ch'era un gran cervello di Principessa*. 'What a valiant woman!' he would exclaim. 'She alone knows how to rule!'

Grand Duke Ferdinand's object, in the face of Pope Clement's *coup* of the Peace of 1598, was to do something to strengthen Tuscany against Spain. And he had a good weapon, his money-bags. Perhaps the wealthiest prince in Europe in *contanti* or ready money, like Elizabeth he had been helping Henri of France with great loans. Now he had a plan: to ally himself with France by marrying his niece Maria de' Medici to the King. Henri wanted two things, money and an heir. The Grand Duke would furnish a dowry large enough not only to cancel the debts but to leave a handsome overplus, and Maria would supply the heir. At the instance of the French envoys, the Pope dissolved Henri's unfruitful marriage with

---

[1] *Letres*, I. 400.

Marguerite of Valois; and Maria's momentous contract was sealed by the Grand Duke and the French envoy in the Palazzo Pitti at the beginning of 1600: witnessed both by the Grand Duke's confidential adviser the Archbishop of Pisa and by Don Virginio Orsino, Duke of Bracciano, before the Secretary of State, Cavaliere Belisario Vinta.

Much as Clement hated to see the Medici gaining a great ally in King Henri, he found himself powerless to prevent this marriage, which he loathed almost as much as the Spaniards did. Next best was to extract as much political advantage out of it as possible. He would send his astute nephew the Cardinal to Florence in overwhelming pomp to solemnize the royal proxy marriage, and let him continue northward to show the Pope's power in arbitrating Henri's war with the Duke of Savoy.

Ferdinand promptly notified Queen Elizabeth of the intended marriage, which could not fail to interest her deeply. She welcomed a Tuscan alliance which enraged the Spaniards: especially its prospect of a French Queen from a house not under the Pope's thumb—the Medici. As for Maria herself, no wife of the libertine Henri IV could be envied. But for a young woman strictly brought up in a dignified and orderly Court like Ferdinand's, to be thrown into the vortex of French palace-intrigue and love-making! Her future was not to be foreseen in detail, but it was certainly not bright.

In Florence, the months preceding the royal espousal in the autumn of 1600 hummed with the most lavish and elaborate preparations for pomp and festivity of every kind. The expense was terrific, but not for nothing had the English given Ferdinand the cipher-name *Riches*. To

give but one illustration of the scale on which the
celebrations were planned, the Cathedral—larger than
London's present-day St. Paul's—was to have its front
completely covered with a new façade of gorgeously-
painted wood, adorned with columns and with portals
before the three great doors, and between them huge
murals picturing the history of the Medici rulers and of
the three Medici Popes; and above were to be painted
grand heraldic achievements—the arms of the Pope, of
the Emperor, of the King of Spain, of the King and
Queen of France, of the Legate, and of the Grand
Duke.

Myriad and magnificent were the entertainments prepared. Tournaments, running at the ring, hunts, splendid
feasts with music, grand balls, scenic masques, comedies,
tragedies. Among them all the most interesting today is
the Grand Duke's requisition of the new form of art:
Jacopo Peri's *dramma per musica*. With the poet Ottavio
Rinuccini writing the libretto, Peri set to work to compose his *Euridice*; and its tremendous success in performance marks the world's first public production of *opera*.

At some time in the winter or spring of this momentous year of 1600, Don Virginio welcomed an important
visitor from England. Mr. William Cecil, heir of Thomas
Lord Burghley and nephew to Queen Elizabeth's chief
minister Sir Robert Cecil, arrived in Florence. He was
cordially entertained at the Palazzo Pitti by Don
Virginio, and not many months later the Cecils were
able to return this courtesy when the Orsino came to
England.

We move forward to the dramatic crisis which was
one cause of his visit to Whitehall: the quarrel between

the Vatican and Virginio. September had come; Florence was decked and ready to receive and reverence the Papal Legate. For a crowning grace and blessing to the royal *sposalizio*, and to make it that much more *papale* and less *mediceo*, the Pope was sending from his treasury his sanctified emblem, the Golden Rose—*la Rosa Benedetta*. And to Don Virginio, chief of the rose-bearing Orsini, was assigned the honour of carrying it at the wedding for all to see in a ceremonial tour of the brilliantly-lighted and crowded Duomo.

Pope Clement sent out his prime minister, his Cardinal-nephew, in royal style: a magnificent cortege of Roman barons, officers, prelates, and train numbering more than a thousand. As the Legate's cavalcade neared Florence, the Grand Duke, with Don Virginio Orsino and the bastard Medici princes Don Giovanni and Don Antonio, attended by the Court in splendid equipage, rode out from the Pitti through the Porta Romana to receive him. Having quitted his state coach, the Cardinal advanced, superb under a rich canopy, clad in his ruby-red pontificals, and riding the white mule, symbol of purity and chastity. A lively sketch of his personal appearance comes from the pen of Guido Bentivoglio—later Cardinal, and Pope Clement's nuncio to Flanders—an intimate friend of Don Virginio, whom he describes as 'a lord of rarest talent and of other most rare qualities'. Of Cardinal Aldobrandino he writes,

Nature had shown him little favour, in making him both small in body and of a countenance of little nobility. His face was left greatly marked with small-pox, and he had also a chest much damaged with asthma; and the defect of this part occasioned another to his voice, which came out thick instead of clear, so that one had to guess at many words instead of hearing them.[1]

This Legate, though not yet thirty, and only a year older than Don Virginio, is already the power behind the Pope. And he is not an Aldobrandino for nothing. Here is his return in triumph to the stronghold of the Medici who banished his family. His plan to humiliate them on their own ground with a *disgrazia* is well-laid and ready. He will enforce the new Papal decree of precedence, issued purposely to degrade Don Virginio from the primacy of place assigned him by Pope Sixtus; show him that his date as *Gonfaloniere della Chiesa* is out, that the Aldobrandini are in the driver's seat; send him forward to troop with the Roman barons; make him yield the place of honour—that of *Antesignano* or Champion, immediately before the cross—to Marzio Colonna.

But Don Virginio knows precisely what is in the wind, and he does not like its smell. His decision is taken. Let the skies fall. They will not find the chief of the Orsini giving way to a minor Colonnese.

Pause. The ceremonial greetings. The Grand Duke turns his mount, and takes position to the left and just behind the white mule. This is the moment. Don Virginio, closely seconded by the two Medici princes, shoulders his horse in between Marzio Colonna's and the cross-bearer, taking the Champion's place as head of the Orsini, in defiance of the Vatican.

Profound sensation. The Legate, outraged, sends his Grand Master of Ceremonies, Paolo Alaleone, to remind

---

[1] Cardinal Guido Bentivoglio, *Memorie e Lettere* (ed. C. Panigada, 1934), 39–40.

the Orsino of the new Papal decree: that his place is forward. Don Virginio replies that any such decree does not apply to him. Checked here, the Legate appeals to the Grand Duke, who manifests surprise, and ignorance of any difficulty. Under the Aldobrandino's angry insistence, however, he can do no less for appearances' sake than send a message by his noble cupbearer, recommending obedience to the Pope's mandate. But he might know that Don Virginio will not obey. And if the Legate imagines that he will, he is deceived. Don Virginio budges not an inch. More than that, reports Bentivoglio, 'in resolute terms he sent to tell the Cardinal that "he [Orsino] was at Florence, and not at Rome. And that even in Rome he would never have submitted himself to this decree." '

Language of this unbending sort angers the Legate still more, and forces his hand; he must play his trump. He calls for his coach. He will return to Rome, and not perform the marriage!

Deadlock; and the situation is deteriorating rapidly. But that able statesman Ferdinand has a formula, even for a case like this. He gives Don Virginio a message for the Princess Maria, publicly desiring that it be conveyed at once to her at the palace. Excellent. The Duke of Bracciano bows to his uncle's wish—'I shall in all my best obey *you*'—and three princely Medici backs are turned on the red-robed Aldobrandino and all his pomp as they ride off.

The Legate is at no pains to conceal his *gran disgusto*. Don Virginio's defiance of the Pope is soon the common talk of Italy, and will be religiously remembered against him in the Vatican. But his brother-in-law Alessandro

Peretti, Cardinal Montalto, carries considerable weight
at Rome, and will do battle for him.

Luckily for us, an Englishman was on the spot at
Florence, and wrote to Queen Elizabeth's Lord Chief
Justice the news of Aldobrandino,

the Cardinal, to whom was given both honour and worship,
and all that might be done either to men or unto gods. Himself should seem much desirous of such reverence, being so
curious that at his very entry of the gates a difference rising
betwixt a Nephew of the Duke's and another Baron one of
his followers, for matter of precedence, he stayed long, and at
last threatened to return to Rome again, unless it might be
yielded unto his follower. To which was answered by the
Great Duke's bastard Brother, that 'every priest was sufficient
to do the same business he came for'. At length it was deter-
mined that neither party had his will.[1]

No question but that Queen Elizabeth—the best-
informed ruler in Europe, with eyes everywhere, and a
particular interest in the Florentines—heard of the incident from various quarters other than her regular newsletters from Italy. (She could, for example, have had it
from Ferdinand's London agent, the rich Florentine merchant Filippo Corsini—cousin to Ottavio Rinuccini the
poet of *Euridice*—who had long lived in a splendid house
opposite St. Bennet's in Gracechurch Street, close to the
playing-inns of the Bell and of the Cross Keys, where
Shakespeare's company acted in the 1590s.) Here then

---

[1] John Hanam to Sir John Popham, Florence, Oct. 17, 1600.
P.R.O., State Papers, Tuscany, S.P. 98/1/149. There are several
other reports of the episode: Roman Newsletters, September 14,
1600, S.P. 101/72; *Diario Alaleonis*, B.M. MS. Add. 8454, f. 178ᵛ;
G. B. Agocchi (Agucchia) *Diario del viaggio . . . Aldobrandini*, B.M.
MS. Add. 20018, f. 9ᵛ.

was this Orsino, who had sent her his earnest and respect-
ful duty, and of late had also charmingly entertained her
travelling courtier Will Cecil, now showing spirit and
virtù against that Pope who imagined her a ruined and
contemptible old hag, a worn-out voluptuary. An interesting prince!

For all his *disgusto*, the Cardinal was evidently not prepared to push matters to an extreme in Florence. There
was a limit to the insults that could safely be offered to
the Medici on their own doorstep. Even after the scene
at the Porta Romana, therefore, the detested Virginio was
not denied the Papal honour of carrying the great golden
Rosa Benedetta at Maria de' Medici's magnificent espousal. As for the ingeniously splendid festivities which
followed upon it, books would be necessary (and they
were written) to describe only a part of them. At the
tilting, Don Virginio gallantly splintered his lance in the
lists like a knight of old, and at the most important entertainments—including the pristine opera, *Euridice*—cut
a brilliant and central figure with his Duchess Flavia.

For an impression of the performance of *Euridice*, we
turn to Bentivoglio:

But a representation recited in music especially succeeded
most famously, through the great diversity of the exquisite in-
ventions which appeared in it, by the singular beauty of the
main scene, frequently most miraculously transformed into
many scenes, as also by the excellence of the intermezzi—of
machines, of songs, of music, and a thousand other entertainments which continually swept the audience into admiration.
And certainly one could not be sure whether these should be
marvels of fancy or realities; or which at that time were
greater: the *gusto* which the stage created with such rare and
well-accompanied shows, or the delight which was born in

the theatre through so lofty and so majestic an assemblage of spectators.

The diarist in Cardinal Aldobrandino's train was less enthusiastic:

That evening was presented the principal comedy in music, which for its scenic arrangements and its intermezzi deserved much praise. But the manner of singing it grew easily displeasing, and moreover the moving of the stage-machines was not always successful. [And the Cardinal] overheated his head by being at the pastoral and the comedy and afterwards going out into the cool air.

But even such pleasures had their end, and the time came for the new Queen of France to go to the husband she had never seen: an active man of forty-eight, as great a fighter as he was a wencher. The war he was waging in Savoy made it unsafe for her to travel overland. Though the alternative sea-transit—by galley from Leghorn to Marseilles—was a dangerous one in the rough October weather, it had to be faced. To waft the young Queen over the water, Ferdinand had constructed an Admiral-galley which for splendour of decoration has perhaps never been paralleled. Of extraordinary length, with twenty-seven sweeps a side manned by slaves all in crimson velvet, the ship was completely covered to the water-line with beaten gold. The cabins in the poop were curtained and hung with gold silk-brocade and gold tissue. Opposite her throne stood jewelled scutcheons of arms, the fleurs-de-lys of diamonds. It was the marvel of Europe. Recent reports of such a Queen's barge gave Shakespeare's audience a realistic point of reference for his famous description of the chronicled Cleopatra—

The barge she sat in, like a burnished throne
Burn'd on the water. The poop was beaten gold . . .
In her pavilion, cloth of gold, of tissue . . .

Besides the French-born Grand Duchess, Queen
Maria was to have her sister the Duchess of Mantua, her
cousin-german Don Virginio Orsino, and her natural
uncle and brother Don Giovanni and Don Antonio de'
Medici for her chief escort to Marseilles, whither King
Henri had promised to come to meet her. By the time her
royal equipage and stately retinue reached the sea at
Leghorn, where the golden Admiral-galley had been
joined by a squadron composed of six Florentine, five
Papal, and five Maltese galleys, Don Virginio had been
doing some hard thinking.

This trip abroad was certainly opportune for him. By
his open defiance of the Pope's mandate he had made
Rome and perhaps Italy itself at the moment somewhat
too hot to hold him. Honour won abroad would however
silence enemies at home. His favour with Cousin Maria
might turn to account in France. Should King Henri look
graciously upon him, there might be some honourable
military command. But the French were always unpredictable, and he would do well to equip himself with an
alternative. If Henri's welcome proved to be but 'from
the teeth outward', what then?

Don Virginio had long desired to see the famous
Elizabeth of England. For him she was far more than a
portrait in the Grand Duke's picture-gallery. She was a
legend: the deathless Phoenix of the Western Ocean,
who had come to the English throne almost a generation
before he was born. Repeated and hopeful rumours of her
sickness or death put about by the Spaniards were belied

by a stream of travellers bringing evidence of her un-
quenchable gaiety and activity in dancing and hunting.
And what fighting-men she had! His uncle the Grand
Duke was an amateur of pirates—making huge profits by
buying their booty cheap in return for protection—but
the English depredations made the roving sea-dogs'
rivals look like rats. Drake was gone, but Howard,
Ralegh, Essex, Cumberland! Spain and the Pope com-
bined could make Tuscany tremble. Elizabeth had de-
feated the one, and scorned the other. As the warrior
King Henri had declared, on sending her the Order of St.
Esprit, 'She is a knight, because of her gay and indomit-
able spirit. She hath defended herself against two of the
greatest kings in the world.'

Without doubt Don Virginio had gathered from visitors and merchants a confidence that he would find no
cold reception if he should cross the Channel. And now
he resolved that if France held nothing for him he would
visit not only the Catholic ducal courts of Flanders and
Lorraine, but Elizabeth's too. He did not have to be told
that a courtesy of this nature to the enemy and heretic
Queen would be a direct flouting both of the Pope and of
the young and touchy Philip III of Spain. If he were not
well received in England, he would be exposed to scorn
in Rome and Madrid. But on the other hand, if he
brought back the accolade of Elizabeth's consideration
and favour, how his value in the eyes of Clement and
Philip would rise! They need not like him: he would
command their respect.

He must however risk the throw single-handed, must
not in any way involve his patron Ferdinand, who already had trouble enough with Rome and Spain. On this

account he was careful to say nothing of his plan at Florence, and only at the last minute did he give his uncle's confidant, the Archbishop of Pisa, a notion of what he intended, and the reasons for it. It is not hard to read between the lines of his first letter to the Grand Duke, dispatched only after the galleys Marseilles-bound had reached Portofino:

At my departure from Leghorn I had not time to impart to your Highness an intent of mine, which had come to me some days before, of making a journey through France and the Low Countries, arriving also in England. Let your Highness excuse the enforced silence, and be certain that I do all in hope to be one day better able to serve you and the Most Excellent Prince [Ferdinand's heir, Cosimo]. With my Lord Archbishop I discussed not only the voyage, but also the causes which moved me to it, and I hope that by now these will have reached the ears of your Highness, whom I pray to believe that I am moved to this determination as well by reason as by sense. To the effecting of this my intent, nothing else is wanting for my entire satisfaction but the consent of your Highness, the which I trust to have before my departure from Marseilles.[1]

That consent he was not destined to get; and he carried out his programme with nothing to sustain him but a faith in the Queen of England.

And so to the magnificence of the royal landing from the galleys at Marseilles—where the King failed to appear to welcome his new Queen to France. It is now 'a kingdom for a stage, princes to act, and monarchs to behold the swelling scene': for Elizabeth, who had eyes every-

---

[1] Archivio di Stato di Firenze. Carteggio Mediceo del Principato, filza no. 6368.

where, was watching from England. Now, having followed Don Virginio until we have fathomed the true cause of a princely visit to the Court at Whitehall which set the Continental capitals buzzing with rumour and dark conjecture, we turn to the great hostess. What was her purpose in welcoming with well-nigh unexampled honour a Duke who bore no embassy from king or emperor?

First, reasons of state. Her war with Spain was expensive; Ferdinand of Tuscany was both *Riches* and opposed to Spain's power in Italy. Elizabeth told Winwood, her agent in France, to suggest to Ferdinand's secretary that Tuscany might contribute to the war-chest 'as one that hath the best power to bear part of the charges, and most cause to suspect the greatness of Spayne'. To make much of Ferdinand's dear nephew Don Virginio and at the same time to manifest her greatness might be an impressive gesture. Again, to suggest some mysterious English *démarche* with Tuscany would seriously disturb both Philip and the Pope, and indicate to Henri that—even though married to Maria de' Medici—he had no monopoly of *Riches*.

Personal reasons, too, some of them interwoven with her policy, were powerful. To an extent unmatched by any of her predecessors, Elizabeth was England; and the newsletters streaming from the Continental capitals were carrying news of her fatal illness or death. From Madrid: *The Queen of England is ill of a serious and very dangerous disease.*—From Rome: *The Queen of England is at the point of death.*—From Constantinople: *Ragusans* [Illyrians!] *bring news that the Queen of England is dead. This latter, however, is not affirmed positively.* 'Mortua *sed non sepulta*' was her ironical comment—'I am dead, but not buried'—and she wrote to James of Scotland of

such usage which too many countries talks of, and I cannot stop mine ears from: . . . though a King I be, yet hath my funeral been prepared (as I hear) long or [*i.e.*, before] I suppose their labour shall be needful; and do hear so much of that daily as I may have a good memorial that I am mortal . . . whereat I smile.

As for Essex, she was ignoring his unbridled ambition to rule England, and in frustration he was running wild. Through the curtains of feigned flattery and appeal in his letters flashed the steel bolt of the remark he let drop, that '*being now an old woman, she was no less crooked and distorted in mind than she was in body*'. The Pope's opinion, too. Very well. She is dead, dying, contemned, crooked, old; what else? And here France is making a huge stir, welcoming a young new Queen, and the espousal at Florence and the marriage at Lyons were the last word in magnificence and Papal display.

Maria is twenty-seven, Elizabeth sixty-seven: a difference of a mere forty years. She is old enough to be Maria's grandmother. What does Winwood write of this girl?

She yet holdeth the Italian fashion in her apparel. Her ruff is of the largest size, which she weareth somewhat carelessly. She useth no attire at all on her head, but her hair plainly and simply bound up, without any disguisement. She weareth no jewels, saving the pendants at her ears, which are of pearl, and a file of pearl about her neck. She is of comely stature, and for her beauty, the commendation which she seemeth most to affect (for she doth use no artifice) is to have *formam uxoriam* [a wifely figure]. The preparations which are made here [at Marseilles] for her entertainment by the King are very small . . . neither exercises of honour to entertain the Princes and

QUEEN ELIZABETH

gentlemen, nor any comedies, tragedies, or public feasts to give entertainment to the ladies, whereof at Florence there was variety, full of many witty and worthy conceits.[1]

Another English reporter at Marseilles sent back this—obviously intended for Elizabeth's eye:

The preparation of the town for her entertainment was so base and beggarly as it is not worth the remembrance. The Queen herself was attired in a purple satin gown, embroidered with gold. On her head she wears no dress nor tiar of pearl or other jewels, which makes her look like a girl; and but for an old damask canopy, which was carried over her by 4 townsmen, she would not have been taken for a Queen of France. The truth is, she hath no grace nor princelike majesty: her gesture and carriage is incomposed, her passings-by without regard, and in all her actions she loseth that state which in such a Princess might be required. Her face is not much unlike her picture in Whitehall gallery, somewhat bottle-nosed, broad chinned, full-faced, of a reasonable personage, out-shouldered [i.e., broad-shouldered], and, taking her all together, she is, as the Italians say, *bona roba*: a good bedfellow, for one that is not over curious. She is for the most part merry, and liketh well of the French fashion of courting. If a man may guess by her fashion, I think she will never prove any great statist or politician like her predecessor.[2]

Discount all the satire of this, and still you have a simple, unformed creature who has not advanced beyond her hornbook in the seven arts of queenliness. This Don Virginio, the interesting Orsino who is said to be escorting his cousin the new Queen—he was brought up with her: if fresh from seeing France's Queen he might see England's, as a latter-day Paris—a Florentine judge! And as though in answer to her thought, Winwood wrote on

[1] P.R.O., State Papers France, S.P. 78/44/338.
[2] P.R.O., Newsletters, S.P. 101/9/264.

November 20 from Lyons to his chief, Sir Henry Neville, on leave in London :

Don Virginio made show to depart with the galleys, but afterward came disguised to Avignon; he hath a purpose to pass through France, and, as I understand, into England, and the Low Countries, in which places he doth desire to pass his time during the time of this Pope; against whom as he hath, and as he pretendeth, just cause of discontents, so for a disgrace which he lately at Florence did offer to Cardinal Aldobrandino, he is willing to retire himself, knowing how unequal a match he is to contest either with the malice of the one or the power of the other. A thing, as it seems, fatal to his house, ever to stand in ill terms with the Popes; for so his father Paulo Jordano, fearing the displeasure of Sixtus Quintus, first retired himself to Padua, and there not finding himself safe, intending to fly into Germany, died at Como by Milan. After whose decease this man, by mediation of the Grand Duke, to make his peace, was contented to marry the sister of Cardinal Montalto. . . .

Now when Cardinal Aldobrandino made his entry of late into Florence, the Duke attending at the gate to receive him, under a *baldachino*, with a solemn procession, Don Virginio, to perform his service to the Legate *Apostolico*, took his place next before the *baldachino* in form and order as *Gonfalonier della Chiesa*. The Great Duke, knowing how ill pleasing this would be to the Cardinal, prayed him to forbear, which at his instance he was content, but refused his attendance otherwise than in his due place, and so went away; and Don Antonio and Giovanni, for these three draw all in one line. Whereupon Don Virginio, presuming that this will be offensively taken, holds it most assured for his safety to absent himself both from their presence and their power.[1]

This letter of Winwood's must have reached London about December 10. It was the first intimation, but it did

---

[1] S.P. 78/44/352.

not say *when* Don Virginio might come. Possibly King
Henri would press him to prolong his stay in France for
some time after the royal marriage on December 3. No
definite plans could be laid at Whitehall until word arrived
that he was on his way.

That news did not reach Neville's hands in London
until Christmas Day; and here is what Winwood had
written from Lyons on the day after the royal wedding:

I have been entreated by a gentleman who doth accompany
Don Virginio into England (whereof in my letter of the 20th
of November I advertised) to address them by some letter to
someone who would vouchsafe to make them have the sight of
the Court, and access to her Majesty. I have given them a
letter to your Lordship.[1]

We shall be returning to this Christmas news, to consider
how Queen Elizabeth acted upon it.

Meanwhile we are at Lyons with Don Virginio, who,
having bidden Cousin Maria farewell, is ready to start on
his journey northward. Henri's welcome had been flatter-
ing enough, but it was clearly 'from the teeth outward'.
Virginio's old friend the Grand Duke's experienced
secretary, Belisario Vinta, advised him strongly to give
up the notion of 'pilgrimaging in these weathers—for
fear of his health, and many other accidents that can hap-
pen in out-of-the-way countries (*paesi stravaganti*)', but
Don Virginio's mind was made up.

He travelled modestly, incognito—a company of five
souls. Two gentlemen: the Grand Duke's *maestro di
stalla* Signore Giulio Riario, and a Spanish youth, Don
Grazia de Montalvo; his secretary, Emilio Fei; and a servant. They had written ahead to the Grand Duke's

---

[1] S.P. 78/44/354.

London agent, the rich Florentine merchant Filippo Corsini, and he was preparing his house in Gracechurch Street, opposite St. Bennet's Church, to receive the ducal party.

Over the December mountains from Lyons, via Tarare, to Roanne. By boat down the Loire to Orleans. Then by the highway to Paris, seeing Fontainebleau and Saint Germain-en-Laye. Then north again, through the Ile de France, Picardy, Artois, to Calais and his friend the French Governor, M. de Vic. Here Don Virginio hears the war news, that the Catholic Archduke Albert 'will proceed in three weeks to the siege of Ostend', and writes his last letter home to Grand Duke Ferdinand before crossing the Channel: 'January 1. . . . after midnight, God willing, I shall embark for England.'

III

SHAKESPEARE'S ARENA STAGE

WHILE waiting for Don Virginio to arrive, we cannot resist the temptation to go ahead of him in imagination to Whitehall, where the play prepared to entertain him will be performed. What will it look like, in production?

'Keep asking ourselves *how the thing was done*.' I had taken Quiller-Couch's words to heart. In the attempt to bring Queen Elizabeth's Twelfth Night out of its centuries-old obscurity, Shakespeare's performance must stand as the prime object. Every slightest clue which might conceivably lead to light in that direction must be intently followed. We are all aware, however, of an everpresent danger: nothing is easier in any kind of investigation than to overlook a vital piece of evidence staring us in the face. For if that piece of evidence does not seem to corroborate or to fall in with our already-settled ideas, our minds either simply ignore it, or else wrest it by 'interpretation' to make it mean what we think it ought to mean. Such behaviour is certainly very human, but it blocks the road to knowledge.

The reader will recall the note added to the Lord Chamberlain's agenda—the note which records the comedy's performance on Twelfth Night at Whitehall: 'In the Hall, which was richly hanged and degrees placed rownd about it, was the play after supper.' This sentence looks harmless enough, even simple. But in fact *it embodies the evidence which for the first time reveals to us Shakespeare's method of staging plays.*

At first, of course, on reading it with a mind controlled by a long-settled preconception of the Elizabethan stage, I could not see what was plain before my eyes. For my mental picture of Shakespeare's stage at the Globe was the familiar one: a large open platform projecting from a scenic wall pierced with doors left and right, and a double-storeyed alcove—for scenes to be shown 'within' and 'above'—between them. This is what we have been taught to visualize. Docile and biddable as we are in such matters, we have even believed it to be an historical fact.

As for the Elizabethan productions in halls at the palaces, the university colleges, or the Inns of Court, we have imagined that here the projecting stages were set against the lower end or 'screen' of the room, employing the main service doors left and right for the characters' exits and entrances. What they did for an 'inner stage' we have not been able to imagine. That problem is left in suspension, while we charm ourselves with the notion of a probable 'minstrels' gallery' above, for 'balcony scenes'.

A fancy picture of this description was firmly in my mind's eye when I began to try to visualize the production of *Twelfth Night* in the great Hall at Whitehall—which was almost ninety feet long. I did not pause to shake my head over the grave acoustical drawback of a vast open beamed roof, and to wonder how, if the players stood down at the screen end, the thronéd Queen—who could not have condescended to sit below the centre of the Hall—could hear anything. As for the awkward question of an inner stage, it did not arise; for *Twelfth Night* contains no 'interior' scenes at all.

And at first the fact that the *degrees*, or scaffolded seats in tiers for the spectators, were said to be 'placed rownd about' did not bother me. I suppose I lightly took *rownd about* as a loose expression, naturally meaning 'on three sides of the room', with the stage inevitably occupying the fourth. Prejudice would allow nothing else. But that is where I was wrong. Certainly I should have known better, for I learned long ago that the Elizabethans did not share our fuzzy mind and our vague use of words. I should have realized that if they said *round about*, they meant round about, which means *on every side*—describing not a horseshoe, but a circle. When, however, I came to Duke Orsino's narrative of what he saw at the performance, his repetition at last drove the startling fact home to my consciousness: for Don Virginio reported that in the Hall the 'degrees with ladies'—*gradi con dame*—stood *atorno atorno*. And when an Italian redoubles *atorno*, he leaves no more doubt than the Frenchman does with *tout autour* that he means *completely around, on every side*.

It was a stunning revelation. For what did it show? If the audience was unquestionably *all around*, the actors could certainly be nowhere but in the centre of the room. Shakespeare's production was therefore *not* against a wall. It was not even against a backcloth, for the spectators on that fourth side, *behind the stage*, had to see the action. What a wrench to our prejudices! The Elizabethans ruthlessly drag us away from our long, long thoughts of a familiar stage in front of a 'scenic wall' with two useful and friendly doors. Facing us about, they show us reality: the play being acted openly *out in the middle of the floor*—an island of drama surrounded by crowded scaffolds on all sides. A cock-pit. A circus. An arena. A wooden O. The first performance of *Twelfth Night*, presented by Shakespeare completely 'in the round'.

This was staggering. How could our fixed ideas have been so utterly wrong, and wrong so long? Perhaps there was a mistake somewhere. Look at it calmly and proceed with caution. Possibly this circus-arrangement was an experiment, an innovation, as our theatre-in-the-round is today? Yet if Shakespeare had been a revolutionary innovator in stage production we should have heard something about it. And Queen Elizabeth is notable for conservatism and moderation. Let us look back to the days of her father and her grandfather. How were plays produced in the halls of Henry VIII and Henry VII?

On turning up the authorities, we find reports of the Tudors' masques, pastorals, and shows being set against the *end* of the hall, with a great curtain stretched in front of them. This curtain was suddenly dropped to the floor, to produce a startling and gorgeous revelation of *tableau*. But we are not now concerned with masques. *Plays* or *disguisings* are what we want; and here we find the evidence—collected and published half a century ago—that for early Tudor Court plays, the halls were arranged precisely as they were for the performance of Shakespeare's *Twelfth Night*. No curtain was used, and we read that the spectator-scaffolds or *degrees* were built 'all Round abowte', 'on all parts', 'on every side'.

Here was precedent, here was corroboration from the reigns which went before. It should no doubt have been enough for me, but rooted prejudice dies hard. I wanted something more. Some unequivocal statement from Shakespeare's own time, and in technical terms more solid than spectators' reports, which would provide the proof to settle the question finally, one way or another. The problem was to find any such statement still undiscovered,

in a field so minutely searched and sifted as that of Elizabethan stage history.

As everybody knows, for plays at Court the Office of
Revels furnished the scenic decorations—the small
structural units of frame and canvas called *mansions* or
houses, beautifully painted to suggest buildings or pavilions of various kinds, with practicable doors, or with curtains to be drawn away to reveal action within the 'building' or tent. *Houses* to represent all the clearly marked
localities in the action were set up before the performance,
and remained unshifted throughout—the so-called 'simul-
taneous' or 'multiple' method of staging a play, handed
down from the Middle Ages.

But the stages on which these *houses* were set, and the
seating for the audience, were both built by the Office of
Works. That being so, one would certainly suppose that
the Works Accounts preserved in the Public Record
Office would have been repeatedly ransacked by generations of mice-eyed detectives for evidence about Shakespeare's stage. Yet on looking into it I could find no in-
dication that any historian of the stage had combed those
Accounts for the period between 1570 and 1603.

A strange oversight, but one soon remedied. The
neglected Accounts proved to contain not only the carpenters' charges for preparing rooms in the various palaces for plays before the Queen, but also vital details of
the stages and the spectator-scaffolds. For example, at
Christmas 1588 in the Great Chamber at Richmond, besides specified platforms and *degrees*, we find that the
Works built '*a newe stage of xiiij* [fourteen] *foote square
for the Plaiors to plaie on*'.[1] Only fourteen foot square!

---

[1] 'Framing postes and Railes for plaies, setting up degrees in the

A nutshell indeed, but expanded into a realm of infinite space by the spoken magic of dramatic poetry. This is the first time we have ever known the size or the shape of an Elizabethan stage at Court.

Yet still more important to us is the *position* of the stages, now revealed in the accounts for the Whitehall seasons 1601–1602 and 1603–1604, at the height of Shakespeare's career. The first of these lists a charge for '*framing & setting up a broad Stage in the middle of the Haull.*'[1] Here we have the unmistakable proof. There across the centre, surrounded by the *degrees* for the spectators, is the stage: a *broad* (that is, a 'deep') one, evidently made so to accommodate larger scenic *houses* or *mansions* at its ends left and right. On that very stage Shakespeare and his fellows played before Elizabeth on December 26 and 27, 1601, on New Year's Day 1602, and on Shrove Sunday six weeks later.

The second account is for the first year of King James, who took Shakespeare's company under royal patronage as the King's Men. They played before him on Shrove Sunday 1604, and the Works charge is not only for '*making readye the haull with degrees . . . with a Stage in the myddle*', but also for '*altering of a Stage in the haull to*

greate chamber, nailinge on Brackettes & boordes for the people to sett on, makeing newe Halpaces there for the Quenes Majesties use, and a newe stage of xiiij foote square for the Plaiors to plaie on, and Halpaces for the Lordes and Ladies to sett on, and iij other Halpaces for the people to stande on.' P.R.O., E351/3223.

[1] '. . . making readye the Haull with degrees, with bourdes on them & footpaces under the State [i.e., platforms under the canopy], framing & setting up a broad Stage in the middle of the Haull, & making a standing for the L. Chamberlaine, framing & setting up of viij partitions within the Haull end and entryes, framing and setting a roome with a Flower [floor] in it in the round windowe in the Haull for the musitions . . .' E101/504/16, mem. 8.

bring it nearer the king'.[1] For quickness of hearing, James could not compare with the lamented Elizabeth; and if that well-graced actor the Sweet Swan of Avon was to reach the new and duller royal ear with those 'flights on Thames, That did so take Eliza, and our James,' his stage must be moved farther up the hall.

If we ask how long this circus-method for plays continued in use at Whitehall—this open central stage set with scenic *houses* painted and curtained, inherited by the Elizabethans and glorified by Shakespeare—the answer is, 'Into the Restoration'. Pepys and Evelyn saw plays given there in the arena-style unaltered from the days of Shakespeare. For it was only in 1665 by order of Charles II that the fundamental revolution in that Hall was made to the modern proscenium arch-and-curtain, with background of movable scenery for legitimate drama.[2] The new stage was built across the lower end of the Hall from wall to wall, and extended in depth more than a third of the length of the room.

But we have not realized what the detailed Works account of that operation plainly shows: namely, that the old stage, standing in the middle of the floor, without being moved was adapted as a platform or dais for the King's central seat—whence he could look through the proscenium-arch of the new stage. Charles's petty generation had little playwrights who busied themselves with 'improving' the dramas of Shakespeare. The scenic designers' similar 'improvement' of the stage brought to a close the Hall's abounding life as an intimate cockpit or circus theatre, with its platform as the heart of massed

----

[1] A.O. 1/2418/36.
[2] Eleanore Boswell, *The Restoration Court Stage* (1932).

and eager hundreds, like those which surrounded Burbage and Shakespeare as they played before their incomparable Queen.

Since that date, nearly three centuries have passed; but at length in our search for the actuality of *Twelfth Night* we have recaptured what has been long lost—the true conception of Shakespeare's stage. The knowledge that it was a supple, open, and intimate arena comes however very late. Someone should have examined the Works Accounts and found the revealing evidence of the *stage in the middle* eighty years ago. We should have been spared much blind groping. Theatrical historians would then have realized that on an arena-stage without a background, the *doors* for entrances mentioned in stage directions must be doors *in the scenic houses standing on the stage*; that that interior action ('within') and balcony action ('above') must also take place in or upon these free-standing units of scenery.

Lacking this one guiding conception, however, and driven to hunt up some accommodation for such necessary action, writers of theatrical history excogitated the theory of an 'inner stage' and an 'upper stage'. Since it was fundamentally mistaken, this theory inevitably encountered difficulties. First, there was nothing to show that any such alcove-stages ever existed in England. It was fancied that such stages might have developed from inn-yard galleries; but the one bit of testimony surviving points to a canvas erection on the stage for an 'interior'. At a play he saw, probably at the Curtain Theatre, Thomas Platter says that 'the "Englishman" went into the tents'— *stige der engellender in die Zelten*. Second, nothing resembling such extraordinary and awkward devices was known on the Continent. Third (and most annoying), the one contemporary piece of ocular evidence—the familiar de Witt drawing of the interior of the Swan Playhouse—not only shows a solid wall where the theoretical 'inner stage' ought to be, but above this central wall *behind the stage* is shown not an 'upper stage', but a row of boxes filled with spectators. As W. J. Lawrence pointed out, 'Of the four known views of early non-scenic theatres, three show incontestably that spectators sat in elevated boxes at the back of the stage'. These box-holders could not possibly see an 'inner stage' directly beneath their seats even if the thing had existed. The large double-doors shown left and right in the back wall led to the property-dock. Through them the stage furnishings—the hangings or the folded or collapsed scenic *houses*—were carried out on the stage to be set up before the performance. And though useful for unlocalized entrance-and-exit, those doors were not treated as *scenic* entrances.

What the de Witt drawing actually proves, with high-paying spectators seated on the *fourth side*, viewing the play from behind the stage, is that the public stage—like the stage at Court—was a complete circus-stage, a theatre-in-the-round, as the Elizabethans have always told us it was: 'the cirque', 'this throngéd round . . . this fair-fill'd Globe', 'this wooden O'. And what could be stranger than the modern notion of the Elizabethan stage as a bare and poverty-stricken affair 'with no scenery'? Even the least-informed reader knows that the players' costumes were rich and gorgeous; and common sense should tell us that the settings in which they acted had to be in keeping. Actually, the *houses* or *mansions*

73

at the Globe—whether it be the palace of Elsinore, the Tower of London, the opposed pavilions of Henry Tudor and Richard Crookback, the Monument of Cleopatra, or the Roman Capitol—were as rich in colour and as graceful in design as those used at Court. *Sejanus* at the Globe is described as 'set with that rich foil'. Would Shakespeare's leading actor Burbage—who was a painter too—or, for that matter, would any audience with the Elizabethan appetite for stately ornament and rich colour put up with anything less?

A wealth of contemporary comment shows us that the decoration of the public stage, so far from being merely passable, was strikingly splendid: 'the sumptuous theatre houses'—'the beauty of the houses and the stages' —'our scene is more stately furnished than ever it was in the time of Roscius'—'our stately stage'—'plays . . . set forth with as much state as can be imagined'—'the stately and our more than Roman city stages'. English travellers on the Continent drew damaging parallels. In 1600 Dudley Carleton wrote home that a play he saw at Amsterdam 'might not be compared to your plays at London for stately setting forth in stage and apparel'; and a Venetian theatre seemed to Tom Coryate 'very beggarly and base in comparison of our stately playhouses in England'. The Scottish chronicler Robert Johnston summed it up: 'For variety and magnificence of plays, England in our age surpassed all nations.'

The modern world has been curiously deluded about the staging of the finest body of dramatic literature produced since the age of Pericles. So far from restoring to this drama its ample open stage upon which the designer is free to mount that stately 'variety and magnificence' for

which it was unequalled, we have not only robbed it of
its decoration but laboured vainly to put much of it into
the strait-jacket of an imaginary, awkward, and remote
double-storeyed alcove. But now that the Works Accounts
have opened our eyes to the fact that Shakespeare's stage,
both on the Bankside and at Whitehall, was a complete
circus or arena stage, nothing is gained by flogging a dead
horse of theory. It is more humane to let the unfortunate
illusion of 'alcove stages' softly and suddenly vanish
away.

From these dark and remote pigeon-holes of myth we
turn with relief to the actual open stage which Shakespeare used. We see the free-standing, painted and stately
mansions or *houses* set well out upon it, where necessary
over traps giving understage communication with the
tiring-house, and artfully placed so as to present the minimum of obstruction to an encircling audience. How
successfully this was done is attested by foreign visitors,
who reported that 'everyone can well see it all', that
'from all parts the spectators most conveniently could see
everything'. At last we understand why the public stage
was forty-three feet long: to provide room to set the
mansions near the ends of the oblong, and yet leave
plenty of neutral acting-space in the middle. With their
curtains drawn away, we see the *mansions* showing the
famous scenes 'within' and 'above' not in a distant alcove
but in the centre of the audience.

We see *Romeo and Juliet*, for example, with all its
scenes ready set in view before the performance begins:
the Capulets' open, pillared hall; their house adjoining,
with a framework room and window somewhat higher,
for Juliet's bedroom 'above', looking out over the orchard

and wall; Friar Laurence's modest cell and the pillared Capulet monument, both standing open, to be enclosed with curtains when their time comes; and at the 'Mantua' end of the stage, the little apothecary's shop. This traditional and age-old staging with *mansions* was so much taken for granted that it was rarely mentioned. I do find it referred to, however, in Ben Jonson. When the rascally Captain Tucca (in *The Poetaster*) vows revenge, should the players satirize him on the public stage, we naturally do not find him threatening to tear down the curtains of their inner stage or to rip out the hangings of their balcony, because those things did not exist. But he does vow to wreck their costly scenic 'mansions' and canvas 'houses': 'And you stage me, stinkard, your *mansions* shall sweat for't, your *tabernacles*, varlets, your Globes . . .'

Aloft and *above* in these small-scale *mansions* need be only a few feet. This is clear both from the speeches and from the stage directions in *Antony and Cleopatra*. Here the boys acting Cleopatra and her maids, *aloft* in the locked monument, help to 'draw up' the dying Antony while the guards heave him from below. Feasible enough, if the *aloft* is no more than some six feet up, and the boys can lean out to draw him in when *They heave Antony aloft to Cleopatra*. But if the operation had involved the problem of hoisting an inert body up to a 'balcony stage' twelve feet above the floor, it is safe to say Shakespeare would never have written the scene.

On an arena stage scenery inevitably takes its proper subordinate place, as little more than large and sightly *properties*. And that is in fact what those small-scale *mansions* were. Not so large as seriously to obstruct the view. Consisting chiefly of pillared open framework, with curtains briefly closed for concealment when required; when drawn away to reveal action 'within'—as the Capulet tomb—or 'above'—as Cleopatra's Monument—the framework is left transpicuous, to be seen through from every side, creating an impression both of reality and evanescence.

Shakespeare's stage must have been a perfect place, both for dramatic poetry and for the player. An intimate centre of the enfolding audience's life, as the warm heart lives, focus of the body. It is no wonder that Elizabethan playhouses were noted rather for music than for scenic effects. For on an arena-stage poetic drama is communicated less like painting and more like music: not an animated picture presented *yonder*, but a harmony of sound, sense, and motion springing *here*, in the very midst. To such a stage, *perspective* is as irrelevant as it is to an orchestra-platform. And like the instrumental soloist, the speaking actor becomes the focal point primarily of ears rather than eyes. On rediscovering him as an executant of dramatic poetry in the centre of his audience, we can at length perceive the force of the contemporary appreciation of the great actor, which saw imaginary 'lines drawn from the circumference of so many ears, whiles the Actor is the *Center*'.

IV

COMEDIA IN THE GREAT CHAMBER

THIS new revelation of Shakespeare's stage makes an impressive addition to our equipment for visualizing *how the thing was done*. Moreover, in studying those rich Works Accounts, I find illuminating details of the arrangement and decoration of particular rooms and buildings in the Palace of Whitehall which permit us to see something of what Shakespeare saw. With such strong encouragement to vividness, I am tempted to embody the fresh material in a piece of imaginative reconstruction: in the mind's eye to follow the players to a command performance at Whitehall.

Two reasons lead me to choose for this attempt Shakespeare's performance on St. Stephen's Night, December 26, 1600: the occasion when Queen Elizabeth interpreted the play to her German guest, Wolfgang Wilhelm. First, because it adds the experience of a play's production in the Great Chamber to the description of *Twelfth Night* in the Hall, to which we are leading up. And second, because I have reason to believe that it was on this very St. Stephen's Night at Whitehall that Shakespeare received the order to prepare a comedy for the coming Twelfth Night, eleven days later.

London, the day after Christmas, 1600. Half-past six o'clock, and a dark winter's night.

We are shivering under the penthouse of a barber's shop just inside Ludgate, when we catch sight of the players we have been waiting for—a compact mounted troop of some twenty, cloaked against the sharp weather, lighted and led by two outriders, each with staff-torch in stirrup-holster, heading towards us from St. Paul's down Bowyers' Row.

Nine months before this evening, a drunken knot of wild young bloods, Sir Edmond Bainham and his Roaring Boys, were wounded and captured on this spot—after leaving the Mermaid Tavern for a midnight battle with the watch.[1] And six short weeks in the future, this same spot will resound with the shots, cries, and clashing steel of the desperate Essex and his rebels in their last fight with soldiers of the Queen: the dangerous *innovation* or rebellion that will result in the *inhibition* of public plays in the City, which Shakespeare will mention in his tragedy of *Hamlet*.

On this St. Stephen's Night, however, our mounted company have enough on their minds without such memories and impossible peeps into the future. Yesterday their Christmas was sacrificed to hard final rehearsing. And today the afternoon performance at the Globe has left scarce time for dressing, and snatching a bite of supper before putting foot in stirrup. Their riding-cloaks cover handsome gold chains and livery coats of fine blue cloth, bearing below the left shoulder their noble master's cognizance, a silver swan flying—the badge which, as well as being 'the proper ensigne of Poetrie ... the swanne', gave their great poet his nickname, the *sweet Swan of Avon*. For these are the Servants of the Right Honourable, the Baron Hunsdon, Lord Chamberlain of Her Majesty's Household, the finest company of actors in Christendom.

---

[1] See my *Shakespeare's Sonnets Dated* (1949), 89–110.

And on this first of the year's high holidays of Christmas, they are off on their two-mile ride to Westminster and the Palace of Whitehall, to play by command before the Queen. Ready waiting for them at Court are their scenes and properties, under the care of the officers of the Revels. Several boys riding quick-stepping little Galloways follow the leaders close. A group of attendants brings up the rear, their nags' cruppers burdened with round-packed cloakbags and awkward hampers, in which the boys' kirtles, farthingales, and dress wigs take up disproportionate room.

As they pass out of the City through the dark and gated arch under Ludgate Prison, with its guardian statues of Queen Elizabeth and 'King Lud', we may allow the wag among the boys to begin on the stale jest—about how it takes two Sovereigns to support the threescore bankrupts caged overhead under the leads of Ludgate. But the attempt is drowned by the loud clapping under their noses of a wooden dish, and the high-whining plain-song of the jail's official beggar—'*Pity the poor prisoners!*' The wail from 'King *Luds* unlucky gate' still hangs in their ears through the squelch of hoofs in the descent to Fleet Bridge past the old playing inn, the Bell Savage.

Climbing Fleet Street hill holds them to a walk. Under the creaking signs on each side of the street, the narrow pavements overflow with foot-passengers. The required candle-lantern glows at every householder's door, but windows alow and aloft are also shining with unwonted light. The many taverns are loud with merry-making and holiday cheer, above all the Greyhound and the Mitre on the left.

Chancery Lane end, and Temple Bar—where the

seasonable Three Kings tavern-sign looks forward to Twelfth Night. Then, on the bridle hand, Essex House at the foot of its courtyard, blazing with lights, its gate busy with horsemen and coaches. Now the thickly-built suburbs are falling behind. The outriders' torches pierce the dark, as they trace the muddy Strand towards Westminster. Cottages backed with sleeping gardens and wintry fields on the right, and a succession of handsome river-palaces and mansions standing in spacious grounds on the left—Somerset House, the Savoy, York House. Then the lofty Charing Cross looms ahead. Wheeling left as the torchlight flickers on that stately and dilapidated memorial, they close ranks, and touch up their mounts for a brisk step southwards down the King's road to Whitehall Palace. Traffic thickens.

As the troop approaches the arch of the Court Gate on their left, flames leaping from the iron ribs of its cressets throw a wavering glare over an indescribable swarm. Coaches, horsemen, and people on foot, worming a slow, painful progress through a beleaguering horde of 'stare-abouts'. A posse of the Knight Marshal's men are laying about them freely to make some way for the traffic. Closing up for protection round the boys and the luggage, the troop of actors by a blend of determination and cajolery can at last press close enough to call out, 'Master Porter, my Lord Chamberlain's Players!' And at that they must throw back their cloaks and show livery and badges before those club-swinging infidels, the porter's men, will suffer them to edge through the opening.

Now, and drawing a freer breath, they are inside the base court—the great flare-lit yard, all its flanking ranges of battlemented buildings gleaming with the Queen's colours: swan-white, trimmed with shining jet black. Immediately on their right hand rises the huge painted Banqueting House, empty and dark—Elizabeth's wooden 'dancing barn'. That was built for masques and banquets, and the Queen does not use it for plays.[1] Before it on the right extends the broad Terrace, adorned with gorgeously coloured and carved heraldic beasts, topped with gilded vanes, and standing on white pillars. In the midst lies the open-air 'preaching place' dominated by its rich and stately pulpit.

Without a pause, the players clatter straight ahead on the causeway, along a gallant file of white masts or flagpoles towards the main range of royal chambers forming the head of the quadrangle. Before they reach the massive stone staircase going up to the Great Chamber and the Court proper, they draw rein and dismount at an archway on the left, leading to the Stables. Here they find the Chamberlain's man and a Groom of the Revels appointed to meet them. By the time the former has summoned stable-boys to take their horses, the actors have their animals ready unloaded. Carrying their baggage, they are led by the Groom through several covered ways threading the Offices, to a chamber not far from the Buttery.

It is certainly a place small enough, but it holds a half-dozen torch-candles, a bright coal fire, benches, and a couple of hand mirrors. They set down their bags and riding-cloaks, take a moment to warm themselves. Then, having posted a guard, out after the Groom and on to

---

[1] There is no evidence that a play was ever presented in the Banqueting House before James's reign. The impression given by page 125 of Miss Marchette Chute's *Shakespeare of London* is erroneous.

the Buttery for their 'bever'. They follow with a cheerful tread, well aware that this is Christmas—that the 'bouche of Court' passed out over the Buttery-bar will be no penny-a-quart dull ale or drowsy beer, sad stuff for sprightly sack-drinkers, but the best revel-ale: a rare brew, strong enough to make a cat speak.

There is passionate crowding at the Buttery hatch, and they watch their Groom with concern as he battles his way through. But when he staggers forth at last, heated from the press, he has a long string of cans round his neck and a huge leathern 'blackjack' in each fist, foaming with as much of the precious liquor as the players dare to drink. While the ale is going down and fetching up their spirits, the Groom unbends sufficiently to impart the immediate gossip of the Court. Her Highness, he tells them, will have a special guest at their play—a young Bavarian Duke or Count Palatine, a Lutheran called Wolfgang Wilhelm, just come back to London from a brief tour to Oxford and Woodstock, where it is said the Queen appointed him to be shown good entertainment and fair usage. This afternoon at the dancing in the Presence Chamber, her Grace conversed with him. And the actors may be interested to learn that, at the Queen's desire, their master my Lord Chamberlain has even now had this Bavarian to a noble supper in his palace lodging, with a number of other lords and persons of mark.

Though Robin Armin would like a look at the German—he might pick up a useful mannerism or two—the prospect of such a guest-spectator with her Majesty before them in the Great Chamber is not the best news for the players. Ten to one the Bavarian has less than a poor pennyworth of English, and someone will be audibly interpreting for him, running over the meaning in short speeches while they perform. But what of that? They are graduates of a stern school, the multitudinous audiences at the Curtain and the Globe. Who but they for triumphing over noise and interruption?

Yet their immediate cue is dispatch, for they must be ready and waiting in the Great Chamber when the Queen comes forth from the Presence before nine o'clock to see the last and choicest of the courtiers' dancing which precedes the play. So, after tossing off a final round to their own success, and knocking on wood to avert the evil eye, they are quickly back, refreshed, in their narrow quarters, pulling off riding-boots and livery, and making themselves ready in the rich costumes. Every detail of the boys' dressing and head-tires in particular receives the closest and most expert attention. The lads are built up into astonishing counterfeits of the Court ladies whose searching scrutiny they will soon undergo. And like magic, with the busks, padding, farthingales, fans, and head-dresses the boys take on the port, the pace, the gestures, smiles, and glances, the very accent of courtly dames and maids—enough to fool their own mothers. As for their improved 'complexions', Burbage is a portrait-painter, and their making-up must pass his inspection.

Meanwhile the business manager, Heminges, as soon as he is dressed has sallied forth on the company's behalf, escorted by the Groom of the Revels, to examine the scenic properties. These have already been moved to the scene of their performance. They are not to act in the Hall—that spacious and massive stone building with lofty beamed roof and tiled floor, standing near the Chapel, below and eastward of the quadrangle, but in the Great

Chamber—the Court's outermost or entrance chamber, reached by the main stairs from the courtyard. This room begins the Court's principal range—the Great, Presence, and Privy Chambers. It is also known as the Guard Chamber,[1] being the appointed post of the seven score huge beef-eating Yeomen under their Captain, Sir Walter Ralegh: red-coated giants 'big enough to throw Charing Cross for a bar'. Though it cannot equal the Hall for size, in other respects the Great or Guard Chamber is better for dancing and plays. In this bitter weather it can be more comfortably heated with a great coal fire. Instead of a cavernous open roof like the Hall's, it is covered by an ornamented and fretted ceiling of hard plaster, excellent for voices. And the floor is of wood: far better for dancing than tiles—even tiles cushioned with rush matting. Seven majestic tapestries adorn the lofty walls, depicting the Seven Deadly Sins,[2] placed there by Queen Elizabeth to give both her staff and her visitors sound matter for reflection before approaching the Presence Chamber within.

What Heminges sees—when the Groom has at last got him up through the crowd thronging the steps before the door, and past the platoon of powerful Yeomen Ushers defending it—is the Great Chamber not only lavishly lighted with hundreds of great candles in branches hung on wires stretched across the room, but transformed by

---

[1] Sir Edmund Chambers (*Elizabethan Stage*, I. 14, 216) mistakenly thought that at Whitehall the Great Chamber and the Guard Chamber were distinct and different rooms. And J. Q. Adams (*Shakespearean Playhouses*, 387) confused the Great Chamber with the Hall.

[2] 'Goe through the great chamber (why is it hung with the seaven deadly sinnes?) . . .'   John Donne, Satyre IV.

the carpenters of the Office of Works into a circus, an amphitheatre. Wooden 'degrees', or tiers of seats covered with green baize, have been erected against all the four walls. Those against the long sides of the Chamber under the Seven Deadly Sins have three banks of seats; but the one at the head of the room has seven, while that against the lower end, where he is standing, towers ten tiers high. Between the scaffolds, space has been left only for the Queen's door near the head on the corridor side, for the majestic mantel enclosing the glowing mass of the coal fire, and for the double entrance door at the lower end. On a carpeted podium in front of the high stand at the head of the chamber is set a rich canopied throne for the Queen, while on the floor red velvet cushions are ready to seat selected ladies. Remaining open in the centre is an oblong about twenty feet wide and some twenty-five feet long. This is the floor for dancing; and when the dancing comes to an end, it will serve as a stage for Burbage, Shakespeare, and their fellows to present the comedy.

It is already nearly half-past eight o'clock, and the stands in the lower half of the room are crowded with courtiers of both sexes glittering in their choicest apparel and jewels, intent on the performance of some of the Court's most skilful dancers—white satin revellers moving in the preliminary stately measures or quick corantos, to the music of a large and excellent consort of viols. The throne and all the scaffolds in the upper part of the room stand empty, guarded by Yeomen with their halberds, awaiting the Queen and her brilliant procession.

Just within the door, and in the shadow of the lofty stand against the lower end of the room, Heminges takes in the position at a practised glance. But his business is to make sure that everything is ready and right for the play; and with the Groom of the Revels he turns in under the high scaffold, into the twilight of a forest of timbers supporting the crowded boards overhead. A half-dozen scene-men in Revels livery are sitting in ambush here. With them Heminges expertly reviews the scenery, propped in a collapsed or folded state against the wall. It consists of cunningly-hinged frames—filled either with painted canvas or with curtains running on rods—fitted with cloth roofs or tops, and measuring about seven or eight feet in height. These light graceful units, when carried out to the acting-floor, opened, set up, and internally braced, will in miniature represent mansions, palaces, pavilions, or whatever definitely localized scenes the play calls for. Every 'place' will be set up before the play begins, to be used when its time in the action comes. Nothing will be shifted during the performance. A scene 'within' will be shown in a curtained unit, the curtains drawn away to reveal the interior from every side. For a scene 'above' at a window, or 'on the walls', small steps or raised platforms will be concealed inside to give additional height. But here the scale of the 'mansions' is small, for they are to be used in a crowded chamber. (In the Great Chamber at Richmond, less spacious than Whitehall's, the players in 1588 had a stage only fourteen feet square.) And these 'mansions' will be set right and left at the edges of the acting-space: for since the floor is cleared for dancing, and the play must follow immediately after, no stage is provided. They must act on the floor, without any advantage of height.

The Groom has meanwhile gone back to fetch the actors, ready waiting in their makeshift green-room; and by the time that Heminges is satisfied that the scene-men understand exactly where and how the 'mansions' and smaller properties are to be set in relation to each other for exits and entrances, and to allow the maximum of neutral acting-space between them, the rest of the company has edged in through the thronged door, and stands attending the entrance of the Queen. Soon the Gentleman Usher sounds a warning; the preliminary dancing is brought to a close, the dancers retire from the floor. A pause of expectancy, then hark, the trumpets! They are coming on: the clang of twelve shrill-tongued trumpets announces the royal approach, and everyone rises to his feet. The procession is advancing from the Presence Chamber along the corridor, and will enter by the Queen's door.

Now the head of it appears: first the trumpets, sounding the flourish; then the heralds in their coats of arms; then the nobles and knights of the Garter, with the Bavarian Wolfgang Wilhelm among them, led by the Lord Chamberlain, marshalling the train with his white staff. He is also Captain of the band of fifty richly-coated Gentlemen Pensioners, the Nearest Guard, who with their gilt poleaxes form the hedge on each side. Immediately before the canopy of the Queen, on whom all eyes are fixed, comes the crimson-sheathed Sword borne by an Earl, and the Great Seal by the Lord Keeper. Following the Queen, and 'keeping their state' two and two, come her white-clad Maids—'Beauties that light the Court, and make it show Like a fair heaven in a frosty night'. Then her Majesty's Ladies of Honour, and other ladies of high mark.

Now the trumpets call a halt, and the Queen is escorted

QUEEN ELIZABETH DANCING

to the throne by the Lord Chamberlain. Then he over-
sees the seating of all on the 'degrees' and cushions according to rank, by his gentlemen ushers. When they
report the room marshalled to his satisfaction, and the
Queen is pleased, he signals the music to play a favour
for the dancing.

Let us seize the moment for an effort to understand
what dancing and the music inseparable from it meant to
these Elizabethans. Unquestionably it stood as their
favourite art, exercise, and pleasure—even surpassing the
drama—and they cultivated it to a degree which made the
English dancers supreme in Europe. 'Amongst pleasures
which ravish [English]men's senses with delight, not
any one is more coveted than that of dancing.' Spaniards
delighted in riding, the French in courtship, and 'the
dancing English, in carrying a fair presence'. The German Hentzner was but one of the travellers who observed
that 'the English excel in dancing and music'.

This national expertness and delight obliged pro-
fessional actors to be dancers first and foremost. From the
start they learned 'to move in music'. Indeed, in the list of
the player's necessary qualities, *elocution* came fifth: 'dancing, activity [acrobatics], music, song, elocution'. And
when the actors appeared at Court, offering dancing and
music in their comedies, they were very much on their
mettle. For not only were they under the eye of Elizabeth, who bodied forth the very spirit of it—danced 'high
and disposedly' from her childhood, and in the last years
of her life would still tread the nimble galliard, five steps
and a leap, in select company with a French duke—but
also they were before a Court which held the flower of a
dancing nation. Theirs was an art as subtle as modern

ballet, and it was not limited to a few practitioners. We find even the critical Ben Jonson sounding its praise :

> For dancing is an exercise
>   Not only shows the mover's wit
> But maketh the beholder wise
>   As he hath power to rise to it.

And Beaumont and Fletcher soar high to describe a lady's exquisite dancing at Court:

> How like the nimble winds, which play upon
> The tender grass, yet press it not; or fly
> Over the crystal face of smoothest streams,
> Leaving no curl behind them . . . Why, she makes
> Motion the god of every excellence,
> And what the Muses would with study find
> She teaches in her dancing.

No wonder that the whole afternoon at Whitehall has been devoted to measures, pavans, galliards, lavoltas, and country dances, which Wolfgang Wilhelm described as 'continued'; or that now after supper come more hours of dancing, with the most skilled taking the floor amid delight and acclaim. 'You shall see the court ladies move like goddesses, as if they trod air. They will swim you their measures'—and with partners such as 'Mr. Palmer, the admirablest dancer of the time' will show *lavoltas high, and swift corantos, telling the music's numbers with their feet.*

The dances flow, change, and follow, with the best reserved to the last, under Elizabeth's keen and appreciative eye. She is in her sixty-eighth year, but *Ever the Same.* Her dancing days are far from done; she not only follows with moving hand and tapping foot, but like a master who demands perfection, exclaims at faults invisible to most eyes. From their corner at the lower end of the room, the players watch absorbed—their souls of harmonious motion drawn away—almost forgetting how soon their own turn will come.

Now the grand final dance is winding to its close. Applause and excited buzz mark the end; the dancers honour the throne and retire to their places, while the Queen chats affably in Latin with the young Bavarian prince standing near her side with Lord Grey. My Lord Chamberlain Hunsdon, who has charge of the room from his 'standing' on her Highness's right hand near the upper door, signs with his staff to the music to play. The actors have pulled themselves together, and made way for the teams of scene-men who have the folded 'mansions' and the properties ready in hand, waiting the word. The watching Chamberlain catches a beck from the Queen, and up goes his staff in a second signal. Instantly the scene-men hasten forward with their burdens. First bowing low to the throne, they swiftly unfold, set, and brace the cunningly-painted and richly-curtained scenes at the sides of the open floor, place the smaller properties, bow again, and withdraw.

Then the Lord Chamberlain cries, 'Sound, trumpets! Sound out!' And with the shrill flourish still ringing in their ears, his players advance up the chamber in a body— to make their three obeisances, and at once to distribute themselves: a few into the 'mansions' for entrances later, others low on the green rush matting at the sides, waiting 'invisible' for their cues to appear. When they are set, the Lord Chamberlain raises his white staff—a touch on the trumpets, and he cries in a loud voice, 'Peace! Ha' peace!'

The universal hum and buzz from the high-encircling audience dies, and the play begins.

What comedy that audience heard, we do not know; and if the Bavarian prince was told its name, he did not record it. But with Shakespeare's and Burbage's next Court performance, eleven days after this night, in the Hall beyond, the case is altered. For with the Queen on Twelfth Night we shall be witnessing nothing else than *Twelfth Night*.

V

MALVOLIO

EVERY play must have some kind of occasion, some-thing to call it into being. And the name and nature of Shakespeare's Duke Orsino must have had a starting-point in time. I strongly suspect that the exciting cause of the play *Twelfth Night* is to be found in the news from Lyons which reached Sir Harry Neville in London on Christmas Day, 1600.

Neville was Queen Elizabeth's ambassador to Henri IV, and in his absence Ralph Winwood was very ably attending the French Court as English agent, and report-ing regularly to Sir Harry. Winwood's news, written on December 4,[1] informed Neville of the imminent depar-ture from Lyons of the Duke of Bracciano, Don Virginio Orsino, with his two gentlemen, to visit the Court of Queen Elizabeth.

Such news must be imparted to her Majesty without de-lay; and we may be certain that she had it by the next morning, December 26, St. Stephen's Day, the first of her Court's twelve days of high Christmas revels and festival. To account for what we shall find was the result, we must here resort to conjecture for an approximate notion of what passed. The Queen would at once set about making plans to entertain the head of the ancient Guelph House of Orsini, with which—as we shall see—she held she was allied by descent: a welcome befitting her princely cousin. Shakespeare later voiced her thought in Olivia's

---

[1] P.R.O., State Papers, France, S.P. 78/44/354.

words: 'he says he'll come. How shall I feast him? what bestow of him?' And Winwood could not fail to have represented to the Italian gentlemen the advantages of arriving at the English Court before the grand close of the Christmas festivities—the Twelfth Day, observed with most imperial state. Four weeks' travel-time from Lyons to London, barring sickness or accident, was ample. A courier covered the distance, when the Channel was favourable, in seventeen days. An excellent chance, therefore, that the noble Orsino might be her guest of honour at banqueting, Court dancing, and comedy on the highest day of all, Twelfth Day, January 6. *For he that mighty states hath feasted, knows Besides their meat, they must be fed with shows.* The Court delights prepared for the Duke, Orsino, must be of the rarest and most fitting, under the direction of the Lord Chamberlain of her Household. This is her favourite cousin 'good George', as she calls him, the fifty-three-year-old Lord Hunsdon, suffering from poor health, but still discharging the exacting duties of his great office.

Time is short, but Elizabeth is a mistress of improvisation, and rises to the challenge. She calls in her Chamberlain and opens the matter to him at once. Her skilled musicians are prepared always, the Court dancers ready; but the play? What fit of mirth, what comedy shall we have to sum the crownéd day? Let it be a play furnished with rich apparel, have great variety and change of music and dances; and let the subject or matter of it be pleasant. For such a feast, the best poets must use choicest and most rare invention to entertain the time. She knows what an ace Hunsdon holds in the person of his servant Shake-speare—at the height of his powers at the age of thirty-six. As we know, Hunsdon's company of players, led by Shakespeare and Burbage, have established a clear supremacy at Court. He will see at once what may be had.

That same St. Stephen's Night, at the close of their comedy well after midnight in the crowded Great Chamber before the Queen and her noble young Bavarian guest, Hunsdon sends for Shakespeare to come to his lodging in the palace. He imparts the information about the Duke, outlining the position which will doubtless face them in ten days' time, and require a suitable play on Twelfth Night. The Court, by special summons, will be so full that several companies will be commanded to perform on that night. Both the Great Chamber and the Hall will be used for plays, the Hall by her Majesty. The Lord Admiral's men plan to present Dekker's *Phaëthon*. This is a piece refurbished by its author, in which the discontented Lord Essex's faction at Court may usefully read a warning against encouraging his exorbitant ambition: the fatal folly of aspiring to guide the heavenly car—the Chariot of the Sun. *These strong court factions, that do brook no checks, In the career oft break the riders' necks.* But this *Phaëthon*, while very timely for Essex's followers at Court who would lend an ear to such sentiments as 'I'll not be coop'd up: room for Phaëthon!' is clearly not the light-hearted thing her Majesty would have to please her guest with.

Shakespeare remarks that for months past Ben Jonson has been in full competition for the Queen's ear on Twelfth Night. For Ben makes no secret that his *Cynthia's Revels*, now in rehearsal with the newly set-up Children of her Majesty's Chapel, has been contrived with no other purpose. It employs Twelfth Night topicalities with its satire on Court abuses, and brings in the Queen as Diana-Cynthia, justifying her punishment of Actæon-Essex's audacity in having rushed into her chamber after deserting his post in Ireland.

Lord Hunsdon replies that Jonson may be 'early up', but is never the nearer for that. Mr. Tilney, the Master of the Revels, has shown him the copy of Jonson's comedy, and they are agreed that it will never do. Not only is there no courtly matter of love in it, but the piece is laboured and tedious. Ben has too arrogantly followed the unsavoury sharpness of his humour; the courtiers and the ladies are very shrewishly handled; his taunts are too salt, too bitter, sure to be distasted. In brief, it is a satire keen and critical, ill sorting with the jovial mirth of Twelfth Night. Shakespeare well knows how deeply the Court's rebuff will wound Ben's vanity, but there is no help for it.

His own company is not unprovided with a recent and cheerful courtly comedy in *As You Like It*; but that has already been exposed to view. As his master says, what is wanted here is something fire-new, full of music and love; something specially designed to please her Majesty and compliment her guest. Shakespeare inquires about this Don Virginio Orsino the Duke, and Hunsdon refers him for information to my Lord of Rutland's brother, Mr. Francis Manners, or to Mr. Secretary's nephew, Mr. William Cecil. They have both lately visited the Tuscan Court at Florence; either of them should be able to give the poet a good description and brief history of the young Duke. But besides courtly love high-fantastical, with well-turned compliment to the Queen and the Duke, the play must have tricks, devices, and mad hieroglyphics which all can read. For Twelfth Night is the golden saturnalia, the ancient feast of liberty when the man changes places with the master, when servants may say what they list of their lords, who must take all in good part; the mad revel when 'they play new pranks and gambols—no man's person, of what degree soever, free from abuses', the hilarious annual test of the orderly world by standing it on its head.

All this is common ground to Lord Hunsdon and Shakespeare. They know, too, that in any domestical merriment the very happiness of the jest lies in the skilful choice and handling of the butt, who must be a 'master' in the Court. Yet if a great man is to be madly flouted and scouted in drollery, the suggestion must come from authority; and Shakespeare waits for the word—the matter for invention to play on. It comes soon enough. Hunsdon suggests some sport with 'Mr. Controller'. When Shakespeare has it written, let him show it to Mr. Tilney and to him. If it is deftly done, the poet need have no uneasiness. Hunsdon will be his warrant with her Majesty.

Shakespeare has no more than this for a start, but it is enough. If he is to offer appropriate flowers of compliment to the Italian duke, he must learn about him with no delay. In ten or eleven days the play must be written and licensed, the parts cast and memorized, the production perfected in rehearsal, and performed. And this was in the festive season of Christmas, between the company's regular daily performances. The feat seems superhuman to our slower minds. But we recall Cleopatra's well-grounded fear—'the quick comedians Extemporally will stage us'—and the tradition that Shakespeare wrote *The*

Merry Wives of Windsor at the Queen's desire in ten days' time. Quicker still, Francis Beaumont's *Knight of the Burning Pestle* was written and performed within eight days. Shakespeare, famed for 'great quickness and invention', was not less able than Beaumont; and Leonard Digges—who, as stepson of Shakespeare's trusted Thomas Russell, knew the poet intimately—testifies that play-making seemed no 'work' to the poet: 'for to contrive a play To him 'twas none'. Feats more astonishing were accomplished by contemporaries. Pérez de Montalbán said he composed five three-act comedies in fifteen days, while Lope de Vega boasted that 'more than a hundred of my comedies have taken only twenty-four hours to pass from my brain to the boards'. The Prologue to *Gl' Ingannati*— the Sienese ancestor of Shakespeare's comedy—tells the audience it was 'put together and shaped' in three days.

As for the personal jesting required to give the play superlative snap and sparkle, it would be solidly in the tradition. The time-honoured saturnalian mockery drew its Christian sanction from combating self-love, 'the most inhibited sin in the canon'. In ridiculing ignorant fantastical pride, it aimed to teach a man to know himself, and to take him a peg lower for his own good. Castiglione had particularly warned the courtier against 'self liking and ignorance', and Jonson's comical Twelfth Night satire on the Court, *The Fountain of Self-love, or Cynthia's Revels*, closed with a prayer against 'all self-loving humours'. Ovid's 'self-lov'd Narcissus' furnished the accepted type, and the daffodil's colour, yellow, symbolized the vice. A Twelfth Night *Narcissus* had been played at Court in 1572, and two years after the date of our story, in 1603, St. John's College, Oxford, put

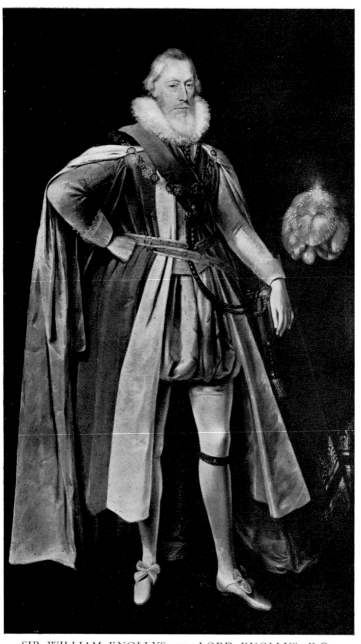

SIR WILLIAM KNOLLYS, 1ST LORD KNOLLYS, K.G.,
EARL OF BANBURY

on their own *Narcissus, A Twelfth Night Merriment*.

To this point we have followed our fresh conjecture about the genesis of Shakespeare's *Twelfth Night*. If that conjecture is sound, the prime jest, pleasant and without scurrility, audacious without impudency, but sharpened with plenty of sportful malice, was to be on the self-conceit of 'Mr. Controller', otherwise Sir William Knollys (pronounced, and often written, *Knowles*), P.C., M.P., Comptroller of her Majesty's Household. The controller, as the name suggests, was the officer who checked expenditure on the Court's diet and other running charges, and acted as chief overseer of all the household servants—took them to task, kept them in order. These servants of the Queen were men of all ranks, and numbered in their hundreds. At this moment Knollys was in fact even more prominent than usual. The five principal officers of the Household, who carried a white staff[1]—both as the symbol of their commission and as a cudgel they did not hesitate to use—were headed by the Lord Steward (the Earl of Nottingham, Lord Admiral), the Lord Chamberlain (Lord Hunsdon), and the Master of the Horse (deputy without staff, Lord Worcester, since the disgrace of Essex). After these came the Treasurer (vacant),[2] and the Controller (Sir William Knollys). But because of the disgrace of Essex and the vacancy of the Treasurership, Knollys at this time wielded the only white staff under the commanding officers Nottingham and Hunsdon, as chief

---

[1] Lord Hunsdon is depicted with his white staff in the painting reproduced opposite page 105. He is the third chief figure from the left.

[2] Roger Lord North, Treasurer of the Household, had died early in December. His office is not to be confused with the greater one of Lord Treasurer, held by Thomas Sackville Lord Buckhurst.

working subordinate in getting things done. Whether or not the access of importance and power—especially during Hunsdon's recent illness—went to his head and made him stubborn and officious, it is certain that the Court would find it delicious to have him singled out for sport: as inevitable a target as a sergeant-major.

Knollys was first cousin to Hunsdon, and both were equally Queen Elizabeth's first cousins once removed: that is, their grandmother, Mary Bullen, was the Queen's aunt. He was also the Earl of Essex's uncle; and though he had been numbered with the Essex faction, he left it in time, and his personal loyalty to the Queen remained unquestionable. For the disgruntled Essex faction, his defection naturally branded him a 'time-pleaser' or time-server.

His father, the godly and puritanical Sir Francis Knollys,[1] though he was no revolutionary, had always been the Puritans' staunch defender, herein stoutly opposing his royal cousin. For the Queen never concealed her strong dislike of innovations and sectaries in religion. Her distaste was heartily shared by most of her Court, who also found the Puritan opposition to dancing, harmless sports, and entertainments, unreasonably sour. Just a year before this Christmas, a courtier had presented a versified New Year's offering to his Queen, embodying 'an invective against the Puritans . . . the danger of innovations, the poison of sectaries, and perilous it is to shake religion at the root by licentious disputes and doctrines' and also 'against the same Puritans, a desire of courtiers, and all ancient courtly usages, devised as well for the public entertainments as for private solaces and disports, not scandalously evil or vicious'.

---

[1] J. E. Neale, *Elizabeth I and her Parliaments* (1952), 57, 300–3.

Now, a most notorious hotbed of Puritans was the parliamentary borough of Banbury in Oxfordshire. Along with the fanatic zeal of its psalm-singing weavers,[1] among the familiar connotations of Banbury were numbered not only its famous cakes and twanging ale, but also the tradition of its terrible rigour in hanging vagrant tinkers—'Tinkers, what a town is't!' 'A tinker . . . If he scape Tyburn and Banbury, he dies a beggar.' The 'memorable execution of Tinkers in this town'[2] had become proverbial at least as early as 1593, when to any tinker the insulting cry, 'To Banbury, tinker!' meant 'Go hang!'[3] As for 'Mr. Controller' and this same hot-Puritan Banbury of soulful singing weavers, cakes and ale, and 'a rope for tinkers', we shall see that Shakespeare made good use of all these topicalities; moreover it is clear that the Banburians were so intimate with Sir William Knollys, the Privy Councillor, important Member of Parliament for Oxfordshire,[4] and their old defender's son, that they later chose him for their High Steward; and when he

---

[1] ' . . . more devout Than a Weaver of Banbury, that hopes to intice Heaven, by singing, to make him lord Of twenty looms.' Davenant, *The Wits* (1636), Act I.

[2] 'Banbury . . . famous for its cakes and ale', J. Muirhead, Baedeker's *Great Britain*. 'Banbury cakes . . . have a reputation of three centuries' standing', *Encycl. Brit.*, art. 'Banbury'. For the 'Brother of Banbury', 'Banbury man', or Banburian baker, Zeal-of-the-Land Busy, and the cakes he made for bride-ales, see Jonson's *Bartholomew Fair*, I. 3, and Herford and Simpson's *Jonson*, 10. 171. For the ale, witness the rousing catch in Ravenscroft's *Pammelia* (1609): *Banbury ale! where, where, where?* Of the quotations on tinkers, the sources are Richard Corbet, *Iter Boreale*; Overbury *Characters*, 1614; *The English Post from severall Parts of the Kingdome*, 1641.

[3] See my *I, William Shakespeare* (1937), 87.

[4] For the Knollys family and the Puritan representation of Banbury in Parliament, see J. E. Neale, *The Elizabethan House of Commons*, 1949.

achieved greatness in the third order of the peerage, it was as the Earl of Banbury.

Another well-known circumstance about Mr. Controller was that his lodging at Whitehall stood at the end of the Tiltyard, which contained the Bear-stake. To this stake was brought the 'royal game'—bears and bulls matched to fight great mastiffs and bulldogs, for the entertainment of foreign ambassadors and the Queen's distinguished visitors. Dangerous accidents at the Tiltyard baitings were not unknown. Only a few seasons before this,

there was a great bull which brake loose from the stake and ran amongst the people, and ran over 300 people; and the Queen, seeing him run amongst them, cried 'Jesus, save my people! Jesus, save my people!' very often; but for all his running over them there was no hurt.[1]

A reporter more religious would have written '*so*, for all his running' etc. The Queen's prayer was granted. The exciting game never failed to attract a huge and tumultuous throng of the populace, far overflowing the Tiltyard, and obstructing all traffic near Mr. Controller's lodging. He need be no Puritan to take a very dark view, both of the yells of 'To head! To head! Fight, dog! Fight, bear!' and of the unruly obstruction which the 'brutish exercise' brought in its train.

But easily the most vulnerable aspect of Knollys at this particular moment was his notorious relation to the latest piquant scandal, which linked Mistress Mary ('Mal' or 'Mall')[2] Fitton with young William Lord Herbert. To

---

[1] Hist. MSS. Comm., *Ninth Report*, App. II, 389.

[2] *Mal* or *Mall*, the common spelling of the nickname for *Mary*, now written *Moll*. The Folio text has 'mistris *Mals* picture'. In

catch the full flavour of the situation, we must recall events of five years before. In 1595 the lovely Mall Fitton was admitted at the age of seventeen as one of the royal Cynthia's Maids of Honour—the band of Court 'glories' dressed all in chaste and virgin white, with whom 'all things must be not only without lust, but without suspicion of lightness'. Sir Edward Fitton entrusted his daughter to the particular care of Sir William Knollys, who was then aged forty-eight and married to a widow even older than himself. And although Knollys promised, as he wrote, to act as a 'father' and to 'defend the innocent lamb from the wolfish cruelty and fox-like subtlety of the tame beasts' of the Court, it was not long before he was himself amorously urging the innocent lamb to marry him when his wife should die. Letters of his, containing extreme expressions of love for the girl, were printed by Lady Newdegate-Newdigate in her able account of Mary Fitton, *Gossip from a Muniment Room* (1897). *Silver hairs delight in golden locks, and frosty years must be thawed by youthful fires.* But his inconsiderate wife persisted in living, and Mr. Controller followed his conspicuous and doting pursuit of the girl, who led her elderly suitor gently by the nose while casting her significant glances elsewhere.

She did not lack present and bad example. Another Maid of Honour, Mistress Bess Vernon, was first courted with too much familiarity by the young Earl of Southampton,

Wager's *Marie Magdalene* (1567), the heroine is addressed as 'little Mall'. About 1573 Lady Southampton refers to her daughter Mary as 'my little Mall' (*Loseley Papers* 4. 19). In Porter's *Two Angry Women* 5. 1, we have 'My name is Mary Barnes. . . . How, wench? Mall Barnes!' Sir John Harington of Kelston brings his wife Mary Rogers into his epigrams as 'My Mall'. And outside the drama Mary Frith appears variously as 'Malcutpurse', 'Mal-cutpurse', and 'Mall cut purse'.

and then hastily married to him in 1598. Taking no warning either by the disgrace visited on these culprits, or by the punishment suffered by other similar offenders against maidhood, honour, and their royal guardian, the sparkish Mistress Mall proceeded boldly to her own 'marring'.

A few months before Shakespeare's *Twelfth Night*, the twenty-two-year-old beauty, then high in favour with the Queen, involved herself with William Lord Herbert, afterwards Earl of Pembroke—who has been fancied as Shakespeare's 'W. H.' He was two years her junior, and is said to have been 'immoderately given up to women'. It is reported that 'she would put off her head tire and tuck up her clothes and take a large white cloak and march as though she had been a man to meet the said Earl out of the Court'. But very little escaped the Queen. Her ear was as quick as her eye, and she plainly heard a bird sing that Mistress Mall Fitton was setting her honesty to the tune of *Greensleeves*.

In the middle of June 1600 her Majesty went in state to Blackfriars to grace the marriage of another of her Maids, Mistress Anne Russell, with Henry Somerset, Lord Herbert of Chepstow. After supper there was a masque of eight Muses, led by Mistress Fitton, dancing to the music brought in by Apollo, with a graceful compliment to her Majesty as the ninth Muse. The Queen chose her moment—after the masque was over, and when the eight dancers had come out to the audience richly-attired in other characters such as Fancy, Desire, Delight, Hope, and the like—to administer her public rebuke to Mistress Mall: 'Mrs. Fitton went to the Queen, and wooed her to dance. Her Majesty asked what she was. "Affection," she

QUEEN ELIZABETH BORNE IN PROCESSION

said. "Affection!" said the Queen. "Affection is false."
Yet her Majesty rose and danced.' *Affection* meant burning or passionate love. 'She loves him with enraged affection.' Ben Jonson describes 'Affection . . . in her hand a
flaming heart', and Marston mentions Venus, 'in her right
hand grasping a heart in flames'.[1]

The Queen was right. Her favourite Mall Fitton was
false to her trust. Nine months later she bore a son to her
lover, who by that time had succeeded his father as Earl
of Pembroke. Again affection proved false, for he utterly
refused to marry her. By Christmas of 1600, then, Mistress Mall was more than six months gone with child.

---

[1] Mary Fitton as 'Affection' raises an interesting question concerning the famous picture attributed to Marcus Gheeraerts, showing the Queen carried in state in a 'curious chair' or litter. It exists
in two copies, one at Melbury, the other at Sherborne Castle. The
first of these is reproduced as the frontispiece to *Shakespeare's England* (1916). The discussions by Sir George Scharf (*Archaeological
Soc.* Vol. 33, p. 131) and the Earl of Ilchester (*Walpole Soc.* Vol. 9,
pp. 1–20) agree that it represents Queen Elizabeth's visit to Blackfriars for the Herbert–Russell wedding of June 16, 1600—on the
evidence of Rowland Whyte's letter (*Sydney Papers* 2. 203). They
also agree that the prominent unmarried young lady following the
Queen's *lectica* is the bride, Anne Russell, and therefore suggest that
the rear bearer, who indicates this lady with a gesture, is the groom,
Henry Somerset, Lord Herbert.

I question the identification of the maiden as the bride. To begin
with, she is not dressed as Elizabethan brides of all ranks customarily
were, with hair hanging loose and crowned with flowers. In the
second place, she is wearing a flaming heart on her sleeve, badge
of Affection or Passionate Love, and is carrying a fan. I will be
judged by a parliament of women whether these are ornaments conceivable for a bride on her wedding day.

It therefore seems to me that this must on the contrary be Mary
Fitton, representing the band of Maids of Honour, in her proper
place after the Queen in procession. In the dance after the wedding
masque she had the character of Affection. If I am right, the young
gentleman pointing to her would be her lover, William Lord Herbert; and this particularity suggests that the picture was painted
either for her or for him.

Besmirching shame lay in wait for her all-admired face. She had therefore withdrawn it, like a curtained picture, from the vulgar gaze, providing Shakespeare's Sir Toby Belch with his passing allusion—'Wherefore are these things hid? . . . Are they like to take dust, like Mistress Mal's picture?' Before the end of January, the very month of Twelfth Night, she was committed to custody.

And what of the fifty-three-year-old Mr. Controller, who, though troubled with a wife, fancied himself a fit husband for the belle of the young Maids of Honour, and longed for Mall while she made an ass of him with a handsome rival less than half his age? If she brought scandal on the Queen's Court, he had brought something worse—ridicule. The favourite refrain to the tune of *Peg a Ramsey* fitted him almost beyond belief:

When I was a bachelor I led a merry life;
But now I am a married man, and troubled with a wife . . .
Give me my yellow hose again, give me my yellow hose!
For now my wife she watcheth me: see yonder where she goes![1]

Yellow hose, or long yellow stockings, are infallibly indicated for this 'Peg a Ramsey' Mr. Controller, the married man who would a-wooing go—in his own conceit a lusty lover, able to 'Please one, and please all'. Or he may be equally mocked by humming

My lady is unkind, perdie!—Alas, why is she so?
She loves another.

---

[1] For *Peg a Ramsey*, see William Chappell, *Popular Music of the Olden Time*, 1. 218. In his *Anatomy of Melancholy* (3. 2. 5. 3) Burton recalls the familiar refrain: 'when we are once tied, and have lost our liberty, marriage is an hell, *give me my yellow hose again*'. *Peg a Ramsey* is the last of five popular tunes listed by Nashe (*Works*, ed. McKerrow, 3. 122): *Rogero, Basilino, Turkelony, Greene sleeues*, and *Peggie Ramsey*.

His fatuous effort to dye his reverend beard 'that did his age bewray' produced the inevitable parti-coloured result—white at the roots where it grew, yellow in the middle, and black at the point: so conspicuously, indeed, as to earn him the derisive nickname of 'Party Beard'. This plainly appears by the widely-known and lewd ballad in which the Knollys–Mall Fitton–Pembroke story was sung to some villainous tune:

> Party beard, party beard . . .
> . . . the white hind was crossed:
> Brave Pembroke struck her down
> And took her from the clown
> Like a good woodman.

A contemporary key leaves the identities in no doubt. The *white hind*, *crossed* or dislodged and *struck down* by the *good woodman* or practised lecher Lord Pembroke, is the fair, white-clad 'M^{ris} Fitton'; and *party beard* and *clown* are each glossed 'Sr Willm Knowles'.[1]

While the conspicuous 'colour of his beard' is therefore the first feature to reproduce if Mr. Controller is to be full-drawn and delineated from the sole of the foot to the crown of his head, the forefront and title of the caricature

---

[1] B.M. MS. Harley 1929, f. 34^v, a copy of this well-known lampoon hitherto unnoticed. For a full text and description of the lampoon, see Mrs. C. C. Stopes, *The Third Earl of Southampton* (1922), 235–42. The *Reindeer*, *embossed* or hunted to exhaustion, is not however (as Mrs. Stopes thought) Queen Elizabeth, but the 'Er. of Essex, out of breathe'. One of Essex's heraldic supporters was 'a raine deere gules, spotted argent' (Bodl. MS. Ashmole 818, f. 2). Compare Peele's *Eclogue Gratulatory* to Essex (1589), line 53: *His Raine Deere racking with proud and stately pace*. The 'Mrs Mary' who danced before the Queen on December 26, 1602 (as Rowland Whyte reported to Sir. Robert Sidney), was Mary Sidney, and not Mary Fitton, as Sir Edmund Chambers mistakenly suggests (*Eliz. Stage*, 4. 115n.). After her disgrace, Mary Fitton was not taken back into favour.

must be the 'jest nominal'—his name in the play. And here Shakespeare's unlooked-for device of wit touches the peak of felicity. For while exposing both the Controller's *ill-will*—towards hilarity and misrule—and his *amorousness* in the name *Mala-voglia* (Ill Will *or* Evil Concupiscence), he also deftly fetches up Knollys's ridiculous love-chase of Mistress Mall by a sly modulation of *Mala-voglia* into '*Mal*'-*voglio*—which means 'I want Mall', 'I wish for Mall', 'I will have Mall'. It is a masterpiece of mockery. Heightened by merciless repetition, with the players ringing the changes of expression on '*Mal*'-*voglio*, while they 'quote his passions and his smiles, his amorous haviour', it will bring down the house.

In their mad 'allowed fooling', old Party Beard is slaughtered in gross and in detail. Sir Toby prepares the unmistakable victim both with ' "*Mal*"-*voglio*'s a Peg a Ramsey', and by singing *There dwelt a man in Babylon*—the ballad of the Elders' lust for the fair young Susanna; Maria makes all sure—'by *the colour of his beard* . . . he shall find himself most feelingly personated'; with 'sheep-biter' and 'hang thee, brock!' Sir Toby holds him up both as a chaser of that innocent lamb Mall Fitton and as a self-swelling old wencher;[1] and finally Feste, covering his own long fool's coat of mingled motley with the clergyman's gown, sternly rebukes the devil of carnal motions

---

[1] For *sheep-biter*, see *O.E.D.*, s.v., 4: 'One who runs after "mutton"; a woman-hunter, whoremonger.' See also Dekker, *2 Honest Whore*, 2. 1. 312.

For *brock* see 'the selfe-swelling Badgerd'—Sylvester's Du Bartas (1608), 514; 'What, with a brace of wenches, I faith olde brock, haue I tane you in the maner?'—John Day, *The Ile of Guls* (1606), H2ᵛ; 'Hang him, badger! There's not a hole free from him; whores and whores' mates Do all pay him obedience.'— Beaumont and Fletcher, *The Mad Lover*, 4. 5. 13-15.

infesting the amorous '*Mal*'-*voglio* with 'Talkest thou nothing but of ladies? . . . Fie, thou dishonest Satan!'

If we may credit the well-known anecdote preserved in L'Estrange's jest-book of about 1650, it illustrates Mr. Controller's unedifying notions of suitable revenge:

The Lord Knolls, in Queen Elizabeth's time, had his lodging at Court, where some of the Ladyes and Maydes of Honour us'd to friske and hey about in the next roome, to his extreame disquiete a nights, though he had often warned them of it; at last he getts one to bolt theire owne backe doore, when they were all in one night at their revells, stripps off to his shirt, and so with a payre of spectacles on his nose, and Aretine in his hand, comes marching in at a posterne doore of his owne chamber, reading very gravely, full upon the faces of them. Now let the reader judge what a sadd spectacle and pittiful sight these poor creatures endur'd, for he fac'd them and often traverst the roome in this posture above an houre.

As long ago as 1916 Sir Edmund Chambers found it 'tempting to compare the scene in which Malvolio breaks in upon the midnight revels of Maria and the riotous knights' with this anecdote. And in 1925, while suggesting that 'the pompous and besotted old Comptroller gave Shakespeare his hint for Malvolio', he followed the clue no farther than to the strange conclusion that by Maria— of whom Malvolio is very far from being enamoured— Shakespeare meant the Mary Fitton with whom Knollys was so notoriously infatuated.

It would be folly to think that we can recover more than a portion of the delicious topical spice with which Shakespeare seasoned his take-off of Mr. Controller. We today can never see what the Twelfth Night revellers saw—a player got up as the image of the Controller, beard, white staff and all, mimicking the familiar Knollys mannerisms to the life; but certainly we can now join them in savouring a good deal more of the 'close mocks and flouts' than ever we could before.

In one speech—'Quenching my familiar smile with an austere regard of *control*'—we now get the *Controller*. And in another—'Truly madam, he [Malvolio] holds Beelzebub at the *stave's* end as well as a man in his case may do'—we get the white *staff* of power granted to him by his royal cousin. Moreover we can now see that the association of Knollys with Puritans and Banbury is hit off again and again: 'Sometimes he is a kind of Puritan. . . . The devil a Puritan that he is, or anything constantly but a time-pleaser.' (Essex's followers saw him not only as a time-server but as an uncourtly 'clown'.) Malvolio's censure of the roisterers—singing the catch 'that will draw three souls out of one weaver'—that they 'gabble like tinkers' (who at Banbury were quite properly hanged by the fanatic weavers) brings Sir Toby's prompt retort in kind: 'Sneck up!' ('*You* be hanged!') For all its holy zeal, is it likely that Banbury will stop producing its famous cakes and ale for more reasonable Christians to make merry with? 'Dost thou think, because thou art virtuous, there shall be no more cakes and ale?' Shakespeare knew his Banbury, its excellent ale and its Puritans. It lay but twenty miles from Stratford, on one of his two main routes to London.

Mr. Controller's importance as a Privy Councillor and Member of Parliament comes in for some rude knocks: 'an affection'd ass, that cons state without book and utters it by great swarths'. 'Let thy tongue tang arguments of state.' 'I will be proud, I will read politic authors.'

Samples of his affection'd terms are 'consonancy', 'in contempt of question', 'a more exalted respect', 'incredulous and unsafe circumstance', and 'a demure travel of regard'. And how neatly Shakespeare makes Malvolio call himself a fool while interpreting the letter—'Why, this is evident to any *formal* capacity.' For the contemptuous sense of *formal* was *foolish and affected*: 'This formal fool', 'this formal ape', 'a weak formal statesman', 'this formal wit . . . for in these outward forms all fools are wise'.[1] Possibly, too, some behaviour of his to the Lord Chamberlain, his cousin and superior officer, is hinted at in 'Be opposite with a kinsman, surly with servants.' And the noxious Tiltyard bear-baitings by his lodging are by no means forgotten: 'You know he brought me out o' favour with my lady about a bear-baiting here.' 'To anger him we'll have the bear again.'

Such pointed play is made with the rare word *obstruction*—which appears three times in *Twelfth Night*, and elsewhere in Shakespeare only once each in *1 Henry IV* and *Measure for Measure*—that it calls for attention. Though its sense of 'a blocking' or 'a stopping up' had begun to spread to other subjects, *obstruction's* main connotation was still the pathological one: obstruction or oppilation of the liver, the spleen, the arteries, the entrails. Old men were regarded as particularly prone to phlegm, which caused 'obstructions', and made them suspicious and niggardly. Obstruction of the spleen resulted in bad temper,

---

[1] Porter, *Two Angry Women*, 2. 1; Dekker and Middleton, *Roaring Girl*, 1. 1; Beaumont, *Woman-Hater*, Lucio in dramatis personae; Sir John Davies, *Works* (ed. Grosart), 2. 55, 218; cf. Littleton's Dict., 'A formal man, *Affectator*'; and Sir W. Cornwallis's *Essays*, Nos. 11 and 35; 'A meer formal man' Earle, *Microcosmographie*; and the fool's 'formall hat' in Donne's Satyre I.

irritability, jealousy, and black jaundice.[1] We find the black-and-yellow of this black jaundice both in Brome's *Antipodes*, 'My husband presents jealousy in the black and yellow jaundied suit there', and in Malvolio's protestation of love free from suspicion—'Not black in my mind, though yellow in my legs.' Obstruction of the arteries, through which the blood carries the vital spirits to the brain, was even more serious. It bound men in fits, like those of epilepsy or of demonic 'possession'.

Though suspicious, and apprehensive of 'obstruction' both from the Tiltyard bear-baiting crowds and in his vital parts, old Knollys-Malvolio is conceited and gullible. Swallowing the fatal baited letter, he believes 'There is no *obstruction* in this.' Then what self-sacrifice he shows in pleasing his lovelorn lady by binding his legs above and below the knee with cross garters—for, as he nervously points out, 'This does make some *obstruction* in the blood, this cross gartering.' And the consequent madness or demonic possession, for which he is so fittingly treated by the conspirators by being 'obstructed'[2] in a dark house, is wickedly underlined by Feste: 'yet complainest thou of *obstruction*?'

When the merciless crew are 'dealing gently' with Malvolio in his dangerous madness and possession, Sir Toby's gambit in handling him like a barnyard fowl is not immediately obvious to us. But his 'How dost thou, chuck? Ay, biddy, come with me' regains its delicious point when we remember that the poor 'mad woman

---

[1] See J. B. Bamborough, *The Little World of Man* (1952), 59, 60, 66, 160.

[2] Compare Claudio's 'To lie in cold obstruction and to rot.' *Measure for Measure*, 3. 1. 119.

which resorted to the Court' was familiar to all as Mother *Chicken*.

The humour of imposing long yellow stockings and cross garters on the self-lov'd Malvolio is more rich, subtle, and various than we have realized. Like Olivia, Queen Elizabeth (whose own personal colours were white and black) abhorred yellow. For six years yellow had been the colour of danger in her Court—being flaunted by the faction of the Duke of Norfolk until his attainder and execution in 1572. And the flag of her arch-enemy, Spain, was yellow. It is still the 'coward's colour' and that of the 'self-lov'd Narcissus'. Yellow was also the proper wear for jealous-foolish husbands. The English byword for 'jealousy' was 'to wear yellow stockings and cross garters'. And by 1600 the fashion of cross garters was outmoded—they were worn 'chiefly by old men, Puritans, pedants, footmen, and rustic bridegrooms'.[1]

As for the long stocking—a style borrowed twenty years before from the French—it was likewise out of date, and a subject of ridicule in contemporary plays and satires. In Queen Elizabeth's own directions, set down by her Chamberlain, for the Court on this very Twelfth Day we read: 'gentlemen to be warned to weare no lo . . .' Here the burnt page reduces us to guesswork to complete the phrase—'long stockings'? 'long hair'? or perhaps 'long cloaks'? A royal decree against long stockings would be Shakespeare's obvious cue for putting them on Malvolio, and, of course, of a disgusting yellow—and having

[1] See M. P. Tilley, *A Dict. of the Proverbs in England* (1950), S868. M. C. Linthicum, *Costume in the Drama of Shakespeare and His Contemporaries* (1936), 264.

that cross-garter'd gull insanely imagine that Olivia-Elizabeth asked for them. Still another delight of Malvolio's Twelfth Night costume emerges when we consider the figure of old Father Christmas in Ben Jonson's Masque for Twelfth Night, 1616: 'Enter Christmas . . . attired in round hose, long stockings . . . and garters tied cross.' To trick the sour almost-Puritan kill-joy into presenting himself hopefully in the garb of merry old Gregory Christmas—it is a masterly stroke.

Maria's calling him '*Monsieur* Malvolio' merely classes him with the contemptible French—held to be an 'inconstant and scambling nation', more especially after the Huguenot Henri IV had turned Catholic, thriftily observing that 'Paris is worth a mass'. Shakespeare reflected the English view of this in *King John*: 'O foul revolt of French inconstancy!' And in *Henry V* he held up the French as despicable boasters. 'Monsieur' Malvolio now joins the other vessels of contempt, called 'Monsieur' in derision—Lavatch, Parolles, Jaques.

Thus the French had been added to the inevitable and hostile Spaniards as the chief foreign objects of ridicule. In *Cynthia's Revels* we find Jonson writing 'Your frenchified fool is your only fool' and appending a prayer for defence not only against 'Spanish shrugs' but also 'French faces, smirks, irps, and all affected humours'. As for the Spaniards, Shakespeare had already got his hand in with the bragging fool Don Adriano de Armado. It would be surprising if he were to neglect them entirely in *Twelfth Night*.

If we may leave Malvolio for a moment, we get our first hint that Shakespeare has not forgotten the Spaniards in the reason which that shark, Sir Toby Belch, gives for cultivating his dear manakin, the weak-witted Ague-cheeke. Like Iago, Sir Toby plans to make his fool his purse; and Aguecheeke, loved more for his wealth than his wit, has an income of three thousand ducats a year. That these are 'castilians'—*Spanish* ducats, legitimate booty of an Englishman like himself—becomes clear when Sir Toby tells Maria, 'What, wench, *castigliano volgo*!'—'I'm thinking of the castilian!'[1]

Since Aguecheeke's income is in castilians, the simpleton must be supposed a Spaniard: and if so, we have hitherto failed to catch his descriptive Spanish name under its anglicized spelling. Does not its sound betray it as *Agu-chica*, Little-wit, shortened from *agucia chica* or *agudeza chica*? We might have known that the English 'ague-cheek' could not be right. It is neither funny nor appropriate to the artless zany, 'always enjoying a joke, never understanding it'. For there is nothing in the least sickly, hectic, or aguish about the agile and quarrelsome Sir Andrew. As Sir Toby notes, diligent dancing has given his legs an 'excellent constitution'—well-ankled, two confident calves. What is more, he is not only a stiff drinker but a great eater of beef—'and I believe that does harm to my wit . . . I knew 'twas I, for many do call me a fool'. Nor need we look for illustration of *Aguchica* to Ben Jonson's John Littlewit, or resort to the imbecile hamlets of Small Witam or Little Brainford: for Sir Andrew's creator was sufficiently fond of the phrase: 'a little tiny wit', 'the little wit that fools have', 'little wit in thy bald crown', 'that little, little, less than little wit'.

---

[1] See *O.E.D.* s.v. Castilian, and my note, 'Sir Toby's *Castiliano vulgo*', *Times Literary Supplement*, Oct. 11, 1947, p. 521.

No doubt Littlewit-Aguchica's Christian name, Andrew, is out of the same bag: an English-looking form of the Spanish *andrajo*, meaning 'rag' or 'despicable person', as in Shakespeare's 'Away, thou rag!' and Jonson's 'Who let in that rag there?' At all events, Sir Toby's 'Agueface' is certainly another jest in Spanish, and a low one, on the toper who is drunk nightly in his company: *Aguafáce*, 'Makes water'—quite in the same vein as his 'I would not so much as make water but in a sink-a-pace'.[1] Having at long last recovered Shakespeare's jest, it is high time that we restored to Sir Andrew the proper Continental pronunciation of his name—Aguchica.

This acquaintance with Spanish is not surprising. One does not fight an enemy for twelve years without learning something of his language. Indeed, it may be suspected that the Elizabethans knew more Spanish than the critics of Shakespeare ever learned. These were nonplussed by Edgar's *Sesey* or *sese* in *Lear*, which is plainly neither a non-existent 'sessa', nor the French fighting cry *çà, çà!*, but the Spanish *ce, ce*, explained in Percivale's dictionary as 'hola, hola . . . a soft calling unto one, that the rest about them may not hear'. Maria shows familiarity with pronunciation of Spanish in terming Malvolio a *Renegatho*, and Shakespeare would never have put into Hamlet's mouth a term like *malhecho*, had it been unintelligible to his audience. In Elizabeth's London there was a Spanish-reading public large enough to justify the issue both of *El testamento nuevo de nuestro señor Iesu Christo* and Spanish translations of the *Catechismus* and the *In-*

---

[1] Compare Shakespeare's 'knight Samingo' or Sir Mingo (2 *Henry IV*, 5. 3. 79) and Nashe's 'Mounsieur Mingo' and 'knight Domingo' (*Works*, ed. McKerrow, 4. 432).

stitutio of Calvin. And it was Richard Field, Shakespeare's fellow-townsman from Stratford, who printed them, signing himself *Ricardo del Campo*.

We should not forget that in Shakespeare's time English was of small importance. On the extensive library-shelves of the Grand Duke of Tuscany there was not a single book in English. The Continentals—even the ambassadors to England—felt no need whatever of learning it. Englishmen, on the other hand, if they were to acquire either trade or cultivation, simply had to know Continental languages. We recall that Queen Elizabeth's accomplished visitor, Don Virginio Orsino, could converse in Spanish and French as well as in his native Italian, but he knew no English. At Whitehall, as we shall see, he was however relieved to find that 'most' of the English courtiers could speak 'Italian, many, French, and some, Spanish'. In fact he found 'only two who knew no other language than the English'.

Shakespeare was writing for the majority of the courtiers, in the knowledge that the humour of his '*Mal*'-*voglio*, *castigliano volgo*, *Agu-chica*, and *Agua-fáce* would be readily understood. What they show us, however, is plain. If the Elizabethans are not to leave us hopelessly behind, we must know a trifle more than Sir Andrew, with his 'What is *pourquoi*? Do, or not do?' For if we come illiterate to a play written to entertain the most quick-witted and well-languaged ruler England has ever had, we may expect to hear her tell us, as the Red Queen told Alice, 'Now, *here*, you see, it takes all the running you can do to keep in the same place. If you want to get somewhere else, you must run at least twice as fast as that!'

But to return to Malvolio. Under the Restoration, it was believed that

> When Shakespeare, Jonson, Fletcher ruled the stage,
> They took so bold a freedom with the age
> That there was scarce a knave or fool in town
> Of any note but had his picture shown.

At all events, satire and libel were notably rife in 1600 and 1601. But we may be very sure that the quick comedians led by Shakespeare would not have dared extempore to stage Mr. Controller Knollys before the Queen without authority. Yet Queen Elizabeth never withheld a trouncing from one who had clearly earned it, even if she called him, as she called Sir William Knollys, 'one that appertaineth to us in blood'. Indeed that very kinship and favour should have restrained him from improper advances to her Maid of Honour, Mall Fitton. As her 'notable wise counsellor' (?Walsingham) remarked, in allowing a comedy of plain personal satire,[1] 'They which do that they should not, should hear that they would not.' And after invention has played on Mr. Controller, how adroitly Shakespeare spikes his guns : 'How with a sportful malice it was follow'd, May rather pluck on laughter than revenge.' Not only does '*Mal*'-*voglio* get some schooling from Lady Olivia on how a sensible man should take a joke, but his furious threats of revenge in the end are laughed out of court. If he is not to advertise himself as flagrantly unjust by being 'both the plaintiff and the judge' of his own cause, what possible course is left Mr. Controller but to bite the lip, play the man, cut his losses, and join in the laugh?

---

[1] *The Cards.* Sir John Harington, qu. *Eliz. Stage*, 4. 238.

VI

MOST PLEASING TO HER MAJESTY

TWELFTH NIGHT'S first-night audience must have found the hilarious baiting of old *I-want-Mal* irresistible. It was 'Sweet Mr. Controller, ho, ho!' with a vengeance. They took it as the cream of the comedy, beyond all the charm of its poetry and its music. Most topical and personal jesting lives only for the day; but so marvellously did Shakespeare fill his mould with deathless character, that long after these topics of 'our giddy times, which gallop by so fast' were grown stale or forgotten, later generations still regarded Malvolio as carrying the play. In 1623—twenty-two years after the first night—the Master of the Revels notes, 'At Candlemas *Malvolio* was acted at Court.' And Leonard Digges, writing about the same time that

> The cock-pit, galleries, boxes, all are full
> To hear Malvoglio, that cross garter'd gull,

shows that the City shared the Court's delight: an enthusiasm illustrated still later by Charles the First's own copy of Shakespeare, in which the royal hand alters the title *Twelfth Night* to *Malvolio*. Many a modern lover of the play would agree with the monarch, and also applaud his renaming *Henry IV* as *Falstaff*. These richly comic figures from the underplots have all but run away with the plays.

Rapidly as he contrived his comedy, Shakespeare did not however fall into the structural fault which makes some Elizabethan plays as badly articulated as a masque—a cleavage between the main plot and the underplot or bustling low-comedy foil. *Twelfth Night* under his hand moves with the smoothest of rhythms, for he knew how to make unity of disparity; how cunningly to weave a rollicking underplot big with topical satire into the main romantic story.

But what main romantic story? Though Shakespeare knew well before Dryden that the story is the least part, a story there must be; and to please the Queen and her ladies, its theme should be the never-failing matter of the Loving and Not Loved, of mistaken cross-wooing, such as John Day's Violetta describes: 'project for a pretty Court comedy . . . my mother dotes upon her for a man'. And since her Highness's guest of honour at the play will be an Italian duke who has no English, the courteous course for Shakespeare is to adapt some piece well-tried and popular in Italy—which the Duke can readily follow through the skilled miming of the players.

It is no problem to find the very thing: *Gl' Ingannati*, a Sienese comedy popular for seventy years in the Duke's own Tuscany, so popular as to be turned by Bandello into a prose tale translated with alterations into English by Barnabe Riche. It even has a pair of indistinguishable boy-and-girl twins in it, ready-made to remind Orsino of his own twin first-born. Not six years before this present 1600, in March 1595, a Latin version of *Gl' Ingannati*—'far-faméd *Laelia*'—had been acted at Cambridge to entertain the Earl of Essex. In taking this framework, Shakespeare will transmute it into gold—not merely by expunging painful or tragic elements, but by infusing its ageing limbs with the poetry of love: love high-fantastical, love surprising and tyrannous, love deep and loyal.

There is a further requisite, as important as dramatic poetry. Elizabeth, expert in music and song, and a handsome performer herself on the lute and virginals, desires a play with great variety and change of music and dances. To give most pleasure to her Italian guest, she would take his eyes with the English dancing—second to none in the world—and his ears with the international language: music. Shakespeare's Robin Armin can sing both high and low; and music and dance are the actors' speciality, vying in attractive power with the drama. Many an Elizabethan must have agreed with their highwayman Ratsey, who is reported as declaring, 'I have often gone to plays more for music' sake than for action.' There will be opportunity in the intermissions and at the close for dances by the actors, and Shakespeare will insert instrumental music to feed Orsino's love both in the beginning of the play and in Act 2 Scene 4. With Armin as the 'excellent breast', he will put in catches, accompanied love songs, a moral ditty, snatches of ballads. For dancing in the play itself, there will be admirable *pas seuls* by Sir Andrew, and Feste's step-dance to his own music of pipe and tabor—making *Twelfth Night* altogether the most musical of Shakespeare's comedies.

Nor has he to be taught how to please her Majesty with words. Indeed in the art of subtle and delicate compliment Shakespeare is able to give the courtiers lessons, as he proves again and again while painting—in that 'virtuous maid' Lady Olivia—a romanticized and youthful shadow of 'the most excellent and glorious person of our sovereign the Queen'. The very choice of *Olivia* shows his purpose to be the same as Spenser's in *The Shepherd's Calendar*:

> Olives bene for peace . . .
> Such for a Princess bene principal.

This dearest praise of Elizabeth found voice even in such plain and hearty lines as

> For such a peace before was never seen
> As we enjoy'd under a Virgin Queen . . .

and Camden went so far as to derive her name from the Hebrew for *Peace of the Lord*. She was presented in 1581 with 'this olive branch . . . in token of your triumphant peace', and two portraits after the Armada show her sceptred with a branch of olive, the 'peaceful', the 'victorious', the 'long-liv'd' olive.

Quick, resourceful, and allusive, the Elizabethan mind can even extract another value from *Olive* for their royal 'mother of peace'. For 'Live!' or 'O live!' is the universal shout of her loving subjects—'*Crying with a voice most shrill, . . . live, live, and God preserve her from all foreign harms!*' '*O live as do the stars, which shine for ever!*' '*Live, Soveraigne Ladie, Live, Elizabeth!*' [1] And every proclamation ended, *Vivat Regina!*

Twelve years before this, in '*The mortall Moone*', his great sonnet on the Armada's eclipse, Shakespeare had already introduced this palmary pun—unnoticed in modern times—to praise that victorious Queen who had used the olive with her sword to make war breed peace. For although the word *Olive* occurs eight times in his works, it is only in Sonnet 107 that the poet wrenches it from its proper accent into *Olives*; and his linking *pro-*

---

[1] J[ames] L[ea], *An Answer to the Untruths*, 1589; T. Bastard, *Chrestoleros*, 1598; Kyd, *Verses of Prayse and Ioye*, 1586.

claims with it—as of a proclamation of peace—betrays
his attendant thought of the royal proclamations' unfailing *vivats*:

And peace proclaimes Oliues of endlesse age.
In *Twelfth Night* without any wrenching the name *Olivia*
gives him the accent he needs to repeat this enriched
meaning: '*O live, Princess of peace!*'

Olivia moreover carries with it a further tribute: to the
wisdom of the Queen called by her ablest minister 'the
wisest woman that ever was': *Olive, due unto the wise.*—
Pansophia's seat, divine Eliza call'd, With Olives deck'd.[1]
And so allusively does the witty Feste compliment Lady
Olivia on her *wisdom* that we have not understood him:
'Thou hast spoken for us [fools], Madonna, as if thy eldest
son should be a fool'—meaning, she has spoken *wisely*;
for the current proverb ran, *A wise man commonly hath a
fool to his heir*: and in 1598 the Queen had been reminded
that 'wise men have fools to their children'.[2] Accordingly,
Feste's *Every wise man's son doth know* means, as we now
see, 'Every fool knows'.

To these lightly-veiled praises of Elizabeth as Lady of
Peace and of Wisdom, Shakespeare adds that of the
goddess Diana—Ben Jonson's contemporary *Queen and
huntress, chaste and fair.* For in the poetic first scene,
Duke Orsino likens himself to Actæon, transformed at
sight of Olivia into a *noble hart*, with an unavoidable play
on *noble heart*:

O, when mine eyes did see Olivia first,
Methought she purg'd the air of pestilence!

[1] Henry Peacham, *Minerva Britanna*, 1612; Lodowick Lloyd,
The Triplicitie of Triumphs, 1591.
[2] Tilley, *op. cit.*, M421; and ?Lyly, *Queen Elizabeth's Entertainment at Mitcham* (Yale, 1953), 22.

> That instant was I turn'd into a hart,
> And my desires, like fell and cruel hounds,
> E'er since pursue me.

The power to purge pestilent air is divine, as the prayer of Leontes in *The Winter's Tale* implies—'The blessèd gods Purge all infection from our air whilst you Do climate here!'

When we recall responsible estimates of Don Virginio's character—such as d'Ossat's 'a young nobleman of very great worth and valour', Bentivoglio's 'a lord of rarest talent and of other most rare qualities', and Contarini's testimony that 'he has every grace, is ingenious, and discourses well on all subjects'—we understand that Shakespeare's inquiries concerning Queen Elizabeth's valorous guest Orsino might well afford him solid ground for writing Lady Olivia's fair opinion of the Illyrian Orsino:

> . . . I suppose him virtuous, know him noble,
> Of great estate, of fresh and stainless youth;
> In voices well divulg'd, free, learn'd, and valiant,
> And in dimension and the shape of nature
> A gracious person.

It has long been common form for critics to take turns dipping into the youthful and noble Orsino's dramatic character and coming up with the same thing: 'sentimental and fancy-sick', 'voluptuous love-languors', 'a thistle-down amorist', 'amorous and sentimental'. This seems a notable case of 'fishing fair and catching a frog'. For when it becomes evident that such rapturous lines as *Now heaven walks on earth* put into Orsino's mouth are *not* dramatic, but transparent lyric worship of the listening Queen—shooting the shuttle of attention from the playing-floor to the throne—these extreme sentiments take their proper place as excellent passages of Elizabethan poetic tribute, of 'writing the Queen anew'. Cavil at them for excrescences we may, but it is too naive to believe them symptoms of reprehensible sentimentality or nerveless amorism in the Duke of Illyria.

Seen in the light of their intention, Orsino's ecstasies fall into line with the effusions addressed to Elizabeth's ear by Essex or Ralegh. The first wrote:

> The two windows of your Privy Chamber shall be the poles of my sphere. . . . While your Majesty gives me leave to say I love you, my fortune is as my affection unmatchable. If ever you deny me that liberty, you may end my life . . .

And Ralegh:

> My heart was never broken till this day, that I hear the Queen goes away so far off, whom I have followed so many years with so great love and desire . . . I that was wont to behold her riding like Alexander, hunting like Diana, walking like Venus . . . sometime singing like an angel, sometime playing like Orpheus: behold the sorrow of this world! One amiss hath bereaved me of all. O Love, that only shineth in misfortune, what is become of thine assurance? All wounds have scars but that of phantasy; all affections their relenting but that of womankind.

It takes but half an eye to perceive that these two soldiers were not 'sentimental and fancy-sick', but Elizabethan courtiers who, like Shakespeare, understood the due decorum of the high-fantastical.

One had indeed to be either simple-minded or frantic to take this courtly convention of being in love with the Queen seriously. We recall Beaumont's lines,

> I would not willingly
> Be pointed at in every company,
> As was that little tailor, who till death
> Was hot in love with Queen Elizabeth

—and the poor distracted veteran William Renoldes, with his belief that the Privy Councillors 'would seem to marvel much why I come not a wooing to the Queen'. As for Shakespeare's Illyrian duke, if Lady Olivia is a shadow of the Queen, he *must* court her, however hopelessly, and in terms of adoration too, until she chooses a husband. Perseverance in his 'dear faith' is not a mark of self-deception, but of the courtier's loyal devotion.

Shakespeare takes little pains to mask his allusions to the listening Sovereign Lady Elizabeth in the person of Lady Olivia, queen in her Illyrian house. He portrays a *sovereign cruelty*, whose heart might be supplied with one self *king*. To both Feste and Viola she is a *princess*. And in matters of state, Lady Olivia falls naturally into the royal *we*: 'We'll once more hear Orsino's embassy', 'Give us the place alone: we will hear this divinity', 'We will draw the curtain and show you the picture', 'But when we know the grounds and authors of it'. Moreover she wields a power of life and death impossible to any countess. Maria warns Feste, 'My lady will hang thee', and Olivia commands, 'Hold, Toby! On thy life I charge thee hold!' And when Malvolio's fantastical ambition pictures himself married to her, we should read '*King* Malvolio' rather than 'Count Malvolio', for he is sitting in his *state*. A *state* is no count's chair, but a canopied royal throne.

As Elizabeth gazes on his feigned Lady Olivia, through the timeless mood induced by music Shakespeare takes his autumnal Queen back to her youth. There was a time when, like the virgin Olivia, she freshly mourned her father, bluff King Harry—the 'count that died'—whose personal magic she alone inherited. There was a sadder time of grieving for her dear young brother Edward, rare and virtuous, who 'still did use to style her his sweet sister Temperance':

> A brother's dead love, which she would keep fresh
> And lasting in her sad remembrance.

A long period of years had witnessed a succession of suitors—'kings, and kings' peers, who have sought her far and nigh' and been sent away with a willow garland. *She will admit no kind of suit* epitomizes the reign of the Virgin Queen. She is married to England.

From this minor key of memory, Shakespeare soon modulates into the life and love-making of high comedy. One of the Queen's own watchwords was *Ad Tartaros eat melancholia*—'To hell with melancholy!'[1] For though her mourning for her brother provides Olivia with reason for admitting no kind of suit until she is brought down by Love's arrow, cursed melancholy has no place in the bright mirth of *Twelfth Night*.

The golden light reveals a Lady Olivia, young, passing fair and imperial, cruelly rejecting the devoted courtship of the youthful Duke, Orsino—who by an amazing coincidence bears the identical name and rank of her Majesty's noble young visitor, standing at her side as she watches the comedians. Yet though this queenly and marble-breasted counterfeit sways her Illyrian house, commands her followers, dispatches affairs with a smooth, discreet, and stable bearing, it appears that even her

---

[1] Letter to Lord Mountjoy, Bodl. MS. Tanner 76, f. 10.

proud heart is subject to Cupid's power. Shakespeare draws the scene straight from Queen Elizabeth's own confession in song:

> When I was fair and young
>> And favour gracëd me,
> Of many was I sought unto,
>> Their mistress for to be.
> But I did scorn them all,
>> And answer'd them therefore,
> 'Go, go! Go seek some otherwhere—
>> Importune me no more.'
>
> But there fair Venus' son—
>> That brave victorious boy—
> Said, 'What! Thou scornful dame,
>> Sith that thou art so coy,
> I will so wound thy heart
>> That thou shalt leave therefore
> "Go, go! Go seek some otherwhere—
>> Importune me no more."'
>
> But then I felt straightway
>> A change within my breast:
> The day unquiet was,
>> The night, I could not rest.
> For I did sore repent
>> That I had said before:
> 'Go, go! Go seek some otherwhere—
>> Importune me no more.'

Shakespeare has made Olivia's case Elizabeth's, pride brought low. 'O divine Love, thou over-reachest the wisest, conquerest the chastest, and dost all things both unlikely and impossible, because thou art Love.' Journeys end in lovers' meeting. The proper business of court comedy is the epigamic: which is to say, efforts to attract a mate—especially so for a comedy in January, the month

Gamelion, sacred to Jupiter and Juno 'because of marriage'. Feste emphasizes this obvious fact not merely with aphrodisiac ginger 'hot in the mouth', but also by invoking Saint Anne—always a great help in finding a husband, as every marriageable girl knows: 'Blessed Saint Anne, send me a man as fast as ye can!' 'Now by Saint Anne, I will not die a maid!'

Before we can properly appreciate the cross-wooing in this play we must first be sure that we have all the significant data in hand. For, as Ben Jonson wisely observes, 'A good play is like a skein of silk: which, if you take by the right end, you may wind off at pleasure.' Already we have been permitted to wind off a pleasurable bobbinful by luckily getting hold of the Malvolio business by the right end.

But perhaps there is another 'right end' still unnoticed in the very date of the performance, 1600. It will not be 1601 until Lady Day, March 25: just as the terrible '*octogesimus octavus*, which would of course begin on 25 March 1588',[1] continued (after the Armada danger had passed) into 1588/9, as Oliver Pygge noted—'March 7. 1588. the meruailous yeere, in respect of the . . . wonderfull deliuerance.'[2] Like 1588, 1600 is leap-year, the year of ladies' law—'What, 'tis women's year! Dian doth rule, and you must domineer.' Leap-year, when the woman chooses, when the woman woos. God forbid that it should be otherwise. And great luck for Shakespeare, whose Dian-Elizabeth-Olivia must rule, must choose for herself.[3]

---

[1] Chambers, *Eliz. Stage*, 3. 415.   [2] *Meditations*, 1589.
[3] For 'leap-year' in other plays of 1600, see *Jack Drum's Entertainment*, 1. 166; *The Maid's Metamorphosis*, 4. 1. 157; and *Patient Grissell*, line 157.

As the fatal consequence of leap-year, *man's* court-ship, the Illyrian Orsino's, is necessarily hopeless from the start, prohibited by the law of 'women's year'. In such a year, his love-making *must* remain ideal, melancholy, in-effectual. 'Now the *melancholy god* protect thee . . . for thy mind is a very opal!' As Thomas Barrington wrote of another leap-year, 1632, 'Women are cruel this year, *Saturn* reigns with strong influence.' *I am slain by a fair cruel maid.*

It must be the women who woo and win. Maria ac-cordingly makes a neat catch of Toby, and we wish her joy of him. Viola's poetry of love, singing the song of truth, charms the mind and wins the heart of Orsino—even through her masculine usurp'd attire and his devo-tion to Olivia-worship. The stately Olivia, conquered by love, 'stoopeth, yieldeth, and fawneth on the strange "boy" '—inadvertently wooed and won *by a woman* in disguise. But since leap-year may not be cheated, and Lady Olivia cannot be offered 'a woman to her lord', the resourceful Saint Anne provides an indistinguishable twin brother, to be wooed and won—*by a woman*—to satisfy all demands. None can deny that this is neat work: that Shakespeare might say with Peter Quince, his carpenter, 'And I hope here is a play fitted'.

There is courtly art in Shakespeare's significant choice of a *Cesario* for the conqueror of Olivia. In the year preceding, the Virgin Queen had been offered a poetic *New-Year's Gift*, expressing the universal wish, 'But had she . . . A *Cæsar* to her husband, and a King to her son!' Nor can anyone complain of inappropriateness in the name *Sebastian* for Viola's twin. His patron, Saint Sebastian, was commonly pictured to the Renaissance as a beautiful young soldier, severely wounded with arrows. The handsome namesake is styled 'my young soldier' by Sir Toby, and his fate it is to be transfixed by Cupid's arrow, shot from the bow of Diana.

Viola, her passionate fidelity finding expression in the poetry which crowns the play, recalls in her Italian name *both* the blue flower 'for faithfulness'—to the Orsino whose motto is *Rather die than break faith*—and the stringed *viola da braccia* 'for passion and chastity' which Raphael pictured as Apollo's instrument.[1] And Shakespeare guards her role from any excess of the plaintive by granting her good measure of spirited confidence and humour.

The modern spectator, seeing Viola-Cesario arrive as ambassador from Duke Orsino, might well misjudge the Illyrian nobleman on the score of his distant and vicarious wooing. Surely a manly suitor would plead his cause in person? No, indeed he would not. European courtship in the sixteenth century between 'great estates' was properly and customarily conducted by envoys. Henri of France both courted and married Maria de' Medici by envoys. And a passage in *The Ambassador* (1603), the translation of an expert treatise by the experienced Jean Hotman, might have been written purposely to illustrate Duke Orsino's embassy to Lady Olivia:

For he that would give commission to an old and melancholy man to treat of a marriage with a young Princess, and make love unto her in the behalf of his Master (a thing which most commonly amongst the Great is done by an Attorney), it is very certain, that naturally she would not so willingly see or hear him as one that were more youthful and gallant. I have sometime seen experience thereof.

---

[1] The studies of Dr. Edgar Wind show us the significance of the *viola da braccia*, as well as of many other symbols.

Shakespeare in writing his play perfectly understood not only this, but also the Florentine custom of 'wooing by picture', to which Lady Olivia charmingly alludes in putting back her veil for the marriage-envoy Viola-Cesario: 'We will draw the curtain and show you the picture.'

In view of the fact that at sixty-seven Queen Elizabeth certainly used artificial complexion, as the mature Court ladies customarily did, the lines which follow might seem of dangerous implication:

Oli. Is't not well done?
Vio. Excellently done, if God did all.
Oli. 'Tis in grain, sir; 'twill endure wind and weather.

But we must remember, first, that the use of cosmetics was very common; and second, that Olivia is a romanticized shadow not of Elizabeth 'today', but of her when like Olivia she was a young and 'virtuous maid', recently bereft of father and brother. The cautious marriage-attorney is in duty bound to make sure that so marvellous a complexion is natural. His remark gives Olivia the opportunity both to remove all doubt, and to leave him astonished at her true loveliness.

To Viola Shakespeare allots one of the neatest topical strokes in the play—a jest of that rare sort which gives the audience great delight, and the butt of the joke nothing he can take hold of. Hitherto we have missed it completely, since the line looks perfectly harmless. Before coming to it, we may offer a latter-day parallel. The reader will agree that in most contexts the line *Nothing but peace* would be neither witty nor funny. But it was certainly both, at a recent London production of *Love's Labour's Lost*. When Boyet asked the lords who arrived disguised like Muscovites, 'What would you with the Princess?' a gale of laughter greeted the assurance, delivered in a strong Russian accent, '*Nossing bot pease.*'

Shakespeare's court-audience had had *their* Russian envoy, Mikulin, under foot for months—ever since the preceding October, when he had been given 'his belly full of garowses' at Richmond. Earlier on this very day of *Twelfth Night* they had him here at Whitehall. And he had been notoriously 'difficult'. Tsar Boris had instructed him to stick out for supremacy in every detail of protocol. If he were at dinner in the Queen's presence, and any other ambassador came in, he was to walk out.[1] The inclusion of any other envoy in an invitation to a royal function was grounds sufficient for his refusing to attend. In accounting to his Tsar, Mikulin carefully reports

---

[1] Instructions of Tsar Boris to Grigori Mikulin and Ivan Zinoviev, Moscow, May 1600. (Translated from *Sbornik*, loc. cit., 283, 290–1.)

'And suppose, please God, Grigori and Ivan shall be on English soil with Elizabeth the Queen, and Queen Elizabeth commands them to her palace on their embassy, then Grigori and Ivan are to go to Queen Elizabeth. But they are to pray the *pristav* that at that time, when they are to be with the Queen, there shall be no ambassadors or envoys of other sovereigns.

'And if Elizabeth the Queen summon Grigori and Ivan to her palace to dine, and if Grigori and Ivan have been told by the *pristav* that at that time with the Queen at dinner there would be no ambassadors or envoys of any other sovereign; if nevertheless with the Queen at dinner there be any other ambassadors or envoys, they are not to go to dinner; but if the Queen command them to dine alone with her, then Grigori and Ivan are to go to the Queen to eat dinner. But if with the Queen at dinner there be ambassadors or envoys of the Turk, or the Pope, or the Emperor, or the Spanish King, or of whatever other sovereign, then at the Queen's palace with those ambassadors or envoys Grigori and Ivan are not to eat, or to go in person to dinner; but at such time if ambassadors or envoys of other sovereigns come to dine, then Grigori and Ivan, rising from the table, are to go to their own lodging.'

how he refused to deal with Elizabeth's advisers anywhere but in her palace; how he would have refused to attend the Queen's State Entry if, as he told the liaison-officer or *pristav*, Sir Jerome Bowes, he and Ivan his secretary were to be offered the 'infamy or disgrace, the *byezchéstiye*, of having any foreigners whatsoever with us'; and how he *did* refuse to dine with the Lord Mayor because he could not be seated at table above his host.

Every ambassador was of course accountable to his master, and had to report any ill-treatment. As Hotman writes,

if he himself receive any injury . . . he ought forthwith to advertise his Master thereof . . . the person of the Prince seemeth to be violated in the person of the Ambassador . . . a scorn or contempt done unto some Ambassadors hath been oftentimes cause of the beginning of war.

But accountability to his terrible Tsar rendered Mikulin so apprehensive of a *byezchéstiye* or 'scorn' as to make him a nuisance. M. de Boissise, indeed, the French ambassador, warned Sir Robert Cecil in plain terms of rocks ahead if the pretentious Muscovite held out for supremacy at the State Entry: 'I should be constrained to trouble the company, and they would see some disorder there.'[1]

This kind of thing made Mikulin amusing to the Court: and the quick comedian Shakespeare was not slow to seize his chance. On Twelfth Day the Muscovite was to consume his bread and salt and down his *garowses* of healths at the State Dinner which confirmed the olive-branch peace with Russia; after which he was to *go away*. He was *not* to be at the play at night. He *couldn't* be, as Don Virginio Orsino was to be the guest of honour.

---

[1] P.R.O., Trans. 3/31. France. Boissise au Roi, Nov. 28, 1600.

Good. To emphasize the Russian's welcome absence, Shakespeare at once scribbled in a part for an ambassador, 'Cesario', who comes on embassy to Lady Olivia's gate, speaks 'very shrewishly', would seem to have 'some hideous matter to deliver, the courtesy of it is so fearful', but—just like the very great fat Muscovite—holds the olive-branch in his hand, brings no overture of war, no taxation of homage. Admitted at length in audience, and primed to the teeth with his memorized speech as full of peace as matter, he is instantly miffed at not being told at once which is 'the honourable Lady of the house'; whereupon, after a step or two with 'gait very majestical', and a hand spread below the chin for the 'round black beard', comes the loaded line, in a Russified and ominous voice—
'*Let me sustain no scorn; I am very comptible* [countable], *even to the least sinister usage.*'[1] And the next speech hits off Mikulin's by-rote answers, dictated by his puppet-master the Tsar: '*I can say little more than I have studied, and that question's out of my part.*' What a delicious drollery we have been missing—the little boy-actress aping that Russian colossus.

Shakespeare's gentle jape reveals the great, fat, and tiresome Grishka Mikulin, hoisted for one brief moment alongside that irresistibly sparkling tun of Englishman, Jack Falstaff, as 'the cause that wit is in other men'. But since he was not there when his leg was pulled, Mikulin could not report Shakespeare's 'least sinister

---

[1] *Comptible* here obviously carries its usual sense of 'account-able': 'I am very accountable [to my master for every insult or *byezchéstiye* offered me], even to [i.e., even including] the least sinister usage.' The passage is mistaken by the commentators and by the *Oxford English Dictionary*.

usage' of him as a *byeʒchéstiye* to the Kremlin. No international incident arose out of *Twelfth Night.*

But it is high time for us to follow Shakespeare, as he goes to look over the scene of the coming jest, the centre of Whitehall's stately Hall, built long ago by Wolsey, the King-Cardinal. We follow him in no delusion of possibly becoming private secretaries to his thoughts; but merely in the belief that by identifying some of his precise conditions—of place, of 'the quality of persons, and the time'—we shall see better what he put into his play.

We follow him back to the Great Chamber. But here, instead of returning to the courtyard stairs, which lead out left to the court entrance, he turns immediately right, out down a stair to ground level at the back of the royal range. The buttressed side of the great stone Hall is directly before us, with a stair climbing to its main floor-level. Up the stair, and we find ourselves entering near the head of the Hall, by the Queen's door. Directly across from this door is a great recessed bay-window in the opposite side, through which we catch a glimpse of the Chapel's flank, rising close by, between us and the river. This Hall is about ninety feet long by forty wide within, built in five bays or structural sections containing windows, the end walls lighted by grand mullioned clerestory windows soaring high towards the huge beams of the open roof.

Destroyed by fire in 1698, this Hall was originally the glory of Wolsey's palace of York Place:

> That proud, ambitious, stately Cardinal
> Did first foundation lay, and built Whitehall.

His Hall's distinguishing feature was its orientation.

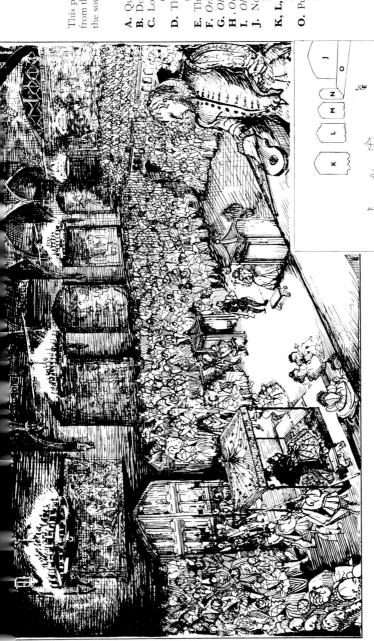

This perspective view is seen from the musicians' gallery in the south-east window.

KEY

A. Queen Elizabeth
B. Don Virginio Orsino
C. Lord Hunsdon, Lord Chamberlain
D. The Gentlemen Pensioners
E. The Yeomen of the Guard
F. *Orsino*
G. *Olivia*
H. *Orsino's house*
I. *Olivia's house*
J. North clerestory window, blocked with tapestry
K, L, M, N. Bay windows, blocked with tapestries
O. Public gallery beyond the permanent screen

RECONSTRUCTION OF THE GREAT HALL OF WHITEHALL PALACE ON THE FIRST NIGHT OF *TWELFTH NIGHT*

Wolsey laid it precisely on the meridian, due South and
North; and because 'there is more holiness and virtue on
the south side than on the north', the dais end, or head of
the Hall where we are standing and where its master sat,
is at the South. Thus its great clerestory window faces
the exact South, the *Midi*, the meridian, noonstead, or
midday—the sun at noon. The proud purpose of its
builder is clear: as he sat at its head, he would be 'super-
illustrated, with a Meridionall light, a South light, the
light of glory'.[1] And if with this circumstance in mind we
now look into Wolsey's tragedy (*Henry VIII*, 3. 2), we
realize that Shakespeare knew and used it:

> Nay then, farewell:
> I have touch'd the highest point of all my greatness,
> And from that full Meridian of my glory
> I haste now to my setting.

This is the only occurrence of *meridian* in all Shakespeare.
The meridian-point gave the building its distinctive name
of *Noon-hall*—as Pepys noted in 1665: 'the first play is
played in White Hall noon-hall'. Back to Shakespeare,
and we shall find that he has not forgotten the Hall's
famous orientation in writing *Twelfth Night*.

Carpenters from the Works have been busy here: the
whole interior is lined with *degrees*, wooden stands rising
in tiers of seats against all the walls. High in the 'round
window' opposite us they have built a 'floor' for the
musicians. Out in front of the lofty stand of *degrees* at
this South or dais end, they have set a large platform for
the Queen's *state* or canopied throne. The oblong of
floor left open in the middle of the room is no more than
twenty feet wide, perhaps less. What Shakespeare must

---

[1] John Donne, *Sermon XLIX*, 28 Jan. 1629/30.

now picture for his coming performance is this Noon-hall at the black 'noon of night': brilliantly lighted with hundreds of giant wax candles, huge fire glowing in its chimney-place, all its windows blocked with rich and heavy hangings to shut out the midnight January cold, its stands crowded with a shining paradise of ladies and courtiers enclosing the players down in the centre, who face the Queen at the South on her canopied throne.

One thing is clear. These intimate surroundings and general lighting rule out any attempt at optical illusion, by scenic means to waft the audience in fancy far away. That must be done with poetry. And for a comedy here, the method by which 'strong imagination works to frame things which are not' should be to create an illusion of actuality by letting parts of the fiction reflect some of the actual surroundings of the production: to make its art at moments join hands with the life which breathes around it.

The room will be crowded, the acting-space limited, and since a grand ball immediately precedes, there will be no stage. The scenic 'mansions' or 'houses' must be held to a minimum, both in number and size. If they are to conceal the chief characters before entrance and after exit, they cannot be opened to the view to show 'interior' action. Very well, we will have no interior scenes. But let the houses each have two doors, to permit two characters to come out *separately* from the same house and then 'meet' on the floor. How many houses? Two: Olivia's and Orsino's, set at the sides, facing each other, the neutral space between them backed by an 'orchard' of low property shrubs, including a 'box-tree' for hiding behind.

Are we assuming too much? On the contrary, I believe
that Shakespeare's text itself shows all this; and in addition it shows that, as Queen Elizabeth saw the play,
Olivia's house was to her right, Orsino's to her left. For
when Olivia dismisses 'Cesario' from her house, sending
him home to Orsino's, she says, 'There lies your way, *due
West.*' In this Noon-hall, on the meridian, as the players
face the Queen at the South, the way across the acting-
space from Olivia's (East) to Orsino's (West), is *due West.*
Again, Fabian tells Sir Andrew, 'You are now sailed into
the North of my lady's opinion'—and with the royal
'Olivia' sitting at the South or Noon, the North—which
the Germans call *Mitternacht*—is the farthest point from
her gracious presence, both by the compass and by the
chronometer. Another delicate touch of the same vivid
sort is Fabian's 'If this were play'd upon a stage now, I
could condemn it as an improbable fiction.' For it is *not*
being played upon a stage. It is *happening* on the floor of
the Hall, which has just been cleared of dancers, and Mr.
Controller Knollys is apprehensively watching '*Mal*'-
voglio being roughly handled under his very nose.

Later, that unfortunate 'madman' is kept in darkness
like a stage-property shut up inside Lady Olivia's close
house. 'They have here propertied me; keep me in darkness.' He speaks through the canvas wall, and cannot see
Feste when the Fool comes to tease him, with Sir Topas's
clerical gown put on over his own long robe of mingled
motley:

Feste. Sayst thou that house is dark?
Mal. As hell, Sir Topas.
Feste [*looking about him, round the brilliantly-lighted Noon-
hall with its bay windows and clerestories blocked with hangings*].

Why, it hath bay windows transparent as barricadoes, and the clerestories to the South North are as lustrous as ebony!

Feste of course names the South first. The South is the Queen's place, and gives the Noon-hall its name. This droll speech of his, far from being the invincible nonsense we have always taken it to be, now leaps to our eyes as a sparkling example of Shakespeare's bringing in the actual surroundings—of wedding fancy to fact. Here in the text he draws to the life the interior of his Twelfth Night arena-theatre in the palace Hall, with its blocked bays, its covered clerestories due South and North, and its two scenic 'houses' set due East and West. What but that precise time and that very room could conceivably give apt significance to these hitherto incomprehensible lines? Nor is this all. We remember that the Chapel Royal stands beside the Hall; Shakespeare employs it in having Olivia bid Sebastian

> Now go with me and with this holy man
> Into the chantry by.   There, before him,
> And underneath that consecrated roof,
> Plight me the full assurance of your faith.

And surrounded as he will be by *degrees with ladies*, the thought of them is already in his mind as he writes: 'I pity you . . . That's a *degree* to love. . . . No, not a *grize*.'

Even the actual scenery, the *houses* or *mansions*, comes to life for us in the text. Olivia's house, in which Malvolio is 'propertied', *is* small and dark. And Orsino's similarly takes shape in the scuffle between Sir Toby and Sebastian, with Sir Toby's 'Hold, sir, or I'll throw your dagger o'er the house.' With modern scenery, an impossible feat. Impossible too with what we have so long and so mistakenly imagined to be the Elizabethan staging at the Globe. In neither case would such an idea have occurred to a playwright's mind. But there in the Noon-hall Shakespeare already sees a little, free-standing, roofed *house*—over which Sir Toby *could* throw a dagger with a simple twist of the wrist. As for smaller properties to be used in the performance, besides the immortal 'box-tree', we need a bench or chair for Olivia near her house, and a bell to be struck inside the house to represent a striking clock: *Clock strikes*. 'The clock upbraids me.'

It makes an absorbing table-game of solitaire—and one anybody can play—to 'produce' *Twelfth Night* for one-self, in the light of our rediscovery of its original and simple production on an arena. Take two sheets of paper for the 'houses'; set one labelled *Orsino's* (*West*) at the left hand, the other, marked *Olivia's* (*East*), at the right. Give each house two doors: one at the front (facing the other house), another at the rear—so that characters can *'enter at several doors'*—appear or come on separately from the same house. (For example, Act 2, Scene 2, when Viola and Malvolio enter separately from Orsino's house.)

I think it will be found that the play can be performed in faithfulness to the text with a company of eighteen: two of them doubling (Sea-Captain and Gentleman, Sailor and Attendant), and one tripling (Sailor, Atten-dant, and Priest). The mariners can 'change' by simply doffing their sea-gowns, and the attendant turn priest by putting on a cassock. Prepare small paper counters marked with the characters' names—distinctive shapes and colours will be useful. Now follow the action of the play, as Shakespeare planned it in his mind's eye, enter-ing the characters as indicated from the sidelines right or left, as from the 'seacoast' or the 'city', or 'near Olivia's' or 'near Orsino's', or out of the houses themselves. As I play it, the greatest number of persons to be accommodated in either 'house' at one time is nine. And since nine persons seems rather a crowd for one of these small constructions, I assume that on occasion some Attendants or Gentlemen, instead of going in, slid beside the house to sink 'invisible' on the matting at the side of the acting-space until needed.

'Producing' the play in this card-table fashion reveals one extraordinarily interesting point, which may remove an old difficulty. At the opening of the fourth scene of Act 2 (at *Orsino's, West*), the Duke asks Viola-Cesario to procure him 'that piece of song . . . we heard last night'. He is told that Feste, who sang it, 'is not here', but 'about the house', and must therefore be sought out by Curio. Some thirty lines later, Curio brings Feste in, and the Duke asks him to repeat the song, urging Viola-Cesario to 'mark it'.

What is the cause of this apparent awkwardness? Critics have assumed that the song was originally meant to be sung by Viola-Cesario, who in the second scene of the play says that she can sing; that by the time of some later performance, this boy-actress's voice had changed, and Feste was substituted as the singer here.

A better clue seems to be offered by Queen Elizabeth's own directions for music and for the play, as set down in Lord Hunsdon's memoranda: '*To appoint Musicke severally for the Queene, and some for the play in the Hall. And Hales to have one place expresly to shewe his owne voyce.*' The lutenist Robert Hales (aged forty-one), 'the Orpheus of the Court', was the most excellent singer in England.

If Shakespeare had to make him one place expressly to show his voice, that place is no doubt this very one; and it was Hales who on Twelfth Night sang the poignant *Come away, come away, death!*

For the public stage, the song had to be transferred to Feste—Robert Armin, the company's best singer. And this transfer necessitated some rewriting of the scene, for the song must be sung at *Orsino's* (*West*). The action of the scene immediately preceding was however at *Olivia's*, (*East*), and Feste was in it. On the Globe's arena stage, he could not walk over to *Orsino's* without some explanation. From *Orsino's*, accordingly, he must be sought out. He proves to be not 'about the house', but still at *Olivia's*, and Curio must go across and fetch him.

But Feste will not thank us for vindicating his original public-stage right to the song if we return it to him maimed and deformed. For in the Folio text Shakespeare's original began

> *Come away, come away death,*
> *And in sad cypresse let me be laide,*
> *Fye away, fie away breath,*
> *I am slaine by a faire cruell maide . . .*

And it stood untampered-with for a century. Then the elegant and refined Nicholas Rowe 'corrected' *Fye away, fie away* to 'Fly away, fly away'; which is just as accurate as Victor Hugo's complacent reading of *The Firth of Forth* as *Le Premier du Quatrième*. (And Hugo stubbornly insisted that he was right.) But there is nothing comic about Rowe's ineptitude, carried into modern circulation by a long sheepish file of editors.

Shakespeare's original expresses grief's paradox with

extreme and powerful contrast. Ugly death is lovely, dear
life hateful. It is 'Come, sweet death!' and 'Get thee gone,
loathsome life!' The passion of self-loathing in 'Fie,
away!' [1] as in Hamlet's 'Fie upon't! Foh!' is of a piece with
Romeo's

> In what vile part of this anatomy
> Doth my name lodge? Tell me, that I may sack
> The hateful mansion.

For passion, the feeble 'Fly away, fly away' substitutes
prettiness, waters down the cry into a fond fanciful adieu,
a sentimental leave-taking of life; offers us Rowe, not
Shakespeare; Queen Anne, not Queen Elizabeth. If we
are satisfied with it, we are certainly getting as much as
we deserve.

But our business is not to look back at blunders, but
forward with Shakespeare to his problem of suiting his
play to the 'quality of persons, and the time'. For its time
will be Epiphany, the high festival of Light, the day of the
Three Kings. How will it be, at Whitehall on that greatest day of Christmas? The symbols and ceremony of
custom will be superb. The Court will all be dressed in
white. For it is the King's day; and in the morning the
Sovereign will come forth; the Court will 'rank to the
Chapel'—the glistening cortege will proceed two by two
through richly-decked and perfumed halls and corridors

---

[1] *Fie, away!* is frequent in Elizabethan English. Florio translates
the Italian *O* as 'an interjection of reproch, as . . . fie, a way a way'.
For the Latin *Vah* and *Apage*, Littleton gives 'Fie! Away for
shame!' and 'Fie Fie Away'. And for the French *Fy*, Cotgrave has
'Fye, away, fye away'. The contrasted *Come away* appears in song
as a favourite for the lover's invitation: '*Sweet, come away, my
darling*'. . . . '*Come away, arm'd with love's delights*'. . . . '*Come
away, come, sweet love.*'

lined with courtiers all in white, beyond the Noon-hall
to the Closet by the Chapel Royal, her Majesty under a
canopy in the midst, attended by the red-coated Yeomen
of her Guard.[1]

The Primate of all England and the Lord Bishop of
London in their white-and-golden copes will conduct the
Epiphany Service, assisted by other bishops and all the
Queen's chaplains. The music of the Chapel Royal will
be magnificent, voices and wind instruments, with Dr.
John Bull at the organ. The most ancient Epiphany hymn
runs, 'Today we are liberated from darkness, and are
illuminated by the light of divine knowledge', and the
Proper Preface in the modern Book of Common Prayer
reads: '*Through Jesus Christ our Lord, who in substance of
our mortal flesh, manifested forth his glory; that he might
bring us out of darkness into his own glorious light.*'
Epiphany reminds us that the way to God is doctrine,
'blind ignorance expelling with that light'.

What wealth of symbol! The white-clad Queen before her priest, Whitgift, whose canting motto is *Post
tenebras spero lucem*—'After darkness, I hope for light'
(the *white gift*):[2]

> Whitegift, whom gracious honour entertains . . .
> The fair Elisa white with heavenly praises
> The God's white church adornèd doth set forth :
> The all-white meaning and excelling worth,
> The virtue white above all honour raises.

On her knees—representing the Wise Men, Kings of
balm-breathing Arabia and sweet Saba, bringing gifts to

---

[1] 'The Guard still takes part in the Epiphany offerings of gold,
frankincense, and myrrh in the Chapel Royal, St. James's Palace.'
Sir Reginald Hennell, *History . . . of the Yeomen of the Guard*, 1904.

[2] 'Motto's . . . Whitgift. Vincit qui patitur. Post tenebras spero
lucem.' Bodl. MS. Sancroft 45, f. 1.

the infant Christ—the wise English 'Queen of Saba'[1] makes her offering of gold, frankincense, and myrrh to God the Triune : gold for the King, the Father; frankincense for the Holy One, the Holy Ghost; myrrh for the Mortal Man, the Son.

Shakespeare knows that so it will be in the solemn morning of Twelfth Day. And at night the joyous Noonhall will hold the same Queen and her prelates, watching his play in a lighter mood. Whitgift has a Fool, and sometimes players, at his own Palaces of Lambeth and Croydon. The Archbishop will be fain to smile at Feste, putting on a curate's gown with the pious wish 'I would I were the first that ever dissembled in such a gown', and then as the learned 'Sir Topas', gravely pressing home the Epiphany lesson to the benighted Malvolio, who imagines that it is the canvas *house* which is dark: 'Madman, thou errest. I say there is no darkness but ignorance.' Malvolio's protest, 'I say this house is as dark as ignorance, though ignorance were as dark as hell,' will leave 'Sir Topas' unmoved. Beyond question, this Malvolio is not merely distempered but possessed. For what says Pythagoras? 'Temperance is that light, which driveth away round about her the darkness and obscurity of passions.' Let us put Malvolio's absurd claim of sanity to the proof with this same philosopher. 'What is the opinion of Pythagoras concerning wild fowl?'

---

[1] *Saba* or *Sheba*, frequently applied to Elizabeth. 'In questioning not inferiour to Nicaulia the Queene of Saba' Lyly, *Euphues and his England*; '*Terralbon*, where *Saba* beholdeth the feeding of hir Lambes' W. Rankins, *A Mirrour of Monsters*, 1587; '. . . under the Gouernment of our prudent *Queene Sheba*' John Speed, *The Historie of Great Britaine*, 1611; '. . . the glory and magnificence of our Quene of Saba' Chamberlain to Carleton, Oct. 15, 1600. S.P. 12/275/94.

With so handsome a body of Clergy present, Shakespeare must give them something more. And he will combine with it another turn of the skilful dancing which delights the Queen. Two birds with one stone. On holidays the country people dance to the music of pipe and tabor in the churchyard; and at every church-stile commonly there's an ale-house. So he brings in the genial Fool with a step-dance to his own piping and drumming, and follows it with this exchange:

> *Vio.* . . . dost thou live by thy Tabor?
> *Feste.* No sir, I live by the Church.
> *Vio.* Art thou a Churchman?
> *Feste.* No such matter, sir; I do live by the Church: For, I do live at my house, and my house doth stand by the Church.

These principal doctors of divinity and homiletics are moreover favoured with this:

> *Oli.* We will hear this divinity. Now, sir, what is your text?
> *Vio. Most sweet Lady—*
> *Oli.* A comfortable doctrine, and much may be said of it. Where lies your text?
> *Vio.* In Orsino's bosom.
> *Oli.* In his bosom? In what chapter of his bosom?
> *Vio.* To answer by the method, in the first of his heart.
> *Oli.* O, I have read it! It is heresy.

And Shakespeare further maintains a strong Gospel flavour in the handling of the 'possessed' Malvolio as though he were the demoniac Gadarene (*Mark* 5. 6). For Sir Toby vows, 'If . . . Legion himself possessed him, yet I'll speak to him', and Feste not only rebukes the 'dishonest Satan', but when asked to read out the message from that unclean spirit, he does it according to Gospel,

147

clamans magna voce, 'crying with a loud voice'. And silenced by Olivia, he very justly protests, 'You must allow *vox*.'

To celebrate the Magi, the term *Wise man* appears more frequently in *Twelfth Night* than in any other of Shakespeare's plays: chiefly, of course, in contrast with *Fool*. The wise Queen herself will be sitting here in her glory at the South, having offered her gifts of 'Sabean odours from the spicy shore Of Araby the blest': that unparalleled Elizabeth, that Phoenix, 'sweet wonder of Arabia', that learned and all-accomplished Saba of the South. On such a day, what could be more pleasing to her Majesty, or more apt, than Viola-Cesario's courtly wish for Olivia, 'Most excellent accomplish'd lady, the heavens rain odours on you'? Or more happy than an allusion to the royal love-song of the Bible—*Come, O South, and on my garden blow, that the spices thereof may flow out*—in Orsino's lines,

> O, it came o'er my ear like the sweet South
> That breathes upon a bank of violets,
> Stealing and giving odour!

And what of the Court—not only the red-coated giants of the Guard, but as many of the 'ordinary', the regular Household staff of ladies and gentlemen, as can be crowded into the scaffolded Hall? Shakespeare must have a touch or two for some of them here and there. In the freedom of Twelfth Night, you do what you will, say what you will. For the courtier's common vice—of pretending to great 'inwardness' at Court—he will have a neat stroke: Sir Toby will make an offhand appointment with Sir Andrew at the *Cubiculum* or Privy Chamber: 'We'll call thee at the *Cubiculo*: go.'

And since Shakespeare and his fellows are *not* members of the Household, he has something further in store for the '*ordinary* men'—gentlemen ordinary, ordinary grooms, yeomen ordinary, ordinary footmen—those privileged mortals on the Queen's check-roll. Her Majesty has some *ordinary* Fools—how did they ever get on the staff?—dunderheads compared to my Robin Armin. Very well. The sour Malvolio shall have a preposterous double-edged line about Feste and Stone the Fool[1]—who was later whipped for calling 'some lord about court, fool', and was held to be a jester 'who could do nought but rail or flatter'—as follows: 'I saw him [Feste] put down the other day with an *ordinary fool* that has no more brain than a *stone*.'

As for the arrogance and emptiness of others of the Queen's ordinary men, Ben Jonson will get nowhere by snarling at their 'essential pride and ignorance', and satirical Jack Donne not much farther by girding at the ordinary Yeomen of the Guard, the one hundred and thirty-eight burly Beefeaters—

> . . . men that do know
> No token of worth but 'Queen's man', and fine
> Living, barrels of beef, flagons of wine.

What will really get home, of course, is the gibe indirect; and Shakespeare puts it into the mouth of the fool Sir Andrew: 'Methinks sometimes I have no more wit than a Christian or an *ordinary man* has. But I am a *great eater of beef*, and I believe that does harm to my wit.'

---

[1] For Stone the Fool see Chambers, *Eliz. Stage*, 3. 369; *Jonson* (ed. Simpson), 9. 701; and *The Odcombian Banquet* (1611), Sig. I4ᵛ.

That's one for the beef-witted Beefeaters, and a jest we could not possibly catch until we identified Shakespeare's first-night audience, which included the Queen's Guard of red-coated Yeomen Ordinary. Another unmistakable allusion to the Guard has lain similarly unsuspected in Feste's remark about the 'Myrmidons'—the third of his trio of cryptic statements, understandable only now in the light of the play's presentation at Whitehall: (*a*) 'Malvolio's nose is no whipstock', (*b*) 'My lady hath a white hand', (*c*) 'and the Myrmidons are no bottle-ale houses'. Feste's knowledge of the limits fixed to unruly behaviour at Court gives him this trio of cautions: (*a*) Liberty may not with impunity make a habit of plucking Authority by the nose—specifically of disdainfully handling that organ of Mr. Controller; (*b*) there is moreover no eluding the justice of what Essex termed the Queen's 'fair correcting hand'; and (*c*) as for her Myrmidons, her red-coated Guard, those 'big-bulk'd painted posts that senseless stand', it is most unsafe to mistake a stationary red coat for the familiar red lattice of an alehouse. Lurch absently into one of them for another drink, and you'll wish you hadn't.[1]

---

[1] *Myrmidons:* 'We are thy Mirmidons, thy Guard'—Beaumont and Fletcher, *Philaster*, 5. 4; 'The Justice and's myrmidons'—John Aubrey, *The Countrys Revell*, 2. 3.

Red lattice for ale-house: 'as well known by my wit as an alehouse by a red lattice'—Martson, *Antonio and Mellida*, 5. 1 ; ''A calls me e'en now, my lord, through a red lattice, and I could discern no part of his face from the window. At last I spied his eyes, and methought he had made two holes in the alewive's new [red] petticoat, and so peep'd through'—*2 Henry IV*, 2. 2.

VII

ILLYRIA FOR WHITEHALL

> The cant of the age, . . . an obscure proverb, an obsolete custom, a hint at a person or fact no longer remembered, hath continually defeated the best of our *guessers*.
>
> Richard Farmer, 1767.

WHY Illyria? Transparent domestic topicalities are always more amusing under the pretence of some distant scene. Ben Jonson set the Whitehall of his *Cynthia's Revels* in Diana's 'fustian country', Gargaphie. What reasons appropriate to Twelfth Night led Shakespeare to choose Illyria—that sea-coast far away, beyond the Adriatic? Were the connotations of *Illyria* for him and his audience the lyric, the idyll, or the illusion which the romantic sound of the name so often suggests in a modern ear?

Far from it. Something more robustious. What the Dalmatian-Croatian *Illyria* brought to mind was thoughts of wild riot and drunkenness, and the lawless profession of piracy. 'Their riotous neighbours, the Illyrians.'[1] 'Of the wine bibbing of the . . . Illyrians: Neither are the Illyrians clear of this beastly abuse.'[2] The Italian byword for a drunken toss-pot or sound quaffer was *un morlacco*— an Illyrian. For sea-thievery, we find Shakespeare elsewhere citing 'Bargulus, the strong Illyrian pirate' and the Ragusan 'Ragozine, a most notorious pirate', and aptly

---

[1] *Nashe* (ed. McKerrow), 3. 367.
[2] A. Fleming, *A Registre of Hystories* (1576), Sig. I2ᵛ.

bringing that 'notable pirate, salt-water thief', Antonio, into *Twelfth Night*'s Illyria.

All in all, a boisterous coast, Illyria. A fit stage for what Dowden happily called 'the reeling heights of Sir Toby's bacchanals'. Its character as 'drunk and disorderly' made it just the Misrulia or Wassailia in which to set the revel-rout, the 'sport, the Devil and all', and the licensed Twelfth Night tippling of spiced ale and burnt sack—fetched from the bar of the wide-open Buttery—to such ditties as

> Lusty, lusty boys and free—
> And very, very lusty boys are we.
> We can drink till all look blue,
> Dance, sing, and roar, never give o'er
> As long as we've e'er an eye to see—

though Sir Toby represents his wassailing as healths to Lady Olivia. 'I'll drink to her as long as there's a passage in my throat and drink in Illyria. He's a coward and a coystrill that will not drink to my niece till his brains turn o' th' toe like a parish top.' His rhetorical demand of Sir Andrew, his fellow-toper, 'Were we not born under Taurus?' is thoroughly sound. For Taurus—'Bull Jove' —governed those avenues of drink, the neck and throat. Jovial by birth, the precious pair are drunkards destined by zodiacal predominance. But to flatter him into show-ing his excellence in capering, Sir Toby assures the simpleton that Taurus governs 'legs and thighs'— blandly passing off *Cen*taurus (Sagittarius) as Taurus.

Slovenly Toby, whom Lady Olivia calls a 'rudesby', found a prompt imitator in Chapman's Sir Cut. Rudesby, who 'will come into the Presence, like your Frenchman, in foul boots'.[1] By brazenly defending his boots as 'good

---

[1] *Sir Giles Goosecap*, I. 2. 126.

enough to drink in', Sir Toby recalls the great leathern blackjacks for drink at Court, or perhaps the heroic boot-carouse—'whole boots-full to their friends' welfare'—achieved by compatriots of Hans van Belch, the drunken Dutchman of *Northward Ho.*

But the prime aura of suggestion clinging to Sir Toby's name and nature is the Biblical one, from the Apocrypha: in itself an affront to Puritan-sympathizers such as '*Mal*'-*voglio* and Mr. Controller Knollys. For the Puritans vehemently rejected the Apocryphal books. As Jonson's Zeal-of-the-land Busy exclaims, 'Peace, with thy Apocry-phall wares, thou prophane Publican : thy *Bells*, thy *Dragons*, and thy *Tobie's Dogges.*' Queen Elizabeth nevertheless had the objectionable Toby—Tobias, son of Tobit or Tobias—actively displayed before the courtiers' eyes. At Hampton Court hung 'two pieces of rich arras of the story of Thobie', and at Westminster, a dozen more 'pieces of tapestry of the story of Tobie'. In 1602 Henry Chettle wrote for the public stage a play (now lost) entitled *Tobias*. Aside from the Angel, and the Devil—who killed his bride's seven previous grooms—, the salient points in Toby's story were two: (*a*) his fish, and (*b*) his postponed wedding-night.

First, the fish. Not forgetting the fumigatory power of the very ancient and fish-like smell, the fishy fume which the devil himself couldn't abide, the fish is firmly held by all devout can-suckers, bang-pitchers, and elbow-lifters to be the happiest of living things—for it can drink at will. It is no accident that the drunken coachman in Fletcher's *Night-walker*, with his 'Give me the bottle! I can drink like a fish', is called Toby; or that Lady Olivia's cousin, who 'is in the third degree of drink—he's drowned', is that deboshed fish, Sir Toby.

As for the Biblical Toby's postponed wedding-night, it became a rule of the Church A.D. 398—marital abstinence for the first night or nights after marriage. The 'Toby-night' custom was so well known to the Elizabethans that Chapman brought it into his play *Alphonsus, Emperor of Germany*. Here the groom is encouraged to console himself on his Toby-night by drinking 'a dozen or two of these bowls', for 'it is the use That the first night the bridegroom spares the bride'.[1]

The trouble with Sir Toby Belch, from Mistress Maria's leap-year point of view, is that this Toby will hardly stop drinking long enough to let her jockey him into the Toby-night situation—turn him from fish into flesh. Feste condoles with her: 'If Sir Toby would leave drinking, thou wert as witty a piece of Eve's flesh as any in Illyria.' With the Toby-night in mind, the audience cannot fail to relish the other meaning of Maria's plea, 'Sweet Sir Toby, be patient for to-night', or to cheer her triumphal progress through Sir Toby's 'I could marry this wench for this device!' to her well-earned success: 'In recompense whereof he hath married her.' But the marriage does not take place until poetic justice, in the shape of bloody coxcombs given them by Sebastian, has sobered both the drunkards, Sir Toby and Sir Andrew. How neatly their punishment fits their crime appears by the contemporary euphemism 'cut in the head' for *drunk*: 'twice cut in the head, once with a pottle-pot, and now with cold iron'.[2]

If Shakespeare fitted his Aguchica and his Toby with

---

[1] See T. M. Parrott's note, *The Tragedies of George Chapman* (1910), 699.

[2] Dekker and Webster, *Westward Ho*, 5. 4.

such well-tailored and significant names, he suited the Illyrian gentleman-reveller who joined them in the mad jest on Malvolio equally well: for we find *Fabian* as a favourite current nickname for 'a riotous, lavish roister, a careless fellow'—'a flaunting fabian'.[1]

Wise men hold that there is no great wit without a mixture of madness. Further, that 'there is a pleasure sure in being mad which none but madmen know'. 'Wild, madding, jocund, and irregular', the world of Twelfth Night is a very mad world, exceeding mad. Small wonder that the epithet *mad* appears here more often than in any other play of Shakespeare's. Sir Toby in drink speaks nothing but madman; witty Maria is a finder of madmen; self-loving Malvolio, both sad-mad and madly-used; Lady Olivia in love, merry-mad; the startled Sebastian not only asks 'Are all the people mad?' but is forced to the conclusion, 'I am mad, or else the lady's mad.' And Feste, mad by vocation, seconds the notion by calling her *Mad-donna*.[2] The piece is shot through with the mad mood of hilarity—only heightened by a humourless Malvolio, who holds with the Preacher: 'I said of laughter, it is mad; and of mirth, what doeth it?'

Twelfth Night's high spirits irresistibly call to mind 'that merry man Rablays'. Like Shakespeare, Rabelais had a mint of phrases in his brain; and it would be strange if he had afforded Shakespeare no suggestion beyond the

---

[1] The *O.E.D.* suggests a probable reference 'to the Fabian priests of Pan, and the licence permitted them at the Lupercalia'. And we may compare Guilpin's *Skialetheia* (1598), sig. D1ᵛ, where an arrogant reveller is reprehended with 'out upon thee *Fabian*'.

[2] Compare 'Mad-dame', in Jonson's *The Devil is an Ass*, 4. 3. 39; *Tale of a Tub*, 3. 5. 4; and in Sir George Buc, *The Third Universitie* —Stow-Howes, *Annals* (1615), 987.

name *Holofernes* for the pedant in *Love's Labour's Lost*, from Gargantua's Latin-master, *Thubal Holoferne*. Swinburne was not alone in finding this affinity strongly in the learned fooling of Feste. The aphorism of Rabelais, *Un fol enseigne bien un sage*—'A fool may teach a wise man wit'—is capped by Feste's 'For what says *Quinapalus*? "Better a witty fool than a foolish wit"'. And as for Feste's Pigrogromitus and his voyaging Vapians, Dr. Furness confessed that

However settled the conviction that these are mere nonsense names invented by the Clown on the spur of a convivial moment, it is vain to deny that a curiosity, almost invincible, possesses us all to know something more of these Vapians, whose passing of the Equinoctial of Queubus was so infinitely droll that the humour thereof permeated even the thin and watery wits of Sir Andrew. Almost instinctively, we all turn to Rabelais; I am sure that I have merely followed many editorial predecessors in reading his volumes from the first line to the last on a keen but futile scent for the possible originals of these fictions of the Clown.

In brief, they *sound* Rabelaisian; but there is no real reason for denying them to Shakespeare's invention, stimulated by that gay companion, the *Curé* of Meudon.

But to call such gracious fooling 'incoherent jargon' or 'mere high-sounding emptiness' is fatally easy for the modern reader nourished on nonsense. It may however be doubted that the Elizabethans could be content with meaningless nonsense. Certainly Rabelais had meaning even in his strangest locutions. And so had Shakespeare. Our failure to find the meaning here is no excuse for continuing to sidle past 'As slyly as any commenter goes by hard words, or sense'. The only respectable course left us is to launch one more assault, for what it is worth, on this *château gaillard*, this *feste Burg* of Feste.

'For what says *Quinapalus?*' Surely the Fool's guide and philosopher, whom he consults for sage corroboration, can be no other than his inseparable bauble, his *marotte*, the absurd little figure on a stick. *That* is Quinapalus. And the form suggests derivation from an Italianate *Quinapalo*—'There on the stick'—on the model of *quina-valle* and *quinamonte*. On his stick, *Quinapalo* is of course in the best position to leap nimbly *di palo in frasca*—from pole to bush—which is the Italian for 'cock-and-bull', skipping, disconnected talk, the Fool's stock-in-trade.[1] As for *Pigrogromitus*, he seems to be compounded of the Italian for *lazy* and *scab or scurf*. *Lazyscurvius* is contemptuous enough, recalling both Sir Toby's 'Out, scab!' and Sir Andrew's 'thou art but a scurvy fellow', but we miss a clear reference.

Can we do better with the *Vapians* passing the equinoctial of *Queubus?* A *Va-pian* should be an Easy-goer, a Leisurely, a Fair-and-softly—from *Chi va pian piano va lontano*: 'Fair and softly goes far in a day'. And the astonishing distance these *Va-pians* cover is beyond the Equinoctial or Equator of *Cubus*—which, in Plato's cosmology, is the Earth: The Easygoers passing the Earth's Equator—below the burning Line. Inevitably there is an ingeniously indecent meaning as well, which however may readily be dispensed with. Stripped of scholarly whimsy, Feste's *festina lente* embodies a sound maxim of statecraft. Queen Elizabeth herself told the French ambassador that 'one should go gently and do nothing in haste'.

---

[1] Compare the French *sauter du coq à l'âne*.

Though the *Va-pians* are Shakespeare's coinage, perhaps the influence of Rabelais is otherwise present in *Twelfth Night, or What You Will*, and in a subtler shape than we have guessed. For the essential spirit of the saturnalian feast of misrule lives in its jovial freedom or licence, well set out by Ben Jonson in his Twelfth Night merriment, *Time Vindicated*:

> O, we shall have his Saturnalia, his days of feast and liberty again: where men might do, and talk all that they list—slaves of their lords, the servants of their masters. . . . Time's come about, and promiseth all liberty—nay, licence. We shall do what we list!

That is, not only 'drink as in the days of Pantagruel' but 'Flout 'em and scout 'em, And scout 'em and flout 'em. Thought is free.' In flouting Sir Andrew, the fair shrew Maria tells him, '*Now*, sir, thought is free.'

Here we find ourselves at the very door of Gargantua's House of Will or Pleasure, the Abbey of Theleme, if not already inside it, among the enviable Thelemites, in whose rule was but this clause—*Fay ce que vouldras*: What you will! From this vantage-point we now see more in Shakespeare's title than 'Call it *Twelfth Night*, or whatever you please'—which is the meaning Marston assigned to his own 'slight-writ' *What You Will*. For Shakespeare's title issues the saturnalian invitation, *Twelfth Night*, or *Fay ce que vouldras*, What you will—Liberty Hall. Do what you list with Mr. Controller or anyone else. No excuse is left for the shallow opinion that the play has no connection with Twelfth Night, or that the added title shows a carelessness of the main one. On the contrary, *What You Will* defines and drives home its rollicking message.

And where did Sir Toby find his ironical and preposterous description of Sir Andrew—'He's as tall a man as any's in Illyria . . . he plays o' th' viol de gamboys, and speaks three or four languages word for word without book'? Where but in the description of Gargantua's Thelemites, the Knights of his Abbey of What You Will? 'Never were seen knights so worthy, so valiant . . . more vigorous, more nimble. . . . So nobly were they taught that there was neither he nor she amongst them but could . . . sing, play on musical instruments, speak five or six languages.'[1]

Since Twelfth Night is the Feast of the Christmas Lord of Misrule, many have joined Quiller-Couch in accepting the festive Feste, with his long green robe of mingled motley and his bauble-sceptre, as 'the master-mind and controller of *Twelfth Night*'. Yet if that were so, Feste would plan and conduct the brilliant campaign against 'Mr. Controller' Malvolio. But no such matter. On the contrary, it is the quick, deviceful, strong-brained little gentlewoman, Maria, whom Shakespeare sets up as rightful ruler of the sport royal, and she richly deserves her crown at the Buttery-bar as a finder of madmen. His excellent ground for this—and, as we have seen, for the choice fitness of the play's main plot as well—is the date of his production, 1600: leap-year, women's year. 'Dian doth rule, and you must domineer.' Inevitably Maria reigns as Lady of Misrule, and inevitably she hooks and lands her fish, Toby. [2]

---

[1] *Gargantua*, Book 1, Chapter 57.
[2] In Ben Jonson's *New Inn*, Prudence, 'The Chambermaid, is elected *Soueraigne* of the *Sports* in the Inne, gouernes all, commands, and so orders, as the *Lord Latimer* is exceedingly taken with her, and takes her to his wife, in conclusion'. The contract of marriage

Sovereign for a night, Maria receives us into her holiday realm—a land teeming with Christmas and Epiphany legend, folk custom, and traditional feasting, dance, jesting, and game. For Twelfth Night is not only the joyful Feast of Light for the returning sun, but also *Le Jour des Rois*, the anniversary of the Three Kings:

> Be merry, all that be presënt,
> Reges de Saba venient—
> Now is the Twelfth Day come—
> God send us good New Year!

According to Florio, the name *Maria* signifies *Illumination*: not inappropriate for the queen of the Feast of Light.

Sir Toby brings in a well-known piece of Twelfth Day folklore by hailing the neat little sovereign's approach with 'Look where the youngest Wren of mine comes'. For the tiny Wren is both universally known as King of the Birds, and connected with this feast in a fashion as familiar as it is baffling. Under 'Wren' in the *Encyclopædia Britannica*, Alfred Newton writes,

> The curious association of this bird with the Feast of the Three Kings, on which day in South Wales—or in Ireland and in the South of France on or about Christmas Day—men and boys used to 'hunt the wren', addressing it in a song as 'the king of the birds', is remarkable.

> *The wren, the wren, the King of all birds*
> *On Saint Stephen's Day he was caught in the fur{e.*

Has anyone ever explained the mystery? Was the Wren King the enemy of the Three Kings? And must he be yearly slain to clear their road, when 'the Kings of Arabia and Saba shall bring gifts'?

---

is here made without a priest, *per verbum de presenti* before witnesses, which no doubt was Toby's and Maria's method too.

Who can tell? But there are some striking coincidences here. 'Happy Arabia, nature's spicery', which as the Elizabethan Fynes Moryson reports 'yields frankincense, myrrh—grains of gold as big as acorns are found here', contained two kingdoms: Saba (Sabæan) and Ma'in (Minæan). *Mineo* and *Minea* are Florio's words for frankincense and myrrh. Here then is *Mine* connected both with the country and with two gifts of the Three Kings. Is the country possibly the original *Mine* of gold or gold-mine as well? Who knows? At all events, it is certain that the ancients called the people of Araby-the-blest 'Troglodytes' or cave-dwellers.[1] Furthermore, the country 'abounds in small birds', and the name of the Wren is *Troglodytes parvulus*, 'the tiny cave-dweller'. However far we may still be from fathoming the mysterious relation of King Wren the cave-dweller to the Three Kings of cave-dwelling Saba and Mine, we can now begin to see light in Sir Toby's 'Wren of Mine'.

Wren Maria discharges her role as mock ruler, Twelfth Night queen, to admiration. But Shakespeare does not therefore neglect two other features of the ancient Christmas folk-play—the sword-dance or sham combat, and the mumming. Of the first he reminds us with the bloodless passage-at-arms between Viola and Sir Andrew, and of the second with Feste's dressing up as a counterfeit Sir Topas the curate 'to visit Malvolio the lunatic'. And Maria, though she put Feste up to this bit of tradition,

---

[1] 'People of Arabia called . . . *Troglodytans*' Topsell, *Four-footed Beasts*, 225; 'Arabia bordering vpon Ethyopia by the auncients called Trogloditick' T. Washington, tr. *Nicholay's Voy.* IV. xi. 122b; 'The Troglodites myne them selues caues in the grounde, wherin to dwell' W. Watreman, *Fardle of Facions*, I. vi. 93; qu. *O.E.D.*

recognizes it as functionless: 'Thou mightst have done this without thy beard and gown. He sees thee not.'

Another Twelfth Night custom of high antiquity which heralds the wassail is *Hunt the Fox*. Obviously a process of 'killing the old Devil for good luck', in former times it was accomplished by the hullabaloo of hunting down and killing a fox or a cat released in the Court. 'The night is our own, for the Devil is dead!' As late as 1572 a fox was killed at Whitehall on Twelfth Night. The death of the devil-fox gave the joyful signal for wassail so notoriously that drunkards were termed *fox-catchers*, and to be drunk was called *to whip the cat, to hunt the fox*, or to be *foxed*. In a less sanguinary form this Twelfth Night custom survived in the rough sport of 'Fox in the Hole', with hue and cry after a luckless human quarry, hunted with yelps of 'Fox, fox, go out of thy hole!' As Herrick has it,

> . . . thy wassail bowl,
> That's toss'd up after Fox-i'-th'-hole.

Hunt the Fox gives point to Feste's defiance of Malvolio: 'Sir Toby will be sworn that I am no *fox*; but he will not pass his word for twopence that you are no fool.' As much as to say, 'I am no Twelfth Night fox to be hunted out; if you are so anxious to chase out a fool, begin with yourself.' And Orsino's banishing of that young fox, 'Cesario', is in the same vein:

> O thou dissembling cub! What wilt thou be
> When time has sow'd a grizzle on thy case?

Once the wassail and catch-singing have been well launched, the natural course is to stretch to the limit the last gaudy night of the holidays, mocking the midnight bell. But Sir Toby's 'Not to be abed after midnight is to

be up betimes' and "Tis too late to go to bed now' inevitably bring the thought of the morning after, when the
world will go back to work. And since the universal,
ceaseless, and typical work was drawing the fibres and
whirling the spindle, the morrow of Twelfth Night was
Saint Distaff's or Rock Day:

> Give Saint Distaff all the right,
> Then bid Christmas sport good night.[1]

This prospect of 'spinning tomorrow' underlies Sir
Toby's broad jest on Sir Andrew's thin and 'flaggy' or
flat-lying hair, which betrays his foolishness—*His thin-set
hair along did sit, Which represents a woodcock's wit* [2] :

To. It hangs like flax on a distaff; and I hope to see a house-
wife take thee between her legs and spin it off.
And. Faith, I'll home tomorrow, Sir Toby.

But tomorrow, Saint Distaff, and the hussy are futurities.
Sir Andrew still has his hair, such as it is, and Twelfth
Night is here—a dancing time of revels. These make
the delight of Sir Andrew, who is good at gambols,
capers, and sprawling 'kickshawses', *quelquechoses* of
papier-maché in Toby's pun, kick-'shows' for show, not
eating (see p. 180). The knightly Aguchica-Littlewit even
claims Illyrian excellence in the acrobatic *salto indietro*
or 'back-trick', of which the Italian masters describe no
fewer than nineteen distinct and astonishing varieties.[3]

General freedom of dicing, under the regulation of her
Majesty's Groom Porter, was a further Court liberty

---

[1] Herrick, *Hesperides* (1648), 'St. Distaff's Day'.
[2] *Bacchus Bountie* (1593), by 'Phillip Foulface'.
[3] Tomaso Garzoni, *La Piazza Universale* (1589), 454.

during Christmas, in which the Queen herself joined. If we think it credible, we may believe what Ben Jonson is reported to have said, that she 'had always about Christmas evens *set dice*, that threw six or five, and *she knew not they were other*, to make her win and esteem herself fortunate'. More credible is the story of Elizabeth's gamester's-humour in calling Pope Sixtus Quintus, her admiring enemy, by the winning nickname of 'Sice-cinq'. A favourite holiday game with the 'square rattling bones' was *trey-trip*, in which a three was the winning throw. *Twelfth Night* brings this in twice. First with Toby's 'Shall I play my freedom at trey-trip, and become thy bond-slave?' and punningly again, when Feste tries to beg a third gold-piece of Orsino (as a Christmas present) with 'Primo, secundo, tertio, is a good play . . . the *tri*plex, sir, is a good *trip*ping measure'—only to be told, 'You can fool no more money out of me at this *throw*.'

Another popular implement for dicing at this feast was the four-sided top, whirligig, or teetotum: which survives in use today at the Hanukah Festival of Lights as the *Drehrädchen* or *Dredel*. When 'Time's come about', and Malvolio's number is up and his luck is out, Feste employs this Twelfth Night teetotum or whirling die to symbolize poetic justice : 'and thus the whirligig of time brings in his revenges.'

As for card-play with the dicing, perhaps the leading Christmas game was what Ben Jonson calls 'the thrifty and right worshipful game of Post and Pair'. The Knave or Jack in this game held an important place under the name of *Pur*:

> Some, having lost the double Post and Pair,
> Make their advantage on the Purs they have.

'Post and Pair' figures as a character in Jonson's *Christmas his Masque*, 'his garment all done over with Pairs and Purs'. So familiar were the Twelfth Night *Post* and *Purs* that they furnished Viola with a scornful pun in her refusal of Olivia's gift of money: 'I am no fee'd *post*, lady; keep your *purse*'—that is, 'your *knavish* gold'.

Turning from gambling to Twelfth Night guessing games, we learn from Drayton and Jonson that the latter included Purposes and Riddles:

> In pretty riddles to bewray our loves,
> In questions, purposes, or drawing gloves.

'At Draw-gloves, Riddles, Dreams, and other pretty Purposes'—'For sport's sake, let's have some riddles, or purposes.' Purposes (a sort of 'Guess what I'm thinking of') receives only passing reference in Maria's admission, 'My *purpose* is indeed a horse of that colour'. But the Riddle takes centre-stage in *Twelfth Night* with Maria's cunningly-prepared 'dish o' poison' for Malvolio: '*M. O. A. I. doth sway my life*'.

Clearly, this fustian riddle must have a simple solution, obvious both to the audience and to all the characters except that dullard, Malvolio. His fatuous, self-absorbed, and fruitless brain-beating furnish the fun:

> What should that alphabetical position portend? If I could make that resemble something in me! Softly! *M. O. A. I.* . . . *M.—Malvolio. M.*, why, that begins my name! . . . *M.* But then there is no consonancy in the sequel. . . . *A.* should follow, but *O.* does.

Can we do any better than Malvolio? Query, what is the most obvious group of four? Answer, the Four Elements—which in her 'Armada' prayer Queen Elizabeth defined as 'serving to continue in orderly government

the whole of all the mass'—and the word *element* comes
more frequently into *Twelfth Night* than into any other
play of Shakespeare's. '*M. O. A. I. doth sway my life*'.[1]
Maria has cleverly chosen those 'fustian' designations of
the elements whose initials appear in his name: *Mare*-Sea,
Orbis-Earth, *Aer*-Air, and *Ignis*-Fire. *M. O. A. I.*

> Fire hot and dry, air moist and hot we call;
> Seas cold and moist, earth dry and cold withal.[2]

Her 'dish o' poison' dupes the self-loved *MALVOLIO*
into imagining himself Controller of Lady Olivia,
although every fool knows that she is swayed only by
*M*are, *O*rbis, *A*er, and *I*gnis. And the order of Maria's
arrangement of the elemental four is thoroughly appropriate. According to accepted theory, Woman is cold
and moist, Man, hot and dry; in the elements swaying
Olivia, therefore, *Mare* must take first place. Also she
commands Malvolio ('*I may command where I adore*'):
consequently *Mare* leads and *Ignis* comes last. Moreover,
in mourning her brother, Olivia's controlling emotion is
grief: and 'Grief like water cold and moist' is again *Mare*.

---

[1] The elements compose the eternal Unity, the controlling, turning Universe:

> 'A man to join himself with th'Universe
> In his main sway, and make (in all things fit)
> One with that All, and go on round with it.'

Chapman, *Revenge of Bussy*, 4. 1. 139–41.

The controlling elements also figure in love lyric:

> 'What else mishap, but longing to aspire,
> To strive against earth, water, fire, and air?'

The Phoenix Nest (1593), ed. H. E. Rollins, 81.

[2] R.C., *The Times' Whistle* (E.E.T.S., 1871), 117. Chapman
likewise employs *Sea* for the element Water—'When sea, fire, air,
in earth were indisposed' *The Shadow of Night* (1594), line 42;
and Feste uses *Orb* for the Earth: 'Foolery, sir, does walk about the
Orb like the Sun' 3. 1. 39–40.

This riddle is an essential part of the practical joke on Malvolio. Elaborate plots to make somebody look a fool constituted a principal Court pastime in the holidays. The current courtier's slang for the jest was to *dor* someone— 'that villain dors me'—or to give someone the *dor*. Like Malvolio's *geck*, the term is obviously borrowed from the Dutch: *een door*, a fool. Jonson's Twelfth Night comedy *Cynthia's Revels* exhibits a deal of this *dor*-ing. In Act 5 Scene 2, a trick is described very similar to the one played on Malvolio: 'He follows the fallacy; comes out accoutred to his believed instructions; your mistress smiles, and you give him the *dor*.' Shakespeare likewise brings in the *dor*-ing, but so lightly and deftly that we have failed to notice it—in the foolish Sir Andrew's innocent echo of Sir Toby's boast of Maria's love for him: 'She's a beagle true bred, and one that adores me: what o' that?'

Sir Andrew: 'I was a-*dor*'d once too.'

To close up the Illyrian revel with music and moral, Shakespeare gives us Feste's celebrated song, *When that I was and a little tiny boy*. For lack of understanding of its drift, this song has naively been received as a tale in rime but little reason: nonsense contemptible or nonsense charming; but nonsense. But is Feste the man to waste his wit in nonsense? He knows precisely what to provide as a fitting farewell to wassail and saturnalian excess: and it is not something adapted to a Christmas party for Victorian young persons. As Rupert Brooke observed, 'The Elizabethans liked obscenity; and the primness and the wickedness that do not like it, have no business with them.'

Must we really be reminded that ribaldry was the proper and age-old function of the Fool? Shakespeare's

colleague Robert Armin played not only Feste but Lear's
Fool as well. Knavish, licentious speech is common to
both roles; and Armin's rendering of Feste's song proved
so popular that an additional stanza was sung in *Lear*—
He that has and a little tiny wit. Historically, the Fool and
indecency cannot be parted. To make up for his mental
shortcomings, Nature was commonly believed to have
endowed the Fool with an excess of virility, symbolized
by his *bauble*. 'Fools please women best.' 'A fool's
bauble is a lady's playfellow.' 'A foolish bed-mate, why,
he hath no peer.' Priapus used to be described as *that
foolish god*; and Mercutio's cynical notion of Love is a
great natural with his *bauble*.

Feste's lascivious lapses earn him Lady Olivia's sharp
reproof—'you grow dishonest'. We realize that he has
not forgotten its sting, when, with the Fool's immemorial
trick of 'box about'—that is, of passing a received blow on
to someone else—he buffets the devil of lechery in Malvolio with this same *dishonest*: 'Talkest thou nothing but
of ladies? . . . Fie, thou dishonest Satan!' His boastful
pun, 'He that is *well hang'd* [i.e., *handsomely furnished or
adorned with virility*] in this world, needs to fear no
colours [*no deceptions or foes*]' is taken up by Maria.[1] She

---

[1] For this sense of *hang'd*, see the fool Pompey in Fletcher and
Massinger's *Wit at Several Weapons*, 2. 2: 'When they saw how I
was hang'd . . .' Compare Cotgrave's *Couillatris*: 'Well hang'd'.
Maria gives Feste the derivation of his byword: 'I can tell thee
where that saying was born, of "I fear no colours" . . . In the wars.'
Colours of course means 'military colours' as well as 'deceptions'.
The historical source would seem to be *La Guerre Folle* of 1485 in
France. And who more expert on the Mad War than that accom-
plished 'finder of madmen', Maria? Sir Walter Ralegh, writing on the
valour of the English fighting man, cites 'another place of the same
Authour [de Serres], where hee tells, how the *Britons* [i.e., Bretons],
being invaded by *Charles* the eight, King of France, thought it good

bids him, 'Make that good [*Prove that statement in a decent sense*].' And Feste's lenten answer blandly reverts to the gallows-meaning, dismal but decent: a man well hang'd *by the neck* 'shall see none to fear'.

As for Lear's Fool, he advertises the Fool's characteristic advantage by announcing, 'Marry, here's grace and a codpiece: that's a wise man and a fool.' To this he adds a complacent boast of his physical irresistibility to the other sex: 'ladies too, they will not let me have all the fool to myself, they'll be snatching.' [1] And he closes the first act of the tragedy with the witty and bawdy tag

> She that's a maid now, and laughs at my *deporter*,
> Shall not be a maid long, unless things be cut shorter.

The text has *departure*, a word unacceptable both for the rime and for the sense. I suggest that Shakespeare must have written *deporter*, which Cotgrave gives as the French for 'a sporting bauble'. What roused the wanton wench to hilarity was not the Fool's vanishing but the

---

policie, to apparell a thousand and two hundred of their owne men in *English* Cassacks; hoping that the very sight of the *English* red Crosse, would be enough to terrifie the *French*.'—*The Historie of the World*. Another writer, Henry Belasyse, employed the same familiar incident, as follows: 'These victoryes [in the Hundred Years' War] made the English so famous, that the Duke of Britanny warring against Charles 8th of France, to strike terror into the French, apparelled fifteen hundred of his owne subjects in English armes and under the English colours. But the asse is never the better for having putt on the lyons skinne, nor the Britons [Bretons] for appearing like English.'—H.M.C., *Various*, 2. 196. Feste may be bold to use a phrase extolling the terrific reputation of English military valour.

[1] Compare the Fool's song in *Volpone*, 1. 2. 71:

> Your Fool, he is your great man's darling,
> And your ladies' sport and pleasure;
> Tongue and bauble are his treasure.

sight of his immoderate 'bauble'.[1] *Thing* in its 'bauble' sense is the key word, not only here, but also in the first stanza of Feste's song. In the Fool's childish state as a little tiny boy, a *foolish thing* was no more than a harmless trifle. Far otherwise, however, when he was grown 'fit for breed'—a lecherous knave and thief of love, on the prowl after other men's wives:

> 'Gainst knaves and thieves men shut their gate.

Having begun by making sure that in listening to Feste's song we are not like that blockish Rosencrantz, with whom a knavish speech sleeps in a foolish ear, we may now look at the 'reason of the rime'—the plan of the ditty as a whole. Feste has already given us his exquisite love songs; now we are to be sent away with 'a song of good life'. What he trolls out is a Drunkard's Progress, an Elizabethan forerunner of such bibulous confessions as *I'm a rambling wreck of poverty* and *I've been a moonshiner for seventeen long years*: a moral and musical reminder that the wassailing of the Twelfth Night saturnalia had better not be followed as a way of life. That is the road to 'wet damnation'. He has already told Lady Olivia—as they contemplate the condition of Sir Toby—that a drunken man is like a fool, a madman, and a drowned man: 'One draught above heat makes him a fool, the second mads him, and a third drowns him.' Now he proceeds to illustration, with a dramatic lyric of rueful reminiscence leading us through the same three familiar degrees—goat-drunk, lion-drunk, and swine-drunk: 'now goatishly to whore, now lion-like to roar, now hoggishly in the mire'

---

[1] 'Shee is enamour'd on the fooles bable' *Jack Drum's Entertainment* (1600), Act 2, line 308.

—whose attendant deadly sins, appropriated to the three ages of manhood (youth, prime, and old age), are Lechery, Wrath, and Sloth.

As we have noticed, in the second stanza—*'Gainst knaves and thieves men shut their gate*—the lecherous knave finds that his goatish vice renders him an outcast, shut out in the rain. In the third stanza, unable to mend his ways on the precept 'Leave thy drink and thy whore, and keep in-a-door', he makes a shiftless, beggarly, wrangling marriage. Lion-drunk, he dings the pots about, swaggers with his own shadow, and his screeching wife drives him forth—out in the rain.

The final phase exhibits him in the torpor, the 'be-numbing apoplectic sleep' of the swine-drunk—*But when I came unto my beds. Beds* is inevitably plural: the various spots where he happened to fall. The abandoned drunk-ard has many beds, as well as a long series of drunken heads in toss-pot company. As John Day puts it, 'The last . . . carry their beds o' their backs . . . and go to bed in the kennel . . . and these we call Swine-drunk'.[1] The grovelling Sly of *The Taming of the Shrew* is either hog or corpse: 'This were a bed but cold to sleep so soundly. O monstrous beast! How like a swine he lies! Grim death, how foul and loathsome is thine image!'

Again, out in the rain. 'Through the sharp hawthorn blows the cold wind.' With a sorrowful hey-ho, the wind and the rain, and the implied early death they bring with them, form the inevitable burden. *A great while ago the world begun;*[2] and for the drunken fool without the wit to

---

[1] 'Peregrinatio Scholastica' *Works* (ed. Bullen, 1880), 51, 52.
[2] Feste's 'A great while ago the world begun' recalls the Eliza-bethan euphemism for coition, 'To dance The Beginning of the World'.

come in out of the rain, it is all but ended. What of it?
But that's all one. . . . Then turning smoothly into Robin
Armin the player, Feste is out of his moral and into an
Epilogue, to beg a gracious *plaudite* of the hearers—

> our Play is done,
> And we'll strive to please you every day.

VIII

THE DAY OF KINGS

Everything has been drawing to the climax, Queen Elizabeth's Twelfth Day—that whole which she has fashioned with perfect art. To follow its glorious and traditional Epiphany Service, she has revived the ancient State Dinner with dazzling splendour and Muscovite features for an immediate end of state—to confirm the league with Russia. Finally, with swift and unerring hand she completes the masterpiece with public entertainment of Don Virginio Orsino: a stroke which achieves every end of policy abroad and at home, of artistic delight and personal pleasure.

The picture calls to mind the triumphs of the Chinese brush. Only genius and long practice lend the sure power to produce a masterpiece in a moment. But one thing is certain. Without Shakespeare, Elizabeth would have missed perfection. None but his incredibly quick imagination and faultless taste, none but his flying pen could 'upon the gad' have produced the radiance of charm and the delight of wit which set the garland on the day —could have launched this 'flight on Thames that did so take Eliza'.

Ideally, we should have the Queen's diary, setting down her secret plans in detail, and recording the events of the day which realized them. But Elizabeth's memory was not (like Spanish Philip's) the plodding daily slave of pen and ink. She saw in her mind's eye, and kept in mind, while she 'gave order'. But now we have found

173

that unexampled Elizabethan record, the compendious list of directions which she had 'good George', her Chamberlain, take down to guide him. We shall return to these orders. To show how they were carried out, we have unearthed three reports: one by a herald or officer of arms, a second by the Russian ambassador Mikulin, a third by Don Virginio Orsino—and each of them, by individual details and cross-lights, lends precision to the picture of the great day at Whitehall.

These are of the highest value; for a careful study of them in conjunction with the Works Accounts reveals for the first time important features of the Whitehall which Shakespeare knew. For example, even that great authority Sir Edmund Chambers did not know that the Palace had *two* Great or Guard Chambers—one on the 'King's side', the other on the 'Queen's'; and that the splendid Council Chamber had formerly been the Presence Chamber, 'Queen's side'. Now these are the very rooms into which we shall soon be following the Queen, the Ambassador, Orsino the Duke, and Shakespeare; and we need not wander in a mental fog if we make an effort to visualize the general scheme of the chief rooms, and their relation to the Hall and the Chapel.

In simplified outline, the main rooms—which were all on the *piano nobile*, one flight up from the ground— formed a right angle, bounding the great courtyard. Draw therefore a capital L; and below the tip of its foot set two short heavy dashes, one below the other—to represent the Hall and the Chapel, which are separate buildings but connected with the tip of the L, the first by stairs, and the second by a long passage.

The foot of the L is the 'King's side', and the upright

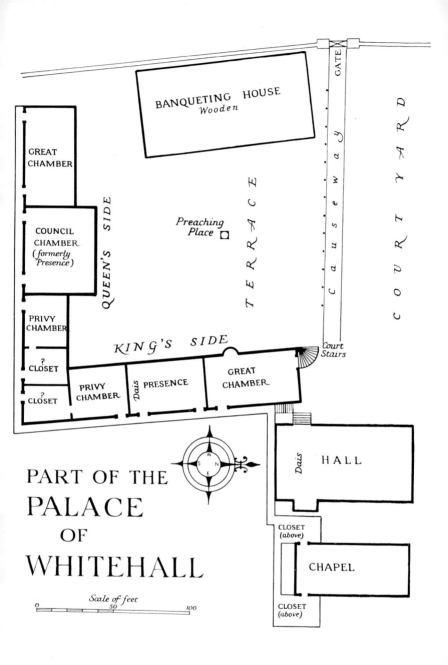

BANQUETING HOUSE
Wooden

GATE

C a u s e w a y

C O U R T Y A R D

GREAT
CHAMBER

QUEEN'S SIDE

COUNCIL
CHAMBER
(*formerly*
Presence)

T E R R A C E

Preaching
Place

PRIVY
CHAMBER

?
CLOSET

?
CLOSET

KING'S SIDE

Court
Stairs

PRIVY
CHAMBER

Dais

PRESENCE

GREAT
CHAMBER

Dais

HALL

CLOSET
(*above*)

CHAPEL

CLOSET
(*above*)

PART OF THE
PALACE
OF
WHITEHALL

Scale of feet
0   50   100

the 'Queen's side'. Queen Elizabeth's private lodging is near the angle where they meet. From it, in order along the foot of the L ('King's side'), and connected by broad corridors, runs the main range: Privy Chamber, Presence Chamber, and Great (Guard) Chamber at the end. This last is the Great Chamber where we saw Shakespeare playing before Queen Elizabeth and Wolfgang Wilhelm on St. Stephen's Day: the outer chamber of the Court, entered from the courtyard by the great stair. Out of it at the rear a stair leads to the Hall—our first little dash; also a corridor out of it, still on the first-floor level, leads on round the end of the Hall to the Closet by the Chapel —our second little dash.

The Epiphany procession will form in the Privy Chamber, 'King's side'; when the Queen comes forth, it will proceed via the Presence and the Great Chamber through the long corridor to the Closet. This Closet is a large room, of a peculiar double shape, built round the upper end and sides of the Chapel. From it one can look down into the Chapel from either side, through openings or windows in the Chapel walls. There the Court will wait, while the Queen, escorted only by Yeomen of the Guard, descends to the Chapel to make her offering in the chancel.

We return to the L, and its upright, representing the 'Queen's side'. Starting again from the Queen's lodging at the angle, we have, in order, another Privy Chamber, the Council Chamber (formerly Presence, 'Queen's side'), and at the tip another Great Chamber. This last will be the scene of the State Dinner; and Don Virginio will dine in the Council Chamber adjoining, guest of the Lord High Steward, Lord Nottingham.

With this introduction we can now better understand that unique revelation from the Duke of Northumberland's library of the Queen's plans and preparations to put her house in order for the magnificent celebration and entertainment. It is several days before Twelfth Day; she summons her Lord Chamberlain to give him specific direction, and the copy of his notes runs as follows:

Noblemen to attend her Ma*j*estie att her
dyning abroad upon Twelfe day
the 6 of January 1600

The Karver The Earle of Sussex [*Robert Radcliffe*]
The Cupbearer The Earle of Darbye [*William Stanley*]
To cast the Surnap and take th'assay The Lord Thomas Howard, The Lord of Effingham [*William Howard*]
The Sewer The Lord Windsor [*Henry, Baron Windsor*]
To cary the Trane The Lord Chamberlain [*George Carey, Baron Hunsdon*] The Lord Cobham [*Henry Brooke*]
[*Edges of paper burnt away*]
    The Earle of W[orcester, *Edward Somerset*]
    The Earle of Rutland [*Roger Manners*]: *to* [   ]
    The Earle of Cumberland [*George Clifford*]: *to give*
    [   ]

To come before the meat
    Admirall The Lord Steward [*Charles Howard, Earl of Nottingham*] Lord Tresorer [*Thomas Sackville, Baron Buckhurst*] The Comptroller [*Sir William Knollys*]

To followe the meat
    All the officers of houshowlde

To say grace
    The Lord Archbishop of Canturbury [*John Whitgift*]
    The Lord Bisshop of London [*Richard Bancroft*]
    The Lord Bisshop of Eely [*Martin Heton*]
    The Lord Bisshop Almoner [*Anthony Watson*]

The Deane of York [*Lancelot Andrewes*]
and all her Majesties chaplains

[*Another page lists the services and their waiters for the close of the Dinner, as follows:*]

Cupbearer Earle of Shrewsbury [*Gilbert Talbot*]
Carver Earle of Sussex
Sewer Lord Henry Seymor or Lord of Effingham
To give the Towell Lord Tresorer
To give the Water Earle of Notingham
To uncover the bason Earle of Shrewsbury
To give the Assaye Earle of Darbye
To cast the Towell Lord Thomas Howard
To cary the Lavor Lord [*not filled in*]
   with two gentlemen Ushers to attend
Knightes to remove the boarde
   Sir Henry Gray
   Sir Thomas Vavasor
   Sir Edward Moore
   Sir John Salisburye
   Sir John Skidmore [*Scudamore*]

Chaplains for grace The Lord Almoner to attend
[*Recorded afterwards:*]
   To attend the Imbassador were apointed two knightes and
   twelve gentlemen [*to match the Muscovite's remaining
   retinue of fourteen. One Russian had succumbed to the
   strain of life in Elizabethan London near Billingsgate*].[1]

---

[1] Three days before Christmas John Chamberlain had written to
Dudley Carleton: 'The Muscovite Ambassador hath buried one of
his men and sent him with a letter to seek St. Nicolas.' On turning
up the register of St. Mary at Hill by Billingsgate we find under date
of December 5, 1600 the burial of 'Annys [?Onesime] Russion'.
As to the manner of his burial, I find a note in MS. Harley 296,
f. 195: 'This order was used by the Ambasador of Muscovye when
he was heare in the tyme of Queene Elizabeth', accompanying an
extract from Anthony Jenkinson's well-known report of Russian
burial customs: 'When any man or woman dieth, they stretch him
out, and put a new paire of shooes on his feete, because he hath a
great journey to goe: then doe they winde him in a sheet, as we doe,

[Programme for the guests: Mikulin is to be brought in from the 'Queen's side'. Don Virginio from the 'King's'.]

The Ambassador resteth first in the Chamber of Presence *[the Council Chamber, Queen's side]*; to go with the Queene to hear service And after dinner *[at midday in the Great Chamber, Queen's side]* to rest in the Closet one the Queenes side *[where*

but they forget not to put a testimonie in his right hand, which the priest giveth him, to testIfie unto S. Nicholas that he died a Christian man or woman. And they put the coarse alwayes in a coffin of wood, although the partie be very poore: and when they goe towards the Church, the friends and kinsemen of the partie departed carrie in their hands small waxe candles, and they weepe and howle, and make much lamentation. They that be hanged or beheaded, or such like, have no testimonie with them: how they are received into heaven, it is a wonder, without their pasport.'

The following, as an example of the kind of passport put into the hand of a more distinguished corpse, with a severe caution to St. Peter, furnishes an extraordinary glimpse of the Russian mind:

'Makarios, by the grace of God Metropolitan of Kiev . . . to our master and friend Saint Peter, High Gatekeeper of almighty God.

'We give thee notice that at this time there ended his days a certain servant of God, Prince Fedor Volodomirski; wherefore we charge thee that without any hindrance and delay thou admit him directly into the Kingdom of God. We have absolved him of all his sins, and given him the benediction. And so thou wilt transgress naught of these, and that worse may not come to pass, we have given him these letters of absolution.

'Given in our High Cloister in Kiev, 30 July 1541.'

('Translated out of the Russian by order of the most Serene Catherine of Austria, Queen of Poland' *[died 1572, wife of Sigismund II]*.)

'Macharius Dei gra*tia* Criofensis Halitrensis et Vniuersae Russiae Archiepiscopus, Domino & amico nostro Sancto Petro supremo Dei omnipotentis Janitori.

'Significamus tibi hoc tempore diem suum obijsse quendam Dei seruum Principem Fedor Volodomirski quamobrem precipimus tibi vt illum sine omni impedimento & cunctatione rectá intromittas in Regnum Dei. Absoluimus eum ab omnibus suis peccatis & dedimus ei benedictionem. Itaque nihil eorum transgredieris atque vt peius non fiat dedimus ei has literas absolutionis. Datum in nostro summo Claustro in Criofa   30. Julij. 1541.'

(*In marg.*: 'Conuersum de Russico ad mandat*um* Serenissimae Catherinae Austriacae Reginae Poloniae'.)

B.M. MS. Cott. Vespasian F. V, f. 189^v.

he had first seen the Queen]. And the Company apointed to wayte one him untell his **departure**. [*He is not invited to stay for supper and the play.*]

The Duke of Brachiana to be brought first to my Lord of Worcesters Chamber, the Master of the Horse; [*The disgraced Essex had been suspended from this office, the third highest in the Household; Worcester was Deputy without staff, his lodging on the ground floor of the Palace*] when the Queene goeth to the [*Chapel*] Closett, if he shall desire, to be sent for. [*Here is the question: will the Catholic Don Virginio desire (or dare) to attend the excommunicate Elizabeth to her heretical service?*] From thence to accompany the Queene to hir sitting downe [*at dinner in the Great Chamber, Queen's side*], and then to retyre to the Councell chamber [*adjoining*], ther to dyne and after dinner to be brought to the place of dawncinge [*?Presence Chamber, King's side*]. And after [*supper*] to be brought to the play in the Hall and conveyed back [*to Corsini's house in Grace-church Street*] by those noblemen and Coaches that brought him thether.

[*Particular matters:*]

To give order for the furnishing of 4 chambers [*?Great Chamber, Council Chamber, and lower chamber by the preaching place, Queen's side, and my Lord of Worcester's uttermost chamber, King's side*] very well & richly and makeing cleane the glas windowes to give good light.

To give order that the Cowncell chamber boord [*for Don Virginio*] be furnished with playted napkins, after the French fashion with a good Su[rnap, *tablecloth*], faire chaires and a Carpett to cover the Table that the oldnes of the boord be not seene.

To proportion the heigth of the Chaire of Estate to be [of a] heigth fitt for her Ma*jestie* to sitt at dinner and to appoint fowre knightes to remove the Table

[*Edges burnt*] gentlemen to be warned to weare no lo[*?ng* stockings, and] to be apparelled in the best sort they canne d[*?evise.*] To warne all the gentlemen ordinary and Ex*traordinary* to attend [her] Ma*jestie* in their best and richest apparell

To Confer with my Lord Admirall and the Master of the Revells for takeing order generally with the players to make choyse of [?the] play that shalbe best furnished with rich apparell, have greate variety and change of Musicke and daunces, and of a Subiect that may be most pleasing to her Majestie

To cause the Wardrop to furnish the lower Chamber [?*under the Council Chamber, Queen's side*] by the preaching place, for entertaining the Muskovitts retinewe, and the Lord of Worcesters uttermost lodging chamber with good hangings fitt for the Receypt of the Duke at Supper

To speake to Mr Comptrouller [*Sir William Knollys*] that the Bankett [*of confections at the Queen's lodging after the play*] be made of better stuffe fitt for men to eate and not of paper shewes as it is wont to be And that he send for John Mushie, Sir Edward Staffordes Cooke [*Stafford had been ambassador to France, and this is evidently a Jean Mouchy he had brought back*] and others to dresse the dinner and supper that is to be made for the *Duke of Brachiana:*

To take order that my Lord Sandes [*William, Baron Sandys*] and Sir Jerome Bowes fetch the Muskovite Embassador, and that my Lord of Bedford [*Edward Russell, Earl of Bedford*], Dr. Parkins [*Christopher Parkins, diplomat*], and some other gentlemen fetch him from the gate and Conducte him up to the Chamber of Presence and accompany him whilst he is here.

That the Lord Darcy [*John, Baron Darcy*] be warned to fetch the *Duke of Brachiana* accompanyed with Mr. William Cicill [*who had visited Don Virginio in Florence*], Mr. Lewkner, Mr Edward Gorge and Mr Bucke [*George Buc, afterwards Master of the Revels*] to bring him to be at the Courte presently after 11 of the Clock.

That he be mett at the gate by my Lord of Rutland and his two brothers [*Sir George Manners, Mr. Francis Manners*], my Lord Darcy [?], Mr Cotton, and Mr. Savadge. And all these required to accompany him during his abode in the Court, and those that brought him to cary him backe that night.

To appoint Musicke severally for the Queene and some for
the play in the Hall. And Hales [*Robert Hales, England's leading singer*] to have one place expresly to shewe his owne voyce.

To send for the Musitions of the Citty to be reddy to attend
[*As we know from Thomas Morley's 'Consort Lessons', the Lord
Mayor's Waits were excellent and expert musicians, and included
viols, flutes, lutes, citterns, and pandoras, as well as 'families' of
hautboys, double-reed instruments brought to a high degree of perfection in Elizabethan England.*]

The Children of the Chappell to come before the Queene
at Dinner with a Caroll.

[*Recorded afterwards:*]

In the Hall which was richly hanged and degrees placed
rownd about it was the play after supper.

[*The Chamberlain's memoranda continue:*]

Noblemen warned to be by x a clock with the Lord
Steward and the Lord Chamberlaine

The Earle of Darby	The Lord Worcester
The Lord Thomas Howard	The Earle of Rutland
The Lord of Effingham	The Earle of Cumberland
The Lord Windsor	

Gentlemen to accompany the embassador with Sir Jerome
Bowes

Mr Hart	Mr Saunders
Mr Leigh	Mr Joanes

[*There follows an impressive list of the Court, on a sheet
damaged by fire. It would have been longer, but at least
four ladies have fallen victim to the flames.*]

The Lo: Archbishop of [Canterbury]	The Countesse of Oxford
	The Countesse of Worcester
The Lo: Keaper	The Countes of Derby the
The Lo: Tresorer	Younger
The Lo: Admirall	The Countes of Derby and
The Lo: of Derby	her daughters
The Lo: of Worcester	The Lady Katherine Howard
The Lo: of Cumberland	The La: of Effingham

The Lo: Henry Seymor

The Lo: Thomas Howard, the Lo: Vicount Bindon

The lo: Cobham

The lo: of Effingham

The Lo: Harbert

The lo: Harbert of Cardiffe

The Lo: Graye

The lo: Henry Howard

The Lo: Windsor

The Lo: Morley

The Lo: Lumley

The Lo: Darcy

The Lo: Cheife Justice

The Bishop of London

S[r] John Fortescue

The La: Harbert

The La: Windsor

The La: Lumley

The La: Willughbey

The Countes of Hertford

The La: Shrewsburye

[*three names missing*]

The La[   ]

The La. Buckley & her [   ]

The La. Hatton

M[ris] Berckley

M[ris] Cicill

Here we have another unique document: a list of the notables of England for an original 'Shakespearean 'first night'. The cream of Shakespeare's actual audience, set down in their order of precedence. And the size of the Court which this array of prelates, councillors, lords, and ladies indicates is exceptional. Since the English custom was to pass the Christmas holidays at home, it represents the impressive result of the Queen's unexpected command, sent post-haste to all the nobility within two days' journey of London.

One lord on the list did not appear, and his name at once catches the eye: 'The lo: Harbert of Cardiffe'—the young and handsome William Lord Herbert, Mistress Mall Fitton's lover, whom in the preceding September the Queen had appointed to receive the Muscovite ambassador at Tower Wharf in her name with great military pomp and ceremonial gunfire. Official cognizance had not yet been taken of Mistress Fitton's case; and though Lord

Herbert was ninety miles away over muddy January roads at Wilton House, by the bedside of his dying father, the urgency of the Queen's wish to fill the Court included him in the summons.

But the Fitton scandal was already abroad; he had no wish to appear, and he did not come. Instead, he sent up an anxious letter of excuse to Sir Robert Cecil, on Monday, Twelfth Eve: 'I was sent unto by a very friend of mine to come post to the Court, and not to fail of being there to wait on Tuesday at dinner, if I would not utterly lose the Queen's favour: a sentence of little more comfort than hanging: and yet if I had made all the haste I could, I should hardly have been there by the time, receiving the letters but this Monday morning about 8 o'clock; and if I could perchance have been there by the time, I leave to your judgment how fit to wait that day.'[1] Had he gone, it is certain that Shakespeare's '*Mal'-voglio* would have given him small joy, and the remark about Mistress Mall's picture 'taking dust' was not one he would gladly listen to in public.

If the nobles were many, courtiers of less exalted station must have thronged the palace in proportionately great numbers. By no means could the stands in the Hall at Shakespeare's play accommodate them all; and we know that two further companies of actors were required to entertain the crowd at night in the chambers at Whitehall.

Queen Elizabeth made it a day high and memorable for everyone, but especially so for her two principal guests—the Muscovite Ambassador and Don Virginio Orsino. Before launching upon their two accounts, we must how-

---

[1] H.M.C., *Cecil Papers*, 11. 3.

ever not miss the beginning of Don Virginio's letter to his wife, recounting his arrival three days before the great day, and the Queen's welcome of him:

My Lady and most beloved Wife

By my last I gave your Excellency word of my having reached this Island. Now I must tell you that on Saturday after dinner I arrived here in London at the house of Signore Corsini, whom presently I sent to her Majesty to let her know of my arrival, and to beg her to be pleased that I might privately kiss her hands. Signore Corsini spoke with Secretary Cecil (*Secil*), who is the one who governs this kingdom, and with the Lord Chamberlain, who replied—after conferring with the Queen—that her Majesty welcomed my coming hither more than that of any gentleman who has ever arrived in her realm; and that for Tuesday (the 16th in our style, in theirs the 6th, Twelfth Day) she would appoint me audience, albeit not so private as I had desired.

On the Sunday morning I went to visit the Ambassador of France, and to hear mass in his house, for here in London mass is said in no other place. Her Majesty has twice a day sent only principal gentlemen to visit me, causing them ever to tell me that I should consider myself not merely at Florence in the house of the Grand Duke, but at Bracciano in my own.

This brings Don Virginio up to Twelfth Day, and before we go with him to Whitehall, let us first take the story of that long-expected day as Grigori Ivanovich Mikulin saw it and reported it to his Tsar. (I confess I find some of his expressions awkward to translate, in particular his term for 'bowed very low'. It is *bil* (or *udáril*) *chelóm*, literally *struck* (the floor) *with his forehead*, *kowtowed*. As the traveller Anthony Jenkinson reported, the Russian people 'doe bowe and knocke their heads . . . that some will have knobbes upon their foreheads with knocking, as great as egges'. The English both served and addressed their Queen upon the knee, and Mikulin must have literally kowtowed to her in true Oriental fashion. No doubt in the eyes of Don Virginio this was one of the Muscovite's 'ridiculous manners'. But then Mikulin reports that Don Virginio *udáril chelóm* too, which cannot be taken literally. Each of them unquestionably made the profoundest reverence of his own country, and we may leave it at that.)

Mikulin prefaces his tale with the arrival of the royal command, brought to the Russians' lodging—Sir Cuthbert Buckle's house in St. Mary at Hill, near Billingsgate —on the Sunday two days before Twelfth Day, by the Latin-speaking diplomatist, Dr. Christopher Parkins:

And on the fourth day of January, from the Queen came the courtier Dokhtur Parkin, and spake from the Queen to Grigori and Ivashko, putting off his hat: 'Our great Lady,' quoth he, 'Elizabeth the Queen, for love of her brother, your great Lord, the Tsar and mighty Prince Boris Fedorovich, absolute Monarch of all Russia, and in grace to you, hath summoned you to her on the Feast of Twelfth Day to eat bread.' And Grigori and Ivashko prostrated themselves (*chelóm bíli*) to her Majesty's favour, and 'presented' [*gave a gift to, tipped*] her Majesty's courtier.

On the morning of Twelfth Day, the Russians put on the finest 'lendings' issued to them by the Tsar. No doubt the colossal Mikulin was wrapped in the same gorgeous pearl-and-gold caftan he had worn to his October audience at Richmond, as we read in the Duke of Northumberland's document:

He had one a gowne of [cloth] of goulde downe to the small of his legge [*i.e. ankle*], made close before with lac[es] of pearle, a great furre Capp upon his head, and underneath that a capp . . . imbrodered very richly with greate pearles, and his buskins were of Redd leather with highe heeles.

With him he had Ivan (Ivashko) Zinoviev, the secretary appointed by his master to watch him, and the other indispensable, his interpreter Andrei Grot, who made communication possible by turning Latin into Russian and Russian into Latin. These three were to dine in the Great Chamber (Queen's side) in the presence of the Queen. His train, a baker's dozen of burly retainers, were to dine below stairs, in a ground-floor chamber by the Terrace.

Queen Elizabeth knew her Russians. What really impressed them was intrepidity, physical size, and strength. Accordingly, she had formerly sent as her envoy to Moscow her most towering gentleman-giant, the bold Sir Jerome Bowes. And Bowes had won the esteem of Ivan the Terrible by thundering back at him in the Kremlin, threatening the tyrant with Elizabeth's revenge for any mistreatment of her ambassador. Eighty years later the legend of Sir Jerome's proficiency in handling Russians still lived in the mouths of London's leading merchants and customs-officers. For Pepys tells how,

among other pretty discourse, some was of Sir Jerom Bowes, Embassador from Queene Elizabeth to the Emperor of Russia; who, because some of the noblemen there would go up the stairs to the Emperor before him, he would not go up till the Emperor had ordered those two men to be dragged downstairs, with their heads knocking upon every stair. . . . And when he was come up, they demanded his sword of him before he entered the room. He told them, if they would have his sword, they should have his boots too. And so caused his boots to be pulled off, and his night-gown and night-cap and slippers to be sent for; and made the Emperor stay till he could

SIR JEROME BOWES

go in his night-dress, since he might not go as a soldier. And lastly, when the Emperor in contempt, to show his command of his subjects, did command one to leap from the window down and broke his neck in the sight of our Embassador, he replied that his mistress did set more by, and did make better use of the necks of her subjects: but said that, to show what her subjects would do for her, he would, and did, fling down his gantlett before the Emperor; and challenged all the nobility there to take it up, in defence of the Emperor against his Queen: for which, at this very day, the name of Sir Jerom Bowes is famous and honoured there.

As tall in body as he was in courage, Bowes was approximately estimated as standing 'three storeys high'. Ben Jonson reports a wit who 'beat once upon Sir J. B.'s breast and asked if Sir Jerome was within'. Tsar Boris would never have selected Mikulin, were he not 'of tall stature very fat'. But Elizabeth had a Boötes, a Bearward for this Bear, and told off her Russian-experienced behemoth Bowes to wait upon Mikulin. When these two stalked out in company, the Cockneys could swear that Corineus and Gogmagog had deserted their posts at Guildhall. Bowes it is, therefore, who comes to take the Muscovites on Twelfth Day from Billingsgate to Whitehall, and here is Mikulin's story, with every point of protocol scrupulously noted:

And on the sixth day of January, to Grigori from the Queen came the liaison-officer Sir Jerome Bowes (*pristav knyaz Yeremie Bous*), and with him fourteen of her Majesty's courtiers, and spake from the Queen to Grigori and Ivashko, putting off his hat: 'Our great Lady,' quoth he, 'Elizabeth the Queen, hath sent me to you, and commanded me to carry you to her to dine; and hath sent here to you her coaches, for you to go in.'

And Grigori and Ivashko prostrated themselves to her Majesty's grace, and taking seats in the coaches, travelled to the Queen; and in the coach, Grigori sat in the chief place, and over against him [*i.e., riding backwards*] sat Sir Jerome Bowes.

When they arrived at her Majesty's Court, and alighted from the coach, at the gate there met Grigori a more exalted (nearer, more inward) courtier, the Lord of Bedford (*Betfort*), for they call him the Queen's cousin by the mother's side, and Lord Windsor (*Vinzor*); and coming to Grigori, shook hands, and went with Grigori to the palace; but they walked on Grigori's left.

And when they came to the principal Chamber [*Council Chamber, Queen's side*] Lord Bedford spake to Grigori: 'Please you,' quoth he, 'to sit here for a little.' And at the same time there came from the Queen a higher person, an earl, the Lord Chamberlain of the Household, and shook hands with Grigori, and spake to Grigori: 'Let it not displease you,' quoth he, 'that I have not yet spoken to the Queen of you' (*or*, 'I am just about to speak to the Queen concerning you'). And the Lord Chamberlain went to the Queen, and Lord Windsor with him; but the Lord of Bedford and Sir Jerome sat with Grigori; and after a little, Lord Windsor arrived from the Queen, and spake from her Majesty, putting off his hat: 'Our Lady,' quoth he, 'Elizabeth the Queen, hath commanded that you go to her.'

And then Grigori and Ivashko entered the Queen's chamber, and prostrated themselves to her Majesty. [*They had been taken from the Council Chamber through the Privy Chamber, Queen's side, to the Closet or first Withdrawing Room.*] And the Queen, rising from her place, bowed, and questioned Grigori about his health, and spake: 'For love of our brother,' quoth she, 'your great Lord, Tsar, and mighty Prince Boris Fedorovich, Monarch of all Russia, and in favour to you, I have this day summoned you to me on this Feast, to eat bread. But now I go to divine service, and you shall go along, and witness our ceremonies and customs, how in our religion we pray to God, and how in our country the Communion Service is sung.' And she bade Grigori go before her with her greatest (nearest) lords. And the Queen passed out of the room to the entry [*i.e., of the Withdrawing Chamber, King's side*].

And at that instant, at the entrance, on the threshold, there bowed low to the Queen an Italian nobleman [*Orsino; and his first glimpse of Elizabeth*]; and the Queen chatted with him, and appointed him to eat bread with her; and the officers said of him that he was an Italian, the Florentine duke Virginio degli Orsini (*Verdzhen Aursinov*), called brother-in-law to the French King; he was come, said they, to make his obeisance to the Queen, to see the English realm, and to observe her Majesty's ceremonies; and the Queen invited him to dine. 'However,' said they, 'he is not to sit together with you at table in the Queen's dining-chamber, but is to dine in another chamber with the lords.'

Then the Queen passed to Chapel; and before the Queen went the courtiers, and after the courtiers the lords, and following the Queen went many ladies and maidens; and in the chambers and the passages people stood on both sides; on the right hand stood courtiers, and on the left ladies and maidens. And the Queen, going out of her chambers, passed to the Chapel. [*From the Great Chamber, along the passage behind the Hall to the Chapel Closet.*] And at that moment in the Chapel they [*Dr. John Bull and the Queen's Music with cornets and sackbuts*] began to play on the organ, and on wind instruments, with much other music and song [*by the Gentlemen and Children of the Chapel Royal*]. The officers said, 'They are singing the psalms of David.' [*Don Virginio had accompanied the Queen, and was now with her at the window in the Closet where she usually sat to hear service, looking down into the Chapel. Mikulin was on the opposite side, looking down through the other window.*]

And in the place where the priests serve is set a dais, and on the dais is placed a table covered with a damask cloth, and on the table lie two books covered with gold, which they call the Apostles and the Gospel; and also on the table are two unlighted candles. The priests were in golden copes, and at the sides stood subdeacons in white surplices. And as they began to celebrate the Eucharist, the Queen, approaching the place where the priests minister, knelt down, and gave the priest a dish with three things in papers; and the officers said that the Queen in her religion at every Feast [*of the Epiphany*] brings as an offering to God gold, and frankincense, and myrrh. And having made her offering, she went back to her lodging.

At this point we may advantageously interrupt the fascinating flow of Mikulin's impressions, to insert the herald's account of the day's ceremony up to this point, preserved in the manuscripts of the Marquis of Ripon, and reproduced here by the generosity of Commander Vyner. It gives us another vivid glimpse of the scene at the Chapel Closet, running as follows:

At the Court at Whitehall 6° of January *anno* 1601, being Twelfth Day, it was ordained that the Embassador for the Marchants of Muscovia should, in confirming the League, Dine or eat bread & Salt with the Queens Majestie. It also then happened that the Duke of Braciano, Virginio Ursino, Cousin Germain to the Duke of Florence and the new Queen of France, arrived in England to see her Majestie, & was appointed at that time to come to the Court.

Sir Heierome Bowes, kn*igh*t, & other gent*lem*en with Coaches were sent to Conducte the Embassador; & at the Court the E*arl* of Bedford, Dr Perkins & others received him & brought him up to the Presence Chamber, where the Council sitt usually.

And for the Duke of Braciano Seign*or* Virginio Ursino were sent the E*arl* of Rutland & his Brethren, the Lord Dacre [?*Darcy*], the Lord Sands, & others, who met him at the Court Gate, he being thither brought by S*ir* [*Mr.*] William Cecil & others.

The Queens Majestie came forth to her Clozet [*or Withdrawing-room*], & after a while proceeded to the Chappel; & then the Duke was placed to see the offering at the Window in the [*Chapel*] Closet on the Queens side, & the Muscovite on the other side at the other Window; and after the Creed Song, Her Majestie went to the offering Down to the Chapell, &

offered the gold, Frankinsence, & Mirrhe; and returned, & so
departed to her Chamber accompanied with the Duke by her
& the Muscovite went by Garter before the Sword. [*Mikulin
was thus ranked with her servant, the chief herald; while Don
Virginio walked with the Queen, like a visiting royalty. Mikulin
is careful not to mention this.*]

In the Interim the great Chamber on the other [*or Queen's*]
side towards the Tarras was prepared with an Estate & two
cupboards of Plate therein, where her Majestie Dined . . .[1]

A picture even more satisfying and detailed of the
stately dress of the Great Chamber for the Treaty Dinner
is the account attached to the Lord Chamberlain's budget
of memoranda—the Duke of Northumberland's document, somewhat damaged by fire:

[?On Twelfth Day the 6 of January 1600, the Queenes]
Ma*jes*tie lying at Whitehall a[ll Christmas, she dined abr]oad
in State: the Muskovy Ambassador ly[ing] in London was
appointed to be ther: and an Italia[n] Duke being the Duke of
Brachiana, who landed some fowre dayes before, as a Traveyl-
ler with a small Traine, haveing [ac]companyed the newe
Queene of Fraunce into her Realme; and from thence came
ouer to see her Ma*jes*tie

Theise States being here present accord[ing] to order taken,
her Ma*jes*tie dyned in the great chamber, which [was] very
richly hanged and a marveislous [*sic*] rich cloth of estate ther
pl[aced], the boord her Ma*jes*tie dyned at being of that length
that the place required. Ther was also one the right side of the
Chamber vnder the windowes a boord placed, wher was appointed to dine the Muskovy Embassador sitting at the
boordes end with two others with him. The *Duke of Brachiana* dined in the Councell cha[mber. And] in the chamber by
the preaching place dined all the Muskovittes retinewe:

The Chambers were richly hanged, and very well and

[1] MSS. of the Marquis of Ripon, Studley Royal, Yorks. Heraldic
Entry Book, collected by Augustine Vincent, f. 139.

richly appointed in all degrees. Also one the other side of the Chamber wher the Queene dined was placed a Cubhard with degrees [*steps*] upon it which were sett full of golde plate: one the lower end the whole length a Cubhord full of silver & g[old vessels]. To this feast ther came from the Tower of London in seven Carres seven great standardes [*i.e.*, *huge chests*] full of plate: Ther were to all services noblemen appointed to wayte . . .

One has only to read the explorer Richard Chancellor's account of the state dinner at which Ivan the Terrible received him in Moscow to understand why Queen Elizabeth set out this amazing show of plate for Mikulin:

in the middes of the roome stood a mightie Cupboord . . . and every steppe rose up more narrow then another. Upon this Cupboorde was placed the Emperours plate, which was so much, that the very Cupboord it selfe was scant able to sustaine the waight of it: the better part of all the vessels, and goblets, was made of very fine gold: and amongst the rest, there were foure pots of very large bignesse, which did adorne the rest . . . for they were so high, that they thought them at the least five foote long.

Now back to the Ambassador for whom all this state has been mounted, the dinner-guest Mikulin. The Queen has vanished into her private lodging; and he and his two companions, nobly attended, are resting in the Closet on the Queen's side.

And to Grigori and Ivashko in the chamber came the nobleman and courtier, the Lord Chamberlain, and spake to Grigori and Ivashko: 'The Queen,' quoth he, 'hath commanded that you go to the dining chamber, and at table await her coming.' [*They are then escorted along the Queen's side, past the Privy Chamber and the Council Chamber, to the Great Chamber.*] And after that, with little delay, the Queen came to the dining chamber, and commanded the Archbishop and the priests to say before dinner 'Our Father'; and she sat down to table; but she gave order for Grigori, Ivashko, and the interpreter Andrei to be seated by themselves at a special table on the left hand. And the Archbishop and the priests, having said 'Our Father', went forth from the chamber. But the nobles and courtiers who waited upon the Queen at table all stood, and sat not, not one. And the Lord of Bedford and Sir Jerome Bowes waited upon Grigori and Ivashko at table, likewise standing, and did not sit down. Lord Windsor [*Sewer*] stood by the Queen at dinner, with other Carvers [*Earl of Sussex Chief Carver*], and some thirty Sewers [*led by Lord Henry Seymor and Lord Effingham*] placed services before the Queen, and five Cupbearers, men of noble rank [*headed by Lord Derby*], poured for the Queen to drink. And before the drink borne by the Cupbearer went the Lord High Admiral [*Lord Nottingham, Lord Steward of the Household, specially commissioned Lord High Steward for this day*]; and the cupboards were two: one silver, the other gold, with many vessels.

And as we sat at dinner, the Queen sent by the Carver [*Lord Sussex*] a gift to Grigori—a white loaf on a dish covered with a napkin, and he spake to Grigori: 'Our great Lady,' quoth he, 'Elizabeth the Queen, of her grace bestows on you this loaf. And moreover,' quoth he, 'she graces you with this napkin.' And Grigori prostrated himself to the Queen's favour in the gift and the napkin.

Here we may note by the way that Queen Elizabeth had evidently learned that this form was 'according to an ancient custome of the kings of Muscovy'; for as Chancellor related of Ivan the Terrible,

the Emperour himselfe . . . doth first bestow a piece of bread upon every one of his ghests, with a loud proclamation of his title, and honour, in this manner: The great Duke of Moscovie, and chiefe Emperour of Russia, John Basiliwich (& then the officer nameth the ghest) doth give thee bread. Whereupon al the ghests rise up, and by & by sit downe againe.

At Whitehall the gift of bread was no doubt followed by the ceremonial eating of bread and salt in confirmation of the league of peace and friendship.

Then drink was brought before the Queen [*by Lord Shrewsbury*]; and her Majesty, rising, drank a cup to the health of the great Lord, Tsar, and mighty Prince Boris Fedorovich, Monarch of all Russia; and having drunk the cup, she commanded the Tsar's cup to be given to Grigori; and Grigori, coming out from the table, drank the Tsar's cup, and having drunk it, said: 'I see, your Majesty, your love to our great Lord, the great Tsar; and when I (which God grant) shall be with the great Tsar, I shall inform his Majesty of your love.' After that, the Queen drank a cup to her Majesty the Tsarina and great Princess Marya Grigorevna; and having drunk, commanded the cup to be given to Grigori; and Grigori, coming out from the table, drank the cup of the great Lady, the Tsarina and Princess Marya Grigorevna.

While the Queen's dinner was going forward, before her many players performed many pieces. [*These were the Children of the Chapel, giving their 'show with music and special songs prepared for the purpose'.*]

And when the Queen's board was removed [*by the four knights*], the Queen rose from table and began to wash her hands; and having washed, she ordered the silver ewer with water to be taken to Grigori; and to her Majesty's favour Grigori prostrated himself, but did not wash his hands, and said, 'Our great Lord the great Tsar calls Elizabeth the Queen his beloved sister; and it doth not befit me, his bond-slave, to wash my hands in her presence.' Thereupon the Queen waxed merry, and commended Grigori in that he honoured her so highly as not to wash his hands before her. [*We need not be as wise as Elizabeth to smile at the speciousness of Mikulin's excuse. Obviously this was a contingency not covered in his instructions; and however much honour and deference he demanded as impersonating the mighty Tsar, Mikulin was in fact a bond-slave, could not wash his hands like a gentleman, and did not dare to*

*try. And of course he missed the humour of his royal citation
'For Remaining Dirty in the Line of Duty'.*]

After that, the Queen summoned Grigori and Ivashko and
the interpreter Andrei to her hand, and commanded them to
go to their house. And Grigori and Ivashko, prostrating
themselves to the Queen, went out of the palace; and her
Majesty's courtiers the Lord of Bedford and Lord Windsor
conducted Grigori and Ivashko to the gate, and Sir Jerome
Bowes carried them to their lodging.

Few rarities from Shakespeare's London can compare
with a Muscovite's view of the great Queen Elizabeth,
sending him presents and then waxing mysteriously merry
over hand-washing. The fascination of it only grows
when we can set it beside its companion-piece—the impression of 'the most brilliant Italian nobleman of his
day'. Here, the ponderous Russian Bear; and here, the
slender-graceful Orsino, carrying the Bear in his ancient
name and crest. The extremes of Europe—the uncivilized
East, and the flower of High-Renaissance western culture.
Mikulin the bond-slave [*kholóp*] reporting to his Tsar, the
princely Orsino to his excellent *consorte amatissima*.

On the morning of *Pifanía*, Twelfth-tide, after break-
fasting in his splendid chambers at the rich merchant
Corsini's house in Gracechurch Street, just round the
corner from Falstaff's Boar's Head in Eastcheap, Don Virginio dressed with particular care. We may be confident
that he chose black. For not only was black the proper
noble wear for an Italian gentleman, but it would please
Queen Elizabeth: her personal colours were white and
black, and her ladies would be in white. He put the last
touch to his costume; joined his companions, the *cavalieri*
Giulio Riario and Grazia de Montalvo, and his secretary,
Emilio Fei; then, like the golden-robed Mikulin three

streets away towards the Thames, wondering just what the fabled Elizabeth had in store for him at Whitehall, he awaited ten o'clock and the Queen's coaches. Striking the three-quarters from the other side of Gracechurch Street, *the bells of Saint Bennet put him in mind—one, two, three.*

While he waits, and before we plunge into his enthralling narrative, we remind ourselves that these two rich stories, Mikulin's and Orsino's, are both in foreign tongues, and are here translated into our modern idiom: two veils interposed between our minds and the reality. Twelfth Day at Whitehall can be conjured up only in the language in which it lived—the tongue of Shakespeare and his fellow-dramatists. Let us take the moment to try, in a patchwork of snatches from them, for a touch of their Whitehall, and of that Elizabeth

> When she did flourish so, as when she was
> The mistress of the Ocëan, her navies
> Putting a girdle round about the world:
> When the Iberian quak'd, her worthies nam'd.

We do observe one day with most imperial state. See the Court made like a paradise, full of fair shows and music. Perfume the rooms With cassia and amber, where they are To feast and revel . . . Feast their eyes With massy plate until your cupboards crack. Where be these knaves? Who serves up all the liveries? Are the best hangings up? And the plate set out?

Come, gentlemen, ye shall go my way, which is to the Court. . . . All access is throng'd. Keep the door there! I will have no such press. Women? As I came hither, there was no pair of stairs, no entry, no lobby, but was pester'd with 'em. What mirth and jollity reigns round about the house! Court revels, antics, and a world of joys. Brave Christmas gambols, therewith open hall kept to the full. What sports are now in season? There's a new comedy afoot. Is't good? Is't good?

What is this Duke? The ladies are low in their courtesies! A Florentine. Fame gives him out for excellent. A prince by birth, and by his trade a soldier. He thinks 'tis not Fitting a prince to tread in beaten paths, But to find out or else make new ones. A delicate handsome man, well seen in languages. A most accomplish'd cómplete gentleman. He's come, you see, and bravely entertain'd. The lip-salute, so much as strangers take acquaintance with. He says our ladies are not match'd in Christendom For graceful and confirm'd behaviours, More than our Court, where they are bred, is equall'd. It did him good, he says, To see the goodly order that they kept. He speaks us nobly. Sound, music! Let choice music speak his welcome. . . . He stands at door, to courtesy to her Highness. The trumpets sound. Stand close! The Queen is coming.

How rarely is she usher'd! Those men are happy, and so are all are near her. She comes herself, attended gloriously with sun-bright beauties. What command she carries! And what a sparkling majesty flies from her! How rich she shows in jewels! Methinks they show like frozen icicles Cold Winter had hung on her.

'*How much my Court is honour'd, princely brother, In your vouchsafing it your long'd-for presence!*'

'*Gracious madam, t'have the happiness to see and hear you, Which by your bounty is conferr'd upon me, I hold too great a blessing.*'

'*I heard, sir, that you desir'd to come to see me.*'

'*It is true, madam: I long'd to journey hither, to see your*

Highness, who for beauty and for wisdom do excel all other princes of the world, and t'have the happiness to kiss your hands.'

'You mean, brave Prince, to show your skill in compliment and courtly talk.'

'Believe it, madam, all my best is humbly vow'd And dedicated to your Grace's service.'

'Do you, sir, come with me. I must talk further with you. . . . Set on.'

Room before there! Set on to the Presence! Forward, and keep your state!

This is but a foretaste; we must go back to the beginning with Don Virginio, and his tale begins in Gracechurch Street with the arrival of the Queen's coaches.

On the Tuesday morning she sent her coaches and two great ones [*Lord Darcy, Mr. William Cecil*] to take me and carry me to court. Arrived there, I found at the gate the Earl of Rutland (*Rotelan*), one of the first nobles of the realm, who assisted me to alight. He received me in her Majesty's name, and led me to a lodging appointed for me [*Lord Worcester's, Deputy Master of the Horse*]. I stayed there very little, and then went abovestairs, where I found a hall [*Presence Chamber, King's side*] all filled with waiting gentlewomen; another within [*Privy Chamber*], full of ladies and gentlemen; in the third [*Withdrawing Chamber, King's side*] were all the officers of the Crown, and the Knights of the Garter, all dressed in white—as was the whole Court that day—but with so much gold and jewels, that it was a marvellous thing.

These all came to greet me, the most part speaking Italian, many, French, and some, Spanish. I answered all as well as I knew how, in the tongue which I heard spoken; and I am sure that at the least I made myself understood. I found no more than two gentlemen who knew no other tongue than the

English; and with these I employed other gentlemen as interpreters. All these brought me near the door where the Queen was to enter. Over against me was the Muscovite Ambassador, who had come as an Extraordinary, to 'compliment with' her Majesty. [*Note the discrepancy with Mikulin's account, which seems to say that he, Mikulin, came out with the Queen, and found the Italian on the threshold.*]

The Queen came to the door, and I presently approached in all humility to do her reverence; and she drew near me with most gracious cheer, speaking Italian so well, uttering withal such fine conceits, that I can maintain that I might have been taking lessons from Boccaccio or the [*Cruscan*] Academy. Her Majesty was dressed all in white, with so many pearls, broideries, and diamonds, that I am amazed how she could carry them. When I had done her reverence, Signore Giulio and Signore Grazia did the like; and then all the Court set forward in order toward the chapel. The order is such that I am having the whole noted in writing; nor do I believe I shall ever see a court which, for order, surpasses this one.

I attended her Majesty to a room next the chapel, where I stayed, in company with many gentlemen; and as we stood in excellent conversation, we heard a wondrous music.

Here we must break in on Don Virginio's letter for a moment. For at this point he smoothly omits to mention a circumstance which soon was common knowledge: namely, that *he looked through the window at the service below, and watched the Queen make her Epiphany offering*. What was this but 'going with the Queen to church'? Was this behaviour proper in a Prince Assistant to the Papal Throne? What the Catholics thought of it may be gathered from a letter of Father Anthony Rivers to Father Robert Parsons:

She invited him to go with her to her closet over the chapel, having before given order that the Communion table should be adorned with basin and ewer of gold and evening tapers and other ornaments (some say also with a crucifix), and that all the ministry should be in rich copes. The Duke, of curiosity, accompanied her, and she was very pleasant thereat, saying she would write to the Pope not to chide him for that fact, with other like discourses; and so, service ended, they returned. But herewithal many Papists are much scandalized.[1]

Scandalous it was, but very human. The Pope's decree had offered him, the Orsino, a shameful public *disgrazia* when he had come out to attend the Cardinal at Florence. Should he now refuse to attend the great Queen who showed him *honori particolarissimi*, out of fear of what that Pope would say? Or of 'a kiss of the Inquisition'? He was very curious, charmed and flattered, and a bit reckless. In his shoes, who would not have been? And Elizabeth dared him. But let him get on with his story:

At the end of half an hour her Majesty returned, with all the Court two by two according to their quality and degrees before her, and all the countesses and ladies after; and while I accompanied her she was ever discoursing with me, as she had also done before.

When her Majesty had entered her chamber, I was conducted into the hall where her Majesty was to dine: the which hall, together with many other rooms, was hanged with tapestries of gold. On a dais at the head was her Majesty's table; at the opposite end, a great court-cupboard all of vessels of gold; on the right hand, a great cupboard of vessels with gold and jewels; and on the left, a low table with three little services for the Muscovite ambassador and two who were with him: it being the custom of Muscovy that if he had not been seen eating in the Queen's presence, his Great Duke would have had him beheaded.

---

[1] Printed by Henry Foley, *Records of the English province of the Society of Jesus*, Vol. I (1877), 5–6.

Meanwhile came the viands of her Majesty, borne by knights, and the Sewer was of the great Order [*i.e., of St. George, the Garter*]. These did the same honour to her Majesty's chair of state as they would have done had she been present; and as soon as the table was prepared came the Queen. I reserve for telling by word of mouth the manner of the many cloths, and of her hand-washing, for this description alone would fill four sheets. Presently after her Majesty had sat down to table, the Muscovite Ambassador (of whose ridiculous manners I shall give an account) fell to dining; and I was conducted to the Lord Admiral (to whom the Queen had given the office of High Steward, but only for that day) and many other great officers of the Crown and Knights of the Order, in a hall [*the Council Chamber, adjoining*] where there was prepared for me a most noble banquet, at the end of which appeared a good music.

As soon as the banquet was ended I rose from the table and went to her Majesty, who was already on her feet; and talking now with me, and now with the Muscovite Ambassador, she tarried a while, and then was attended by me to her room. Those gentlemen who were appointed to wait upon me, with many others whose acquaintance I had made, conducted me to my lodging [*Lord Worcester's*] so that I might rest myself; but after a little the chief among them began coming to visit me; and then there was music, of some instruments to my belief never heard in Italy, but miraculous ones [*pandoras and citterns, played no doubt by the Waits of London*]; so that with good entertainment we came to the hour of supper, which was made ready in a hall in my own lodging [*the Queen had provided Jean Mouchy, Stafford's French cook*]. To sup with me came the Master of the Horse [*Lord Worcester*], and also the Earl of Cumberland (*Comberlan*); and with him I had some speech which will be to the taste of his Highness [*the Grand Duke, his uncle Ferdinand*], since that man is the greatest corsair in the world. Presently after supper I was taken to the lodgings of her Majesty, where in a hall [*the Closet, or Withdrawing Room?*] the Secretary of State [*Sir Robert Cecil*] caused me to salute all the ladies of title after the French fashion [*first, kiss the fingers; next, kiss the lips; then embrace the waist*]. With one I spoke Italian, with divers French; and with the rest he himself played the interpreter for me.

Hereupon the Queen came in, and commanded me to go along discoursing with her. [*Along the King's side, and down out, back of the Great Chamber, to the Hall stairs.*] Her Majesty mounted the stairs, amid such sounding of trumpets that methought I was on the field of war, and entered a public hall [*the Noon-hall*], where all round about were rising steps with ladies, and diverse consorts of music. As soon as her Majesty was set at her place [*the canopied throne on the dais before the grandstand at the South*], many ladies and knights began a Grand Ball. When this came to an end, there was acted a mingled comedy, with pieces of music and dances (*una commedia mescolata, con musiche e balli*), and this too I am keeping to tell by word of mouth [*Alas!*]. The Muscovite Ambassador was not present. I stood ever near her Majesty, who bade me cover, and withal caused a stool to be fetched for me; and although she willed me a thousand times to sit, I would however never obey her. She conversed continually with me; and when the comedy was finished . . .

Here we must beg to interrupt Don Virginio: to remind ourselves that for him this was the grand climax. The greatest Queen in the world had *publicly ranked him as her peer* by bidding him wear his hat in her presence. He accepted that rare honour; but courteously declined the still greater one—to be seated in public by her side. *She conversed continually with me*. Besides pointing out the deft and ingeniously-contrived compliments in Shakespeare's comedy, what did Queen Elizabeth chat about in her skilful Italian with Don Virginio? I find evidence of one topic at least: her own relationship with his ancient House, the Casa Orsina. She said that her Tudor Rose, embroidered in gold and silver on the scarlet coats of her Guard, and the Rose in the Orsini coat of arms were one and the same. For an Italian heraldic manuscript in the British Museum contains the following memorandum, based obviously on Don Virginio's own report:

In the presence of Queen Elizabeth of England, at a public ball, it was given to the Duke, Virginio Orsini, to sit under the state; and the Queen said that the Rose, which is in her royal arms, took its origin from the House of Orsini, and treated him as kin (*lo trattò come parente*); and afterwards had her Historiographer (*Archevesta*) send the Duke an au-thentical certificate (*fede autentica*) of her descent.[1]

I have seen a copy (Archivio di Stato, Florence) of this Orsini-Tudor genealogical tree. The original, engrossed especially for Don Virginio, is carefully preserved among the muniments of Prince Virginio Orsini, 21st Duke of Gravina. Little wonder that Don Virginio felt even Shakespeare's graceful compliments surpassed by Queen Elizabeth's claiming him for her cousin. But we have interrupted his letter long enough, and must go back to allow him to follow the glorious thread.

She conversed continually with me; and when the comedy was finished, I waited upon her to her lodgings, where there was made ready for her Majesty and for the ladies a most fair collation, all of confections. [*Mr. Controller Knollys had seen to it that it was 'made of better stuff fit for men to eat, and not of*

---

[1] 'Dalla Regina Elisabetta d'Inghilterra in una danza publica al Duca Virginio Orsini gli fu dato da sedere sotto il trono, e La Regina disse de la Rosa, che si trovano [*sic*] nelle armi Regi originava dalla Casa Orsina, e lo trattò come parente, fece poi mandare fede autentica della sua descendenza al Duca dal suo Archevesta, di si consemo da' descendenti in Bracciano in grande col quarto Orsini . . .' B.M. MS. Harl. 3546, f. 4ᵛ.

paper shows as it is wont to be'.] The Queen, having first taken but two morsels, gave order that it should all be put to the spoil (*tutta saccheggiata*); which was done amid a graceful confusion (*con una confusione galante*). After the Queen had gone into her chamber, those ladies who could speak Italian and French fell into conversation with me, and at the end of half an hour we took our leave of one another, and I went away home, it being already two hours after midnight.

On seeing Don Virginio to bed—to the passing bellman's cry, 'Past two o'clock and almost three, My masters all, good day to ye!'—one's first unregenerate impulse is to wring his neck for not planning to put more about the comedy into his letter. But second thought reminds us that he acted precisely as we should have done in his place: that is, he saved the best and most fascinating detail—such as the Muscovite's *costumi ridicolosi*, the Queen's rare dinner-ceremony, and the *commedia mescolata* in which the quick comedians extemporally had staged him to the life—to tell to his wife by gesture and by word of mouth.

Sentimentally, of course, we would have the delighted Elizabeth call up the modest poet-player for commendation, and present this Sciecspir, this *Vibralancia*, to the Duke. But alas for our dreams—not a word, not a hint of any such matter. We may be confident, however, that a man of Don Virginio's curiosity and cultivation, with such a Queen, bent on charming, to interpret for him, did not miss much that was written to his address in the play. And it was clear that the English *comedista*—who must have worked this piece up with astonishing speed—showed himself uncannily clever. What had he not got into it?

He had presented him, Orsino, as 'A noble duke, in
nature as in name', desperately and poetically in love with
the queenly-fair 'Olivia', and had her compliment him in
the action with a plainly recognizable description, both
handsome and not undeserved:

> . . . I suppose him virtuous, know him noble,
> Of great estate, of fresh and stainless youth;
> In voices well divulg'd, free, learn'd, and valiant,
> And in dimension and the shape of nature
> A gracious person.

He had mentioned his galleys and the sea-fight. He
had included the pair of boy-and-girl twins, like his own
eldest children. With 'the bells of Saint Bennet, sir, may
put you in mind—one, two, three', he had even recalled
this very lodging at Corsini's in Gracechurch Street opposite Saint Bennet's, whose unaccustomed and unavoidable English bells clanged in his ears.

As for his famous crest, the *Orsa* or Bear, and the
proud, historic Orsini motto *Prius mori quam fidem fal-
lere*—*Rather die than break faith*—the Bear was lugged in
twice: first as a type of danger, 'Pants and looks pale, as if
a bear were at his heels', and again as the symbol of
Olivia's own honour, 'Have you not set mine honour at
the stake And baited it with all th'unmuzzled thoughts
That tyrannous heart can think?' And the Orsini *faith
dearer than life* repeatedly appeared in the Illyrian Orsino's
lines where one would expect to find the word *love*: 'Surprise her with discourse of *my dear faith*', '*the faithfull'st
off'rings*, and 'Since you to non-regardance cast *my
faith*'.

It was a happy man who fell asleep in the small hours

in Gracechurch Street, amid thoughts of all he would have
to tell

> When he returns into his native home,
> Sits down among his friends, and with delight
> Declares the travels he hath overpast.

IX

ENCHANTED PALACES

SHAKESPEARE'S part was played. An amazing feat of swift creation of characters dressed in topicality, personal compliment, and allusion: its genius manifest by the vigour in which those characters live, centuries after all topicalities and even the connotations of their names have been forgotten. How rare a privilege, to have been enabled to restore to Shakespeare—though he has no need of them—a few of the lost 'advantages he might once derive from personal allusions, local customs, or temporary opinions'. For in doing so we reach a juster appreciation of his insight, his knowledge, and his humour.

Shakespeare had done his part: but for Elizabeth this was but Act One. Don Virginio, well aware that his unauthorized visit to the Queen was a ground of disquiet to his uncle the Grand Duke, because of repercussions from the Spaniards, was anxious to cut it short: having plucked bright Honour's golden apple in the Hesperian garden of England, to get over the wall or moat defensive and back to the envy of less happier lands without delay. Yet he found himself powerless to resist Elizabeth's persuasion.

She had set out to charm Don Virginio, and her plan was both conceived and laid with an art which he could appreciate. On the great festival day she had been Gloriana-Cynthia, resplendent in the stately ceremony and public delights of her glittering, white-clad Court. Cynthia, sending her conqueror of the Armada to feast him, and her greatest corsair in the world as a supper-guest.

At night, Gloriana, magnificent in her brilliant Hall, not only bringing the first poet of England to compliment him, but placing him, Orsino, by her side, telling him to put on his hat, and to call her Cousin.

The next vision would be a more intimate one: a party of dance with some select nymphs and courtiers in her chamber, where as Diana-Erato she would take his senses with the music of her grace in moving and in gesture. Reserved to the last is the best. Then would he find her alone, a Laura-Polyhymnia-Terpsichore, winning him with her wit, delighting him with playing on her instruments, and singing to him. An ambitious programme for a lady of sixty-seven (reported at death's door) to perform for a young man of twenty-eight? Not for Elizabeth Tudor.

In reading Don Virginio's narrative of what happened to him, we remind ourselves that this is a private letter to his wife. Had the Queen failed in her attempt to charm him, he would as a gentleman have passed it over, without a word; but here is how he closes his letter, finished on Thursday morning, January 8:

Her Majesty told me that before I depart she wishes to enjoy me again, in private; and I hope from the speech I have had with her that she will favour me by playing and singing. In the mean time I will see two of her country palaces to speed me as soon as may be, albeit her Majesty is very earnest with me that I remain some days more; but I have shown her so many reasons, that I hold it certain she will give me leave to depart within four or five days. This morning I am invited to the house of the Cecils (*Siçils*), where I understand all the principal ladies will be present, and that there will be a goodly feast.

I would not for a great matter have missed seeing this kingdom. Nor do I believe that many Italians have found themselves an opportunity like this, for I hear from everyone that her Majesty, to do me greater honour, made all the ladies and lords that could come in two days return from their seats, and to this end she skilfully delayed my audience.

I have written so badly and confusedly partly by reason of great haste, and partly because I wish to save the better part for word of mouth. In imparting thereof to their Highnesses, instead of reading the letter, let your Excellency report it orally, which will be with fewer mistakes, and impart the substance to the Lord Cardinal [*her brother, Alessandro Peretti, Cardinal Montalto*] by letter. I am writing somewhat to Vettori; but since I have reason to fear that he may be in Rome, I do not make use of the cipher, sending the letter to your Excellency open. I shall take the highway of Flanders, Lorraine, and Milan. I am in health, and kiss your hand.

18 [8] January 1600   Your Excellency's most affectionate
Husband and Servant
V. O.

The sequel followed nearly two weeks later, when Don Virginio had reached Ghent in Catholic Flanders, on his way to Antwerp:

My Lady and most beloved Wife

I wrote at length to your Excellency from London, giving you a minute account of whatever had passed up to that moment. Not having had time hitherto to pursue the description, I do so now that I have a little opportunity.

I told you that I was to go the following morning [*Thursday, the 8th*] to dine with my Lord Cecil [*Thomas Cecil, Lord Burghley, father of William*], and now I let you know that I went, where I found all the first ladies of the Court, and gentlemen infinite. I received a most sumptuous banquet, and after the repast we danced with the greatest mirth.

The next morning came my Lord Cobham (*Cubano*) and the Captain of the Guard [*Sir Walter Ralegh*] to take me to see the finest palace that the Queen has, called Hampton Court

(*Antoncurt*). Arrived thither, I found the son of the Lord Admiral [*i.e.*, *William Howard, Lord Effingham*], who had prepared a Hunt, after her Majesty's custom. First I viewed the palace, of which I shall tell you many things by word of mouth, and then we all went to dine with the son of the Admiral. Afterwards we took horse, witnessed most handsome coursing of bucks and of hares, and returned in the evening to London.

The day following I spent in seeing the Tower, the Arsenal, and the Wardrobe; and on the next [*Sunday, the 11th*] I went to mass and to dine with the Ambassador of France. After dinner her Majesty sent to fetch me, by three gentlemen and her coaches, to give me the audience which I desired for my leave-taking.

As soon as I came, her Majesty received me with so gracious a countenance that I could not ask more, and led me into a chamber with all the ladies and gentlemen, where a most beautiful ball took place. Her Majesty was pleased to dance, which is the greatest honour that she could do me, according to the word of those informed of this court; for they assure me that her Majesty has not danced in fifteen years. [*Don Virginio misunderstood; what they assured him was that she had not danced as much as this in fifteen years*.] She had me view all the ladies and gentlemen who danced well in couples; willed me also to stay ever near to entertain her, making me be covered and to be seated, under compulsion of express command.

The morning after [*Monday, the 12th*], it was signified me that her Majesty wished to enjoy me in private, to use her own word; and after dinner she dispatched two of her most confidential gentlemen to fetch me and convey me in a close carriage; and by way of a back garden gate they brought me in to her Majesty. What the Queen did I am saving for you at my return; but I shall only say that it seemed to me I had become one of the paladins who used to enter those enchanted palaces.

These are not expressions of an English courtier or poet, intended to please the Queen's ear, but a cultivated foreign nobleman's confidences to his wife. Their sincerity is unmistakable.

Don Virginio left London the next day; and before coming to the rest of his letter we should note the impression his visit made on the French Ambassador, on John Chamberlain the gifted gossip, and on Dr. John Herbert, P.C., second Secretary of State. First, then, M. de Boissise writes to Henri IV:

The Sieur Dom Virginio Orsino has been here for a couple of days, wherein I strove to do him all the best offices I could, not only for the honour that he has in belonging to the Queen [*Maria de' Medici*], but also for the friendship he shows towards your Majesty, and for his own virtues and merits, in which he seems to me well accomplished. He offered all possible honour and submission to the Queen of England, and more than foreigners, even of his rank, have used. The said Lady likewise looked most favourably upon him, feasted him, danced, played, and sang for love of him. He has passed into Flanders towards the Archduke and the Infanta.[1]

John Chamberlain writes the news to Dudley Carleton, who was abroad learning diplomacy:

During the holydayes here was the Duke of Bracciano (chiefe of the familie of the Orsini by Rome) that came into Fraunce with the new Quene his cousen germane. The Quene entertained him very graciously, and to shew that she is not so

---

[1] Le Sr Dom Virginio Orsino a esté icy deux jours, où je me suis efforcé de luy rendre tous les meilleurs offices que j'ay peu, non-seulement pour l'honneur qu'il a d'appartenir à la Royne, mais aussy pour l'amityé qu'il tesmoigne envers Vostre Majesté et ses vertus et mérites, dont il me semble bien accomply. Il a rendu tout l'honneur et submission qu'il est possible à la Royne d'Angleterre, et plus que les estrangers, mesmes de sa qualité, ont accoustumé. Ladicte Dame aussy l'a veu de très bon oeil, l'a festoyé, a dansé, sonné, chanté pour l'amour de luy. Il est passé en Flandres vers l'Archiduc et l'Infante. P.R.O., Paris Archives, Transcripts 3/32/6.

old as some wold have her, daunced both measures and galliards in his presence. He was feasted by the Lord Burleigh for
some favor shewed to Will: Cecil & his other sonnes at theyre
being in Italie: and shold have ben by the Lord Treasurer
[*Thomas Sackville, Lord Buckhurst*] and by Grayes Ynne, that
made preparation of shewes to entertain him, but he made such
haste away that they were disappointed. The Quene at his
parting sent him a cup of gold of sixescore pound and a jewell,
for the which he gave the bringer Michaell Stanhop a chaine of
fowrescore pound. He went hence to visite the Archduke and
Infanta, leaving behinde him a generall report of a very court-
like and compleat gentleman.[1]

Finally, Secretary Herbert writes to Sir George Carew
in Ireland that

Virginio Ursini . . . came over, to the outward show only
to visit the court of England, allured thereto by the report of
the singular gifts wherewith her Majesty was endowed. The
entertainment her Majesty gave him was rare and princely; his
carriage answerable to his birth and place. It seemeth he
parted marvellously well content, and satisfied to his expecta-
tion; yet here are [some] that conjecture his coming to tend to
some other purpose.[2]

Conjectures in England, head-shakings in France, dark
suspicions in Flanders, Rome, and Spain. But both Elizabeth and Virginio were content. The Queen had dis-
quieted England's enemies and thereby encouraged her
friends. She had made any comparison between herself
and the plodding Maria de' Medici preposterous. She
had shown the sulking and restive Essex not merely how
wrong he was in supposing her decrepit, but also that
there were better-conditioned young noblemen in the
world whom she could grace when she chose. In short,

---

[1] P.R.O., State Papers, Domestic. S.P. 12/278/223.
[2] *Cal. Carew MSS. 1601–1603*, p. 8.

she had shown the world, England, and best of all, herself, that she was the unmatchable Elizabeth, *Ever the Same*. As for Don Virginio, he had seen the Phoenix, rendered honour where it was due; in return he had received his reward, of which the world must take note—in particular the world of Rome and Madrid, most material to him. And now it is farewell, London. There shall be no louder trump that may sound out Elizabeth's praise, commend and extol her above the skies, than he shall blast in the courts of the Continent:

On the following morning [*January 13*] I departed by river; and the Earl of Rutland (*Rotelando*) came with the Queen's barges, and together with a dozen gentlemen accompanied me as far as Gravesend (*Gravesine*). There I found Sir Walter Ralegh (*Guatterrali*) [*and the Devon man matches him by writing 'Dun Virginia Ursene'*] who—together with me furnished horse by the postmaster—took me to see her Majesty's galleons and ships, which are on the Thames many miles below London.

During their fifteen miles to Rochester, and while their post-horses are walking up Falstaff's lofty Gadshill, we take the time to speculate on the kind of talk which the tall, dark, and handsome 'Sir Guatterrali' held in his high tenor voice with 'Dun Virginia'. We know that the Florentine told him that if the peace of Savoy were concluded, he would see Holland and Zeeland. If Don Virginio asked for an opinion on the Armada, Sir Walter would have observed that before Gravelines it 'was suddenly driven away with squibs': that if the Spaniards had kept better guard, with towing-barges manned and out, they could have avoided all danger from the fireships. And he may have regaled Don Virginio with the Navy's tale of

Queen Elizabeth some four years before. She took barge at Greenwich and went aboard the great new warship *Dieu Repoulse* at Woolwich, attended only by her cousin, Lord Chamberlain Hunsdon, and two ladies. The Earl of Essex, its captain, was ashore.

To clear the ship, all the mariners, three hundred men, went afore the mast and into the shrouds and tops before her barge boarded the ship, in which she was pleased. The master presented a very rich jewel; and she called by name Matthew Baker to her, and reasoned with him, hoping she will prove a well-conditioned ship. He was principal shipwright and built the ship. Going to see the Earl's cabin, which arises to the steerage, the Lord Chamberlain said, 'Your Majesty must stoop.' She replied presently, 'It is more than the King of Spain can make me do.'[1]

When our riders reached the Medway, they were met by Sir Fulke Greville, Sir Philip Sidney's friend, Treasurer of the Navy:

At the river's bank I found the Treasurer of the Navy, who was awaiting me with a vessel like a galliot, which I went aboard; and in the passage which I made among them, the ships saluted me with all their guns, and going aboard some of the finest, I saw craft of such a kind that I do not think their like exist on the sea.

I took leave of those who had had the charge of showing me the ships, and together with Signore William Cecil (commanded by the Queen to keep me company to the embarking-place), and with three other gentlemen my friends, I went forward in a day and a half to Dover. Her Majesty had given order that the chief ship of her vanguard [*H.M.S. Vanguard, 500 tons, 250 men, in the Armada fight and at the sack of Cadiz*] should come to ferry me over to France. But as the weather showed favourable, and this ship was not yet come, I deter-

---

[1] Bodl. MS. Rawl. A173, f. 11.

mined to cross in an Antwerp ship of the States of Holland. Hardly was I embarked, when her Majesty's ship came up; but not to lose time, I would not change. The Queen's ship kept me company for a space; then, having very handsomely shot off all her guns, she turned back.

That night I fell in with twenty ships, part of the fleet of the States, which in the English Channel were awaiting four thousand Spaniards bound in to Flanders, to fight them; and since the wind was not fair, and the tide contrary, I was forced to tarry among them. Presently the Admiral [*Justinus, natural brother of Maurice of Nassau*]—who is very close kin to Count Maurice (*Maurizio*)—having sent to take knowledge of the ship, and learned that I was aboard of her, sent twice to visit me; causing them each time to offer me himself and the fleet, and having me told that he came not in person because it was night and with the fear which I have already mentioned, but that on the morrow he would present his compliments. I did not wish to delay myself further, but so soon as the weather allowed, I had sail made, and got within two miles of Calais (*Cales*). Since more was not possible, I had two cannon-shots fired. Those of Calais, surmising that it was I, came to fetch me, with boats excellently fitted out, and brought me to the Town two hours before dawn. Had I not seized that occasion, I should yet be either at sea or in England, for the wind has been still contrary.

I omitted to say that her Majesty had me presented at my parting with a jewel to wear on my breast, and a cup of gold: the which I trust your Excellency will willingly look upon at my return. At Calais I stayed but a single day, to find horse, and I went hunting with Monsieur de Vic (*di Vich*) [*Dominique de Vic, Vice-Admiral of France, Governor of Calais*].

I have taken the Antwerp road [*Chemin de Flandre–Calais, St. Omer, Armentières, Courtrai, Ghent*], lodging every night in very fine towns, and God willing I hope to arrive there this evening. Signore Giulio Riario finds himself with a bad cold; the rest of us are all well, and I in particular.

Supposing that your Excellency will be able to give a report

of everything to their Highnesses orally, and by letter to the
Lord Cardinal, I hope in Antwerp to find letters from your
Excellency, for which I continue in the greatest longing. If
your Excellency has given birth to a daughter, and she is not
yet christened, I desire that she be called Cammilla [*it was a
boy, and his sixth son*]; and in conclusion I kiss your hands.

From Ghent (*Gantes*) 31 [21] January 1600

Your Excellency's most affectionate
Husband and devoted Servant,
V. O.

[*Endorsed*]

To the Most Illustrious and Excellent-Honourable Lady,
The Lady Flavia Orsini
Florence

X

THE HARVEST OF THE
QUEEN'S DAY

WHAT were the consequences, what the Continental reverberations of Queen Elizabeth's Twelfth Night? Documented detail is already at hand to weave them into a very absorbing tale. We must here content ourselves with a mere outline of what could be told:

How Don Virginio came down at Antwerp with a terrific attack of his gout; how during his convalescence came the strange news of the London *romori*—the hurly-burly of Essex's mutiny, with the very Lord 'Rotelando' who had attended him at Whitehall deeply involved. How in all companies, in Brussels, Paris, Nancy, he spread abroad the praise of Queen Elizabeth, her magnificence, her wisdom, her learning, her dancing, her singing, the unexampled honour she had shown him. How the newsletters carried his story, to the annoyance of France, Spain, and Rome. How the French said that she had honoured him above his desert; how the College of Rome was much displeased, and Philip of Spain so infuriated that he moved to cut off Don Virginio's Spanish pension, and was only dissuaded from it by his ambassador in Rome. How the general voice whispered that Don Virginio had been entrusted by his uncle or by Henri of France with a secret diplomatic mission to Elizabeth; how the Spaniards tormented Ferdinand about it—gave him 'many blows' while he swore that his nephew's visit had borne no official character, and had actually displeased him.

How Virginio came home to find that in spite of all his able Cardinal brother-in-law could do he had to face the music for his crime committed at Whitehall Chapel Royal. As Feste had told 'Duke Orsino' at Whitehall, 'Pleasure will be paid, one time or another.' How he humbled himself, repented, and was given a public penance to perform in the Duomo at Florence. Yet how he was so heartened by Queen Elizabeth's reception—for she had not only told him to put on his hat in the Hall at Shakespeare's public play, but also urged him a thousand times to sit beside her—that he took the bull by the horns and went to Spain. How the Spaniards all accused him of having dealt with the enemy, but how his original judgment was vindicated: they hated him for going, but Elizabeth's *cachet* had added to his stature. How he kept aloof from the Court until authorized by Philip, with the words *Cobred os*, to wear his *sombrero* in the royal presence. How (now 'most royally received') he wore it, created a *Grande de España* of the first class; and to crown all, how Philip, instead of cutting off his stipend, increased it by three thousand *escudos*, and sent him the Order of the Golden Fleece. The royal hands which Don Virginio had kissed at Whitehall were not only white, but very long.

Such then was the success of Queen Elizabeth's favourite guest on Twelfth Night. What became of the Muscovite ambassador Grishka—Grigori Mikulin? His simple story deserves to be recorded. For after all, Shakespeare in his line *I can say little more than I have studied* was essentially poking fun not at him, but at the tyrant behind him, the fear-ridden Tsar who made such puppets of his slaves.

In reading Mikulin's report to Boris of what happened in London only a month after the great State Dinner on Twelfth Day, I suddenly found myself seeing Essex's rebellion through Russian eyes: how the tumult in Elizabeth's peaceable kingdom amazed his mind; how Francis Cherry and John Merrick (the Russian-speaking merchants assigned to look after him) narrated the events as they occurred.

What endears Grigori is his behaviour in the crisis. It seems that, upon the first uproar, he bravely offered to go out and fight the enemies of her Majesty. Was she not his great Tsar's beloved sister? But having no instructions to cover a contingency so unforeseen, he felt uncertain how the Tsar would take such a spontaneous gesture on the part of his *kholóp*, and so said not a word in his report of what he had done.

We learn of it only through Elizabeth's own letter to Boris Godunov. She remembered, both to be grateful and to do the loyal Grigori all the good in her power with his master. She wrote:

We have remitted your Majesty's Ambassador, Gregore Evanowich Mekulyne, by the first opportunity of passage that hath bin offered for his safe conveyance . . . who, being before us at several times, hath carefully and respectively performed the charge of his ambassage, omitting no opportunity to persuade and assure us of your Majesty's great and exceeding love and affection towards us and desire to be advertised of our good health and prosperous estate; and not only that, but upon an occasion of some rebellious attempts against the peace of our government happening at his being here, was ready to have come forth and to have put himself in danger against the undertakers thereof; all which though thanked be God was so soon ended as in 12 hours space almost all the actors were in our hands, yet could we not but take it in very kind and thankful part; and I think it worthy your Majesty's knowledge and due respect.[1]

When after the long and hazardous Arctic voyage round the North Cape in the English ships the returning Mikulin reached Archangel at the mouth of the Dvina, he stayed there at least a month before starting on his journey south via Vologda and Yaroslavl, a thousand five hundred versts to Moscow. Grigori was grateful too. What he said and did at Archangel is described in a report from Robert Barne, the English agent there, as follows:

The entertainment given in so gracious manner, and so honourable, by her Majesty unto the Russ Ambassador was done to very good purpose; and I do not think but that he [*Mikulin*] enlargeth it to the uttermost, for more he reporteth than I understand by letters or speech of any man. There come many to him, to whom he imparteth at large every particular of his entertainment; in which discourse he intermingleth commendations of our country and people, withal showeth the plate given him by her Majesty, with that likewise which other noblemen and others bestowed upon him; which doth very much increase the reputation of our country among the Russes.[2]

It is a pleasant picture, and we wish that we could imagine Mikulin still enjoying his English presents after he had at length reached Moscow and beaten the pavement with his brow before his master in the Kremlin. But on reading the following passage in Hotman's *Ambassador* (1603), so fair a fortune for the faithful Grishka does not seem likely:

---

[1] P.R.O. State Papers, Russia. S.P. 91/1/160.
[2] H.M.C., *Cecil Papers*, 13. 386–7.

I have observed [*writes Hotman*] two other antient privileges: the one, that the chaines of gold and other gifts and presents that had been given unto them in regards of their Ambassage should remaine unto themselves, and I beleeve that no man would now make any question thereof, provided that it be without suspition, and in such sort as I have before shewed. For the incivilitie & barbarousnesse of the Duke of Moscovie is not to be approved, who taketh away, not onely the habites and ornaments which hee giveth them at their departure, but also the giftes and presents which have beene bestowed upon them in their Ambassages, which he converteth to his owne profit. It is true that the Muscovites are not simply subjects (as those [*i.e., Pisemsky and Khovralev, sent by Ivan the Terrible*] which were in England in the behalfe of their Prince about 18 yeares past did shewe unto mee) but slaves unto their Prince.

XI

EPILOGUE

WE have followed the reaching consequences of that memorable Twelfth Day at Whitehall north to Archangel and south to Rome and Madrid. Notable abroad, it was unluckily obscured on its home soil in England by the rebellion of Essex, which 'followed hard upon'. The rude shock of the Sunday hurly-burly in London, and the tragic end of that spoiled darling of the populace on Tower Hill a few weeks after Twelfth Night, at once threw present memory of that high feast and genial entertainment into shadow.

Latter-day historians have been so absorbed in tracing the imminent crisis of conspiracy as to neglect the two significant events of state on Twelfth Day 1600/1: the League with Russia, and the visit of the sovereign of Tuscany's chief assistant. And modern students of Shakespeare are more likely to have heard of the examination of the player Augustine Phillips—on how Shakespeare's company came to revive the stale *Richard II* at the Globe the very day before Essex's rising—than to be aware that Don Virginio Orsino, the Duke, was entertained on the preceding Twelfth Night at Whitehall.[1] Our fresh

---

[1] Don Virginio Orsino has been either overlooked or strangely handled by the Shakespeareans. Neither Sir Sidney Lee nor Dr. J. Q. Adams mentioned him in their lives of the poet. Sir Edmund Chambers (*William Shakespeare*, 1. 406), with 'Orsino, Duke of Bracciano', vouchsafed him no Christian name, and Professor J. Dover Wilson (ed. *Twelfth Night*, Cambridge, 1949) not only gives him a spurious one, naming him 'one Don Valentino Orsino', but refers his arrival to 1600, a twelvemonth too early. The character of

contemporary materials—the memoranda of Shakespeare's master Lord Hunsdon, the report of the Russian ambassador to his Tsar, and Don Virginio's letters to his wife—however redress the balance. They remind us that Queen Elizabeth was not to be frightened by a knot of conspirators into suspending either divine service, state ceremonial, or high-hearted revel.

Lifting the curtain of oblivion on that 'first night', our discovery reveals Shakespeare's *Twelfth Night* in something of its original glow, shows us for the first time the rare and happy fitness of each part. Because her Majesty desired a play with variety of music and dances, *Twelfth Night* is Shakespeare's most musical comedy. Because Queen Elizabeth and Don Virginio must be complimented, Lady Olivia is a shadow of the Queen in her youth, and the Illyrian Orsino a portrait of her valorous and courtly guest, Orsino. Because the time is leap-year, Shakespeare gracefully gives the ladies control : they all must woo and win, and Maria must rule as Sovereign of the Sports. Because the occasion is Epiphany, the piece abounds in Twelfth Night topicalities.

Because Twelfth Night is the licensed saturnalia, whose watchword is *What You Will* or Liberty, the comedians are officially encouraged to make some sport with the 'sergeant-major' of the Household, Mr. Controller Knollys—for this is the very moment when that elderly married man's disgraceful infatuation with young Mistress

---

his visit to Queen Elizabeth has also been mistaken. Following Sarrazin, who assumed that Don Virginio was 'Florentine ambassador at the English Court', C. E. Vaughan (*Camb. Hist. of Eng. Lit.*, 6. 175) declared that Virginio 'had been sent as envoy to England by his uncle Ferdinand', and Professor J. W. Draper (*op. cit.*, 113) speaks of his 'embassy from Florence'.

Mall Fitton looks most absurd. Mall not only 'loves another', but is so far gone with child by Lord Herbert that her picture is inevitably 'like to take dust'; yet the 'rascally sheep-biter' is still pursuing the 'innocent lamb', old Party-Beard Knollys's cry is still *Mal-voglio —I want Mal!*

Because the colossal Muscovite ambassador (that uncouth and apprehensive marionette) has just spent hours at the Palace, a bit of byplay to celebrate his absence is on the cards. Because the audience comprises her Majesty's prelates and chaplains from 'the chantry by' as well as the 'ordinary' of her *Cubiculo* and Outer Chamber, Shakespeare includes ecclesiastical pleasantries, and some sharper gibes at the 'ordinary men', an 'ordinary fool', and the beef-eating Myrmidons of the Guard. And finally, because the comedy is presented in the usual arena-fashion— two 'houses' set on the floor due East and West for scenery, completely surrounded by stands crowded with courtiers glistening in white—in the centre of the Whitehall Noon-hall, its bays as well as its clerestories at the South–North blocked with hangings, the actual room, transformed into an amphitheatre, can be conjured up before our eyes by the witty words of Feste.

The new documents have given us an unprecedented point of vantage. As Ben Jonson would put it, we have 'got the hill', and can see things we could never see before. Now for the first time, in looking at an Elizabethan play of Shakespeare's, we command a firm ground for understanding. We know the exact date and the occasion of the First Night of *Twelfth Night*, which reveal 'the quality of the time'. We also know 'the quality of persons'—the composition, character, and mood of the audience, which show the tone of the piece : its purpose, execution, and reception. Finally, we know not only the very room in which it was presented, but its amphitheatrical, circus-theatre arrangement in detail, affording us our first and only unmistakable view of Shakespeare's method of staging and acting a play.

ORIGINAL DOCUMENTS

Letters of Don Virginio Orsini, Duke of Bracciano, to his Wife, Duchess Flavia

I

Signora Consorte amat*issi*ma

Diedi conto a V*ostra Celsità* con altra mia d'esser giunto in questa Isola. Hora le dico, che sabato doppo desinare arrivai qui in Londra in casa del S*igno*r Corsini; il quale mandai subito da S*ua* M*aestà* per farle sapere il mio arrivo, e supplicarla di contentarsi, che io privatamente le potessi bacciar le mani; parlò il S*igno*r Corsini al secretario Secil,[1] che è quello che governa questo reg*no*, et al gran camberlano, i quali risposero, doppo haver trattato con la Regina, che S*ua* M*aestà* aggradiva la mia venuta, più che d'altro cav*alie*re che sia mai arrivato nel suo Regno, e che il martedì a 16 alla n*os*tra usanza, et alla loro a 6, giorno della Pifania, m'havria data audienza, ma non tanto privata quanto io desideravo. La domenica mattina me ne andai a visitare il S*igno*r Ambasciator di Francia, et a udir la messa in casa sua, poi che qui in Londra non si dice in altro loco messa. S*ua* M*aestà* ha mandato dui volte il giorno a visitarmi sempre Cav*alie*ri principali, facendomi sempre dire che io faccia non solo conto di essere a Fioren*z*a nella Casa del Granduca, ma a Bracc*ia*no nella mia propria. Il martedì mattina mandò sue carrozze, e dui principali a pigliarmi, e menarmi a

---

[1] Sir Robert Cecil, Secretary of State.

palazzo, dove arrivato trovai alla porta il conte di Rotelan,[1] uno de' primi signori del Regno, il quale mi assiste
s[c]endere; questo mi riceve in nome di *Sua Maestà*, e mi
menò in una appartamento disegniato per me; stetti lì
molto poco, e poi salii di sopra, dove trovai una sala tutta
piena di damigelle; l'altra appresso piena di Dame e
Cavalieri; nella terza erano tutti gl'ufiziali della Corona,
et i cavalieri della giarrattera, tutti vestiti di bianco, come
era quel giorno tutta la corte, ma con tanto oro e gioie,
che era cosa maravigliosa; questi tutti mi vennero a salutare, parlando la più parte Italiano, molti Franzese, et
alcuni Spagniolo; io risposi a tutti nel modo che sapevo,
nella lingua che mi sentivo parlare, e sono certo, che al
meno mi sono fatto intendere; non ho trovato altro, che
dui Cavalieri che non sappino altra lingua, che l'Inghlese,
e con questi ho adoperato altri Cavalieri per Interpetri
[*sic*]. Questi tutti mi menarno [*written* menorno] vicino
alla porta dove doveva venir la Regina, essendo incontro
a me l'Imbasciator moscovito, venuto strasordinario a
complire con *Sua Maestà*; venne la regina sopra la porta,
et io subito m'accostai con ogni humiltà a farle reverenza,
et ella [*written* elle] mi s'accesse con gratissima cera, parlando così bene Italiano, e dicendo tanti belli concetti, che
io posso dire d'haver preso lezioni dal Boccaccio, o nella
Accademia. Era *Sua Maestà* tutta vestita di bianco, con
tante perle, ricami, e diamanti, che io son stupito come
ella gli potesse portare. Come io gl'ebbi fatta reverenza,
fecero l'istesso il *Signo*r Giulio et il *Signo*r Grazia, e poi
tutta la corte s'incamminò per ordine alla volta della
cappella. L'ordine è tale che io lo fò tutto notare per
scritto; ne credo haver a veder mai corte che di ordine

---

[1] Roger Manners, Earl of Rutland.

passi questa. Io servi Sua Maestà fino a una stanza
presso la cappella, dove mi fermai in compagnia di molti
Cavalieri, e mentre stavamo in bonissima conversazione,
sentimo una musica stupenda. Sua Maestà ritornò in capo
a mezza hora, havendo tutta la corte di mano in mano
secondo la qualità e gradi innanzi, e tutte le Signore e
Dame appresso, e mentre io l'accompagnava venne
sempre discorrendo con me, si come haveva ancora fatto
prima, entrata Sua Maestà nella sua camera, io fui condotto alla sala dove Sua Maestà doveva mangiare, la qual
sala, insieme con molte altre stanze, era parata di razzi
d'oro; era nella testa sopra un solio la tavola di Sua
Maestà, dal lato opposto una gran credenza tutta di vasi
d'oro, dal canto destro una gran bottiglieria di vasi con
oro, e gioie, e dal sinistro una bassa tavola con tre piccoli
servizi, per l'imbasciatore Moscovito, e per dui che
erano seco, essendo il costume di Moscovia, che se
egli non fussi stato visto mangiare dalla Regina, il suo
Granduca gl'haveria fatta tagliare la testa; venne intanto
la vivanda di Sua Maestà portata da cavalieri, e lo scalco
era del Gran Ordine, facevano questi l'istesso ossequio
alla sedia di Sua Maestà, che haveriano fatto se ella fussi
stata presente, e subito che la tavola fù apprestata venne la
Regina, et io mi riserbo a dire in voce il portamento dei
molti strascichi, et il suo lavar de mano, per che questa
sola discrizione impirebbe quattro fogli; subito che Sua
Maestà fù entrata a tavola, l'ambasciator Moscovito, del
quale accontrò costumi ridicolosi, andò a desinare, et io
fui condotto dal Gran Ammiraglio,[1] al quale la Regina
haveva dato l'ufizio di Mairdomo maggiore, ma solo per
quel giorno, e da molti altri grandi ufiziali della Corona e

---

[1] Charles Howard, Earl of Nottingham, Lord Admiral.

Cavalieri del Ordine, in una sala dove era apparechiato per me un bellissimo banchetto, nel fine del quale comparse una buona musica; subito finito il banchetto mi levai da tavola, et andai da *Sua Maestà*, la quale stava di già in piedi, e parlando hora con me, et hora con l'Ambasciatore Moscovito, si trattenne un pezzo, e poi fù da me servita fino alla sua stanza; quei Cavalieri che havono cura di assistermi e molti altri con i quali havevo fatto conoscenza mi condussero al mio appartamento, perchè io mi riposassi, ma in capo a poco cominciorno a venire di questi principali a visitarmi, e poi musica di alcuni instrumenti a mio credere non mai sentiti in Italia, ma miracolosi, sichè con buono trattenimento facemo hora di cena, la quale fù apparechiata in una sala nel mio proprio appartamento; vennero a cenar con me il Cavallerizzo Maggiore,[1] et il Conte di Comberlan,[2] con il quale hebbi alcuni ragionamenti che sarranno di gusto a *Sua Altezza* poi chè egli è il più gran Corsaro del mondo; subito cenato fui condotto all'appartamento di *Sua Maestà*, dove in una sala il Gran Secretario mi fece salutare alla Franzese tutte le signore titolate; parlai con una Italiano, con alcune Franzese, e con l'altre egli medesimo mi fece l'interpetre; venne in questo la Regina, e mi comandò d'andare discorrendo con lei, sale *Sua Maestà* la scala, con tanti suoni che mi pareva di essere alla guerra, et entrò in una sala pubblica, dove atorno atorno erano gradi con dame, e variati cori di musica; subito che *Sua Maestà* fù messa al suo loco, cominciorno molte Dame e Cavalieri un Granballo, e come questo fù finito, si rappresentò una com-

---

[1] Edward Somerset, Earl of Worcester, Deputy Master of the Horse.
[2] George Clifford, Earl of Cumberland.

media mescolata, con musiche e balli, e questa ancora mi
riserbo a dire in voce. L'Ambasciatore Moscovito non fù
presente; io stetti sempre appresso a Sua Maestà, la quale
mi comandò di coprire, e mi fece portare uno sgabello,
e se bene mi comandò mille volte di sedere, non volsi
però mai ubbidirla, discorse di continuo con me, e finita la
commedia, la servi fino alle sue stanze dove era apparechiata, per Sua Maestà e per le dame, una belissima cola-
zione tutta di confetture; la Regina, preso prima dui soli
bocconi, comandò, che fusse tutta saccheggiata; il chè
fù fatto con una confusione galante; entrata la regina in
camera, quelle dame che sapevano parlare Italiano e
Franzese si messero a discorrere con me, et in capo a
mezz'ora ci licenziamo di sieme, et io me ne andai a casa,
essendo di già dui hore doppo la mezza notte. Sua
Maestà mi ha detto, che prima che io parta, mi vol godere
ancora in privato, et io spero per quello che ho discorso
seco, che mi favorira di sonare, e cantare; io vederò intanto dui sue ville per spedirmi quanto prima, se bene Sua
Maestà mi fa grande instanza io mi fermi qualche giorno di
più ~~se bene~~ ma io gl'ho mostrato tante ragioni, che tengo
sicuro, che mi lascerà partire fra quattro, o cinque
giorni; questa mattina sono convitato in casa de' Signori
Sizil, dove intendo che saranno tutte le dame principali, e
che si farà una bella festa, io non vorrei per grancosa
haver lassato di veder questo regno, ne credo che molti
Italiani si siono trovato una occasione come questa,
poichè intendo da tutti che Sua Maestà per farmi maggiore
honore ha fatto tornar da i loro luoghi tutte le Signore e
Signori che potevano venire in dui giorni, e perciò con
arte haveva trattenuta la mia audienza. Io ho scritto così
male, e confuso, parte per la granfretta, e parte perchè

voglio serbare la miglior parte alla voce, Vostra Celsità nel darne parte a loro Altezze, incambio di legger la lettera faccia relazione in voce, che sarà con meno errori, et al Signor Cardinale dia parte per lettera della sustanza, qualche cosa scrivo al Vettori, ma perchè posso temer che sia a Roma non mi vaglio della cifra per mandar la lettera a Vostra Celsità aperta; farò la strada di Fiandra, Loreno, e Milano; Sto sano, è le bacio la mano.

li 18 [8 *written over* 7] di Gennaro 1600

Di Vostra Celsità Affettionatissimo Consorte e Servitore

Virginio Orsini

[*Endorsed*]

All'Illustrissima et Eccellentissima Signora Osservandissima la Signora Flavia Orsini

Fiorenza

II

Signora Consorte amatissima

[Scrissi] lungamente a Vostra Celsità di Londra dandole minuto conto di quanto [fino] a quell'ora era passato, et non havendo hauto tempo di seguitare la [discrizi]one prima, lo fò adesso, che ho un poco di comodità; le dissi [che] dovevo andare la mattina seguente a desinare con Milor [Cicil], et hora le dice, che andai, dove trovai tutte le prime dame [della] corte, et infiniti Cavalieri; ricevei un bellissimo banchetto, e dopo [pran]zo ballamo con grandissima allegria; La mattina appresso venne [Mi]lor Cubano [1] et il Capitano delle guiardie [2] a menarmi a veder il [p]iù bel palazzo, che habbia la Regina, chiamato

---

[1] Henry Brooke, Lord Cobham.
[2] Captain of the Guard, Sir Walter Ralegh.

Antoncurt,[1] dove arrivato trovai il fig*liuòl*o del Grand'
Amiraglio,[2] il quale haveva preparato una caccia secondo
il costume di S*ua Maestà*. [V]idi prima il palazzo, del
quale dirò molte cose in voce, e [p]oi andamo a desinare
tutti con il fig*liuòl*o dell'Ami*raglio*: doppo montamo a
cavallo, e vedemo belliss*ime* carriere di daini, e di lepre, e
tornamo la sera in Londra; il giorno seguente lo spesi in
vedere la fortezza, l'arsenale, e la guardaroba; e l'altro
appresso andai a la messa, et a desinare con l'Ambasciator
di Francia; e doppo pranzo S*ua Maestà* mandò a levarmi
per tre Cav*ali*eri con le sue carrozze, per darmi l'audienza
che io desideravo nel partire: subito giunto, S*ua Maestà*
mi riceve con tanta genta cera che io non potevo desiderar
più, e mi menò in una sala con tutte le dame e Cav*ali*eri,
dove si fece un belliss*imo* festino. S*ua Maestà* fù contenta
di ballare, che è il maggiore onore, che ella mi potessi
fare, secondo il detto di questi informati di questa corte,
poichè m'accertano che sono 15 anni, che S*ua Maestà*
non ha ballato; mi fece vedere tutte le Dame, et i Cav*ali*eri
che ballano bene a coppia a coppia, e volse che io le stessi
sempre appresso per intrattenerla, facendomi coprire,
e sedere a forza d'e[spresso] comandamento.   La mattina
seguente mi fece sapere, che [S*ua Maestà* mi] voleva
godere in privato, per usar la sua propria [parola], e
doppo pranzo mandò dui Cav*ali*eri i più suoi confidenti[ali
a levar]mi, e menarmi in una carrozzetta serrata, e per
una po[rta secreta] d'un giardino m'introdussero da S*ua
Maestà*. Quello che fec[e] le riserbo al mio ritorno, ma
solo dirò, che mi p[arve di] essere diventato un di quei
paladini, che andavan[o in] quei palazzi incantati. La

---

[1] Hampton Court.
[2] William Howard, Lord Effingham.

mattina seguente partiss[i per] fiume, e venne il conte di
Rotelando con le barche da[lla] Regina, et insieme con una
dozzina di Cavalieri m'accom[pagnò] fino a Gravesine,[1]
dove trovai il Signor Guatterrali,[2] che [mon]tato per la
posta con me, mi menò per vedere i Ga[leoni] e le navi di
Sua Maestà, che sono nel Tamigi molte miglia [giù] da
Londra, alla riva del fiume trovai il tesoriero [della]
armata,[3] che mi aspettava con un vascello simile [ad] una
Galeotta, dove montai, e nel passare che feci t[ra] le navi
mi salutorno con tutti i pezzi, et io montando sopra
alcune delle più belle, viddi vascelli d'una maniera, che
non penso, che sopra al mare ne siono de simili; licenziai
quelli che haveriano hauto cura di mostrarmi le navi, et
insieme con il Signor Guglielmo Cicil,[4] comandato dalla
Regina per tenermi compagnia fino all'imbarco, e con tre
altri cavalieri miei amici, me ne andai in un giorno e mezzo
a Dovere.[5] Sua Maestà [hav]eva comandato, che venissi
la nave, capo della sua van[gu]iardia,[6] a passarmi in
Francia, ma perche la mattina [il] tempo si mostrò buono,
e questa nave non era ancora arrivata, mi risolvei di
passare sopra una nave da [An]versa[7] delli stati d'Olanda,[8]
subito che io fui imbarcato [ve]nne il vascello di Sua
Maestà, ma io per non perder tempo [no]n volsi cambiare;
la nave della Regina mi tenne un pezzo compagnia, e poi
fatta una bellissima salva se ne tornò. La notte trovai 20
nave, che sono parte [de]lla armata delli stati, che as-
pettano nel canale di Inghilterra quattro mila Spagnioli

---

[1] Gravesend.   [2] Sir Walter Ralegh.
[3] Sir Fulke Greville, Treasurer of the Navy.
[4] William Cecil, son of Thomas Lord Burghley.
[5] Dover.   [6] H.M.S. *Vanguard*.
[7] Antwerp.   [8] Holland.

che passano in Fiandra per combattergli, e per che il vento non era buono, e la marea contraria, fui forzato di fermarmi tra loro; subito l'Amirraglio,[1] che è strettissimo parente del Conte Maurizio, mandata a riconoscer la nave, e saputo che io ci ero sopra, inviò dui volte a visitarmi, facendomi sempre offerire la sua persona e l'Armata, facendomi dire, che non veniva in persona, per esser notte, con il sospetto, che ho di già detto, ma che la mattina haveria complito; io non volsi altrimente trattenermi, ma subito che il tempo lo concede feci far vela, et accostavomi a Cales [2] a dui miglia, che più non era possibile, feci tirar dui cannonate; quelli di Cales immaginatosi che io ero, vennero con barche bonissime armate a levarmi, e mi condussero dui hore innanzi giorno alla Città; e se io non pigliavo quel tempo, sarei ancora o nel mare, o in Inghi[lterra], perchè il vento e stato sempre contrario. Ho l[asciato] di dire, che *Sua Maestà* mi fece presentar [nel] mio partire un gioiello da portare al pett[o], et un vaso d'oro, quali spero, che *Vostra Celsità* v[edrà] volontieri al miò ritorno. A Cales mi f[ermai] un giorno solo, per trovar cavalli, et andai [a] la caccia con *Monsieur* di Vich.[3] Ho poi piglia[to il] cammino d'Anversa, alloggiando ogni se[ra in] bellissime città, e piacendo a Dio spero [che] da sera di arrivarci. Il *Signor* Giu[lio] Riario si trova con una cattiva rifreddat[ura]; noi altri stiamo tutti bene, et io in part[ico]lare. Parendo a *Vostra Celsità* potrà dare di t[utto] ragguaglio in voce a lore *Altezze*, e per *lettera* al *Signor* Cardi*nale*, spero in Anversa trovar *lettere* di *Vostra Celsità* delle quali sto con grandiss*imo* desiderio; se *Vostra Celsità* havesse fatta

---

[1] Justinus of Nassau.   [2] Calais.
[3] Dominique de Vic, Governor of Calais.

una fig*liuò*la, e non fusse ancora battezzata, desidero, che si chiami Cammilla; e perfine le bacio le mani.

Di Gantes [1] li 31 di Genn*aro* 1600

Di V*ostra* C*elsità*

Aff*ettionatissi*mo C*onsorte* e Serv*ito*re di core

V*irginio* O*rsini*

[*Endorsed*]

All'Ill*ustrissi*ma et Ecc*ellentissi*ma Sig*nora* Oss*ervand*issi*ma la Sig*nora* Flavia Orsini

Fiorenza

Roma.   Archivio Storico Capitolino.
Archivio Orsini, Corrispondenza di Virginio II,
Fasc. 109,

nri. 0395, 0394

---

[1] Ghent.

Kindlichen gehorsam auch was ich mehr liebs und
guetes vermeg neben windschung von Gott dem all mech-
tigen eines Glüchseligen freudenreichen neuen Jares
und aller bestendiger wollfart seij E[w.] W[ohlachtbaren]
G[naden] aus kindlichem getreuem hertzen und gemuet
Zuvor. Durchleuchtiger hochgeborner Fürst gnediger
geliebter Herr Vatter, aus meinem schreiben so an
E. W. G. ich aus Londra vom 17. 10br des nunmehr ver-
loffenen 160ots Jares gethan, und sie von Köln aus empfangen haben werden, werden dieselben verhoffentlich
verstanden haben, wie glükhlich ich in Engellandt angelanget, wie Ich mit einem *Catharro* und bakhengeschwulst
uberfallen worden, wie es sich mit demselben wüder ge-
bessert, wie Ich beij Ihr königliche M[ajestä]t in Engellandt
audientz gehabt, auch wie gnedig sie ~~anfänglich meines
grosherren Vatter Pfalzgraven darauf~~ auf mein Vorbring-
en erkläret und sowol gegen E. W. G. alss mir erbotten, Wie nun E. W. G. ich hernacher wüderum auss Londra under dem *dato* 3ts *Januarij* diss iezt laufenden Jares
~~vertröstet~~ durch ein schreiben so Ich durch dero Rath *Theo-
dorico Hesso* auf Paris geschikht, vertröstet ds Ich dieselbe
was sich weiter ~~daselbsten~~ zue Engellandt sonderlich auch
beij der mir nach Oxenfurt[1] bewilligten reise zuegetragen
worde, wie Ich, von Ihr königliche Mt. abge~~schiden~~fert-
iget worden, abgeschiden, In Seelandt[2] ankommen undt
zue Vlissing,[3] welche Stadt mehrgemelte Ire Kö. Mt: /

---

[1] Oxford. [2] Zeeland. [3] Flushing.

(allss E. W. G. Ich euch zum nehnermaln angedeutet *Page 2*
Pfandsweis Innen hatt) empfangen worden, berichten
wolle ~~vertröstet~~, alss soll deroselben, ~~zweifellen~~ solchem
Zuvolg Ich gehorsamlich anzumelden nit únderlassen, ds
Ich den 18ts. 10br vergangenen Jars mich sambt dem kö-
niglichen *comissario Stephano Losiero*[1] (von welchem Ich
auch nehnermaln meldung gethan)und denbeij mir wesen-
den auf den weg gemacht uf Wekham,[2] und den 19. uf
Oxenfurt geraiset, daselbsten von dem *Vice cancellario* (*D.
Abbote*[3]), ~~und andern~~ *Decano* (*Dg. Ravisio*[4]), *Presidenten*
(*D. Bondo*[5] genant), und schulverwanten, under dessen
jurisdiction die gantze statt begriffen, uf dem blaz mit
Fakheln weil es spet worden in ihrem roten habit mit einer
langen lateinischen *oration* empfangen biss in ds Wirtshaus

comitieret worden, ~~mich~~ auch selbigen abents der ~~rector~~ *vice
kanzler* sambt zweien ~~anderen~~ von der universitet *procura-
toren* ~~beigewohnet~~ von welchen die *Universitet* mir einem
par handschuh mit golt gestikht vermög alten gebrauches
verehret und zum nachtessen beij mir gebliben, weil Ich
aber von I. K. Mt. auch erlaubnusse bekommen auf dero
Schlösser eines Wodstokh[6] genant, darin sie ein zeitlang
gefangen gelegen, zue zihen, alss bin ich volgendten
tages daselbst hin geraiset, zuenechst dabeij von ettlichen
Englischen herren und vom adel wegen des daselbsten
wohneten ambtmans welcher *Heinrich* Lee[7] des *Georgia-
ner* ordens ritter, ~~heiset~~ *intituliret* würd (so sich wegen

---

[1] Stephen Lesieur. [2] High Wycombe.
[3] George Abbot, Deputy Vice-Chancellor.
[4] Thomas Ravis, Dean of Christ Church.
[5] Nicholas Bond, President of Magdalen College.
[6] Woodstock.
[7] Sir Henry Lee, K.G., Comptroller of Woodstock.

seines zuegestandenen leibsscherenheit, das er nit selbsten, wie er von I. K. Mt. befeliht, herauskomme, entschuldigen lassen) empfangen und durch den Thiergarten In dsselbe Schloss gefueret worden dasselbe *perlustrieret*, hernacher in ein ander heislein darinnen gemelter ambtman sich uffhelt, in dem Thürgarten gelegen gefueret und von selbigem ambtman uf ds stattlichest *tractieret* worden. /

Page 3 Nach dem gehaltenem Panget hatt sie er mich in den thiergarten hinaus füren lassen und ds wildbret, von mehrertheils den hirschen, mir zuetreiben lassen, und ob wol ein gröste anzahl desselben sich sehen lassen erzeigt hab ich doch keines ds der zeit zu schiessen recht war, zue schuss bringen können, alss ich nun nach solchem allem mich hinein zue mehrgemeltem *Cavalliero* begeben, und ihnen für solchem vilweg erzeigte *favor* und guetwillikheit gedankht hatt er zum mehrmalen gemeltet ds er noch vil ein mehres von Ihr K. Mt. im bevelch auch sich ds er nit selber mir beij wohnen nach vermög ihr K. Mt. bevelch mich tractieren könne entschuldiget, darneben seine Pferd Vogel falknereij oder warinnen mich gedienet sein möge mir angebotten.   Weil ich aber noch selbigen abent zue dem *Vice Kantzler* von Oxenfurt zum nachtessen gebodten, alss hab Ich den abschid von Ihnen genohmen und mich wüder nach Oxenfurt begeben, und beij dem *Vice Kantzler* in dem *collegio Universitatis* (da ich zum andermahl widerumb mit einer lateinischen *oration salutiret* worden) die nacht malzeit eingenohmmen.   Den 21. Ist ein lateinische Predig (so der unsern augspurgisch *confession* im wenigsten nit zu wider gewesen) gehalten worden, wie dass E. W. G. auss deren *copia* sie ins künftig so bald sie wie hernach geschikhet würd zum Verlesen haben sollen vernehmen werden, und bin hernacher von dem *Decano in*

collegio Ecclesiæ Christi (in welchem mich abermahl mit
einer schönen lateinischen *oration salutiret* worden) zum
morgenessen stattlich *tractieret*, nach vollendung desselben in ettliche der fürnembsten *collegien*, weil in solcher
zeit alle zu sehen unmöglich, durch den *vice Kantzler* gefüret, auch deren ettlichen underschidlich mit schönen
orationen angeredet. / Zu dem nachtessen hab Ich beij dem *Page 4*
D. Bondo præside in dem *collegio Magdelanensi* nach gehabter *oration* und gehaltener *Music* zu gastgehalten worden,
stattliche *tractation* empfangen, und nach dem nachtessen
~~stattliche~~ lustige lateinische *colloquia orationes* und erzelung
schöner *carmina* angestellet, auch von gemeltem *præside*
ds *Theatrum Mundi* so uf ettliche und dreisig cronen
taxieret würd verehret, und daselbsten in vilweg aus anstellung ihr Kön. Mt. so grosse ehr *cortesia* und *liberalitet*
mir e[r]messen worden ds ich solches E. W. G. nit gnugsam zue *commendiren* weise. Des andern tages nemlich
des 22. haben mehrgemelte *Vice Kantzler, Decanus* und
præses nach dem sie mit mir ds suppe geessen, mich hinauss so weit ihr *Jurisdiction* ~~und frontier (da sie mich
abermahlen mit Musie dahin und~~ gehet (welche sich uf 5.
Englische oder 1. Teutsche meil zu rings umb die statt
hero erstrekhen solle) mit ettlichen anderen schulverwanten begleidet uf die *frontier* & vil leut hingestellet und
mich neben vilfeltiger glükhwindschung ge*valediciret*.
Hernacher bin Ich zurükh sambt meinem zuegeordneten
comissario wüder uf Wekham[1] den 23. uf Winser,[2] daselbstèn ds schöne königliche hauss und die stifftkirchen
(derinnen die ritter des hosenbandes zum theil ihre begrebnuss) besehen, und nach gehaltenem morgenessen durch

---

[1] High Wycombe.   [2] Windsor.

den thirgarten uf Ginsthunn,[1] den 24. uf Handencurt [2]
(welches hauss mit tapyeinereien über die massen stattlich gezieret) Und wüder auf Ginsthunn und Londra gereiset deselbsten Gott lob abermahl frisch und gesund
ankommen, Weil sich aber vermög Landgebrauchs auf
dem christagfest iederman zue hauss ~~still~~ und ~~eingezo[gen]~~
still halten thuet, alss hab ich ~~aus rath des mir Zuegeordne-~~
~~ten~~ auch selbigen tages mich einsambs halten und nit

Page 5 nacher hoff / mich begeben wollen, und den volgenden tag
nemlich den 26. mich nacher hoff gefueret, die königin für
die gnedige *comission* und anordnung neben ~~schuldigem~~
gewehnlichem erbieten gedankhet; darauf I. K. Mt. ds
ihro gar lieb were, wann Ich zue meinem *contentament*
tractieret auch gefüeret war worden, und da es anders
geschehen es wüder dero befelch gethan seij, sich erkleret,
auch ds ~~ich~~ mir weiter wo es mir gefällig hinzureisen ~~mich~~
freij stehe, Ja alles was in dero königreich mir zum besten
sein solle, g[nedig] anerbotten: hernacher habe sie auch
beij werendem tantz der gleich damals angestellet gewesen
gantz gnedig von aller handt sachen (wie E. W. G. ins künftig ~~gnedig~~ zue meiner Gott geb glüchlichen anhaimbs
kunft ~~gnedig~~ auf dero g[nedig] begeren mundlich von mir
zuvernehmen haben werden) *discuriret*, und nach dem der
tantz ausgewesen ~~mich gnedig wüder zue~~ ds ich beij der
nach dem nacht essen angestelleten *comoedia* wüder zue der
selben mich verfüege solle, mich g[nedig] erinnert; zue
dem nacht essen hatt mich der oberste Kemerling [3] auss
sonderbarem geheiss I. K. Mt. wüder zue sich beruffen
und neben anderen Graflichen und herrnstandes Personen
stattlich *tractieret*, und nach dem nachtessen wüder in die

---

[1] Kingston.   [2] Hampton Court.
[3] George Carey, K.G., Baron Hunsdon, Lord Chamberlain.

presentz kammer gefüeret, darinnen Ich von den fürnemsten herren, deren iederzeit ettliche mir gesellschafft
zueleisten bestellet gewesen, biss zue der königin herauss-
kunft *interteniret* worden alss nun die königin herauss
kommen hab Ich diselbe neben anderen herrn in den saal
darin getantzet und *comedia* gehalten würd / *comitiret*, da- *Page* 6
selbsten ist anfenglich ein tantz und hernacher die *comoedia tractieret* gehalten worden. Da ~~mich~~ insonde[r]heit
die Königin einen herrn *Melard Gre*[1] genant ds er mir der
comoedianten propositum (Vorbringen) ˙ verdolmetschen
solle bevelch geben, ~~selbsten~~ zue Zeiten auch selbsten verdolmetschet, und sondsten mit gnedigem gesprech so wol
alss vor dem essen ~~mich interteniret~~ sich gegen mir erzeiget, weil Ich aber vermerkhen können ds I. K. Mt., vil-
leicht in denen gedenkhen stehen ds ich noch ein mehrere
Zeit ~~daselbsten~~ in dem königreich mich ufhalten und noch
ettliche statt und örter zu besehen willens seije wie sie
dann dazue fast anlautung gegeben; aber ohne ds sich
mein darinnen sein etwas lenger alss ich verhoffet verweil-
et, auch der arten ein zimliches grossen Unkosten darauf
gehet, so hab Ich neben den mir zuegeordneten ~~für rathsam gehalten~~ ds es nimmehr zuefrie auch zue ersparung
des Unkostens, rathsam seije erachtet, die *licentia* einmahl
zue begeren dieweil sich ohne ds noch ettliche tag mit Ver-
fertigung eines und des andern, insonderheit aber der
königliche pasporte ~~darauf gehen~~ verweilen werden, damit auch nach erlangter erlaubnuss und abschid mir be-
forstehe meine fernere reise zu *continuiren* und die geleg-
enheit des windes in acht zuenehmen, hab derowegen
alss die *comedia* ein end gehabt I. K. Mt. nochmaln angeredet ds ich von E. W. G. den ~~gnedigen~~ Vatterlichen

---

[1] Thomas, Lord Grey of Wilton.

bevelch meine reise zue *maturiren* derselben angedeutet ~~ds~~
und weil ich nit wisse worin ich mit meine gegenwart I. K.
Page 7 Mt. dienen könne / und demnech[s]t noch ein zimliche reise
vor der hand habe, alss wolte Ich ~~dieselben~~ I. K. Mt. gehorsamlich gebetten ~~haben~~ ds sie (da es anderst mit dero
gnedigem *consens* und willen geschehen möge) mir nunmehr meinen wege weiter zue nehmen und auss dero königreich zue reisen g[nedig] bewilligen wolten, darauf sie
sich gleichsam anfenglich etwas befremdet und ds ihr K. Mt.
meine gegenwart gern lenger, ja auch so lang es mir gefällig leiden möchte und nochmaln ds alles so in dero königreich seij, mir zum besten sein solle, ~~gedacht~~ auch noch
in vill weg alle gnad und guetes sich erbotten. Über ds
hab Ich zum andern maln *repliciret* ds Ich nit ursach hette
wekh zue eilen sondern vil mehr I. K. Mt. so lang es ihr
gefällig uf zu warten mich schuldig erkennete, aber weil
E. W. G. so Vatterlich mir *injungiret,* ds Ich mich so vil
möglich befürderen solt, so wolte Ich verhoffen, I. K. Mt.
wurden mir g[nedig] erlauben und ds ich iezmals etwas
eilete g[nedig] mich für entschuldiget halten, so haben sie
auf mein so instendig auch zum drittenmal anhalten
versuhch endlich gleich darein bewilliget, darauf sich be-
denkhet ds ~~ich~~ Ir hette zuegefallen, ich auch beij diser so
ungelegenen Zeit meine reise vor die hand genohmen,
und ds ihr derab ein guetes gefallen geschehen und sie
~~meiner iederzeit~~ iederzeit E. W. G. und mir, dem gantzen
hauss Pfalz und meinem gantzen geschlecht alles Ange-
Page 8 nehmes liebes und guetes zue erzeigen / ve[r]bint[l]ig seij,
mir von Gott alle bestendige wollfart, glükh zue meiner
noch vorstehenden reise und ein fröliche wüder heimkunft
zue E. W. G. und den meinen wündsche, und was derglei-
chen g[nedig] erbieten und glükhwindschung mehr ge-

wesen ~~sich erkleret~~ darneben erinnert E. W. G. Iren gruess
zuevermelden, für die abordnung zue dankhen, ~~sie~~ I. K.
Mt. seien auch willens deroselben selber zueschreiben und
mit mehrerem ihre gedenkhen und meinung ~~deroselben~~
anzuedeuten ~~desselbe~~ welches schreiben ~~selbe~~ deroselben
(wie darin solches hiemit beschicht) Ich zueordnen ~~lassen~~
solte welches alles ich mich zue verrichten erbotten für die
vilfeltige ~~deselber~~ I. K. Mt. gueden gedankhet, und E. W.
G. mich und meine geschwisterten ~~zue~~ derselbe ~~gueden~~
im besten *recommendiret*, ~~und~~ bin also meines theils,
verhoffentlich auch mit der Königin und iedermenniglich
guetem *contento* und *satisfaction* von hoff geschiden.
Den 27. ~~und 28.~~ wie auch noch ettliche nachvolgende tag
habe Ich mich zu hauss gehalten der königlichen ~~abferti-~~
~~gung~~ *Patent* ~~und des köni~~ an E. W. G. vertresten schrei-
bens ~~erwartet~~ und sonderlich weil der *Admiral*[1] und der
Melar Cobam[2] bevelch bekommen mir ein kriegschif zue
bestellen der ander aber durch seine anbevelchen ambt
mir guete befürderung zu leisten sollen, ~~also hab ich~~ auch
auf deroselben schreiben biss sie gefertiget worden ~~noch~~
~~ein tag oder zw ettlich~~ warten müess[en] damit ich mit desto
besser *commoditet* fortkommen möge, in welcher Zeit mir
zuegefallen behren und ochsen hetz[3] angelle[g]t worden
auch von der Königin die anordnung beschehen ds ich uf
den ~~neuen~~ letsten tag von dem Burgemeister[4] neben
andern fürnehmen Englisch herrn zue gastgebotten und
stattlich *tractieret* worden, biss Endlich den 4. *Januarij* diss
iezt laufenten Jares ~~und monats Ich~~ hatt sich offtgemelter

---

[1] Charles Howard, Earl of Nottingham.
[2] Henry Brooke, Baron Cobham.
[3] Bear and bull baiting.
[4] The Lord Mayor of London.

mir zuegeordneter *commissarius* Löser[1] ~~sambt~~ neben
einem der königin kammerdiener und *Jubilierer* zu mir
verfüeget, nochmaln von der königlich Mt. wegen für die
von mir fürgenohmene reise gedankhet, und neben allerhandt erbieten ~~von Ihr Königliche Mt. wegen~~ ein kleinot
so sich meines ermessens über die 1000 taler ~~erstrekhe~~
Page 9 anlaufe / thuet zue *demonstrierung* I. K. Mt. gegen mir tra-
gender g[nedig] *affection* ~~verehret~~ *presentiret*, gegenwerti-
ges schreiben an E. W. G. stendig so dieselbe hiemit g[ne-
dig] zuempfeh[l]en, und eine Pasporten deren *copia* wie
sie von dem mir zugeordneten verteutschet worden
E. W. G. ebenmessig *sub litera A* ich hiemit überschikhe,
~~zue~~ mir uberlifert ~~worden~~ lassen Ich mich gebürlich be-
dankhet ~~neben schuldigem erbieten~~ solche vilfeltig gnad
ehr und ~~freigeblikheit~~ *liberalitet* E. W. G. und meinen Ver-
wanten im besten zue rhüemen erbotten die sich dann
verhoffentlich neben mir dahin befleisen werden umb
I. K. Mt. solches anderwerts wüder zue *meritiren* bin also
Page 10 den 5. neben dem auch vor disem / ~~umb besserer comoditet~~
~~willen~~ von I. K. Mt. mir zuegeordneten *comissario* und
den beij mir wesenden wüder zu wasser, von hinnen
wekht und auf Grenewitsch[2] dasselbe haus zue besehen,
Gravesin[3] und *Rochester* zue gefahren hab aber den
Lemblein[4] sambt meinem Jungen dem helmstetter mit
den Pferden (welche ich nottwendig, meine vorstehenden
reise halben in die niderlandt weil man ~~nit leuchtlich~~ von
eines in des anderen kriegenden theils landt keine lehen
Pferdt oder gut zue wegen bringen kan, hab kaufen mües-
sen und man in Selandt[5] nit wol mit ihnen fortkommen
kann) ~~den~~ auf hohlandt zue den nechsten geschikhet, ~~da sie~~

---

[1] Stephen Lesieur.   [2] Greenwich.   [3] Gravesend.
[4] The Councillor, Wolf Heinrich Lemble.   [5] Zeeland.

244

meiner ~~vorsehentlich~~ ~~erwarten~~ ~~werden~~, alss Ich nun ge-
melten 5ts zue *Rochester* glükhlich angelanget, hab ich
den 6ts Vormittag der Königin ~~fornemste~~ kriegschiff be-
suhtiget, in die fornemste 3. gestigen und *perlustriret*,
nach mittag uf Sittigborn,[1] den 7ts uf *Cantaburi* und
Sandwizt,[2] gereist, den 8ts. vormittag hinauss an die
Dühnen[3] ~~genant~~ da sich die zuegeriste Kriegsschiff ufgehalten seij mich verfueget, weil aber mehr nit alles eines
welches erst zu land ankommen, und nit nach notturft
proviantiret ~~gefunden~~ dagewesen, die Ubrige aber auf der
Französischen cost sich ufgehalten / alss hab Ich demselben *Page* 11
tag wüder nach Sandwiz mich begeben und damit sich dieselbe *nave* so *Quittanʒa*[4] genant würd, wüder mit *proviant*
und anderem zugerüsten möge daselbsten stilligen mües-
sen.   Und weil sich des volgenden tagens ds schiff von
den Dhünen[5] auf Marget[6] begeben, alss bin ich den
selbigen tag von Sandewiz auch dorthin gereist. Den 10ts
nach mittag hab Ich mich uf ds schiff in dem nahmen
Gottes begeben, den 11. vor tags umb 2 uhr ausgeankhert
und fort gesegelt, ~~nachmittags~~ gegen abent ungefehrlich
von vier uhr an biss das andern morgens umb 6. uhr in
Calma gestanden, hernacher aber sobald wir windt bekommen wüder fortgesegelt und umb 2. uhr nachmittag
Gott lob frisch und gesund zue flüssigen[7] angelanget da
sich alsobaldt *Constantinus* [error for *Justinus*] von Nassau
des Prinz Morizen bastardt brueder ~~damahliger~~ Admiral
über die ~~hinaus~~ ~~geriste~~ ~~zwelf~~ kriegschiff sambt dem Königlichen *luogotenente Gubernator*[8] weil sich der *Gubernator*[9]

---

[1] Sittingbourne.   [2] Sandwich.   [3] The Downs.
[4] H.M.S. *Quittance*.   [5] The Downs.   [6] Margate.
[7] Flushing.   [8] Sir William Browne.
[9] Sir Robert Sidney.

iezt in Engellandt befunden, der *Staten Tresor[ir]* [1]
sambt noch ettlichen andern *capitainen* und befelchhabern
erzeiget, mich ~~ganz~~ *salutiret* empfangen und ihro dienst
presentiret der Gemelte *luogo tenente* sambt einen Englisch
capitain beij mir zum nacht essen gebliben ~~Gemelte~~ der
von Nassaue aber, deme die *expedition* wüder die Span-
ischen anbevelchen hatt sich neben dem *tresorir* also bald
hinauss auf die schif begeben. Volgenden tagens nemlich
den 13ts vormittag bin ich neben gedachtem Englischen
Page 12 *Gubernators* leutenant / und den fürnemsten *Capitainen* und
befelch habern uff dem wahl umb die statt herumb, auch auf
ds Rathauss ~~gefueret~~, durch die statt zue den häfen und in
ds Zeughauss gangen, welcher *Logotenente* die anordnung
gethan ds auf dem wahl sowol mit grossem geschiz alss
auch mit handristen mihr zuegefallen geschoss gethan
wurde welches nit weniger alss ich auss anordnung derer
Raths und Stat zu wasser hin wekh gefähret worden geschehen, also ds ich ~~auch~~ so wol daselbsten als auch auss
dem ganzen Englischen *jurisdiction* mit guetem *contento*
abgeschiden. Wie ich nun zue flüssingen ganz wol
empfangen und angenohmen worden also ist mir auch
ebenmessiges Zu Mittelburg [2] wüderfahren denn Ich von
denen des Raths als ich den 13ts daselbst ankommen den
14ts neben willigem erbieten wol *salutiret* und mit einem
schuss von 20 verehrt worden welche auch wie dero orlo-
ger oder Jagte schiff nacher *Dortmund* [3] mich zuefüren
verordnet haben, den 15ts früe hab auf *Travera* [4] zue fuess
mich verfüeret, daselbsten bin Ich abermaln von burge-
meistern und 2en *capitainen* so bald sie meiner ankunft
inne worden [5] *salutiret* empfangt und ausgeleset

---

[1] Jakob van Valcke, Treasurer of Zeeland.   [2] Middelburg.
[3] *Error for* Dordrecht. [4] Veere in Walcheren. [5] Became aware of.

worden. Welche mich hernacher biss in ds von Mittelburg mir bestelte schiff begleidet und ihren abschid von Mir genohmmen. Von denen bin Ich demselben t[agen]s nachmittag auf *Dortrecht* daselbsten den 16 umb 11. uhr angelanget. Von den Burgemeister und andern 2 des Raths, so bald sie meine ankunft vernommen, empfangen, in die Zeugheuser und durch die fürnemste gassen gefüeret, stattlich *tractieret* und ausgelöset worden, nach dem morgenessen bin ich wüder der wekh uf Roterdam gereiset, dieselbe statt den siebenzehn vor mittag besehen, nachmittag uf Delft, und den Hag[1] zuegereiset. Daselbsten die vorgemelte mit Pferden geschikhte und alles wol befunden, biss morgen bin Ich willens beij Prinz Morizen mich anmelden zulassen und was sich wieter zutregt das werden E. W. G. mit nehster bottschafft zuevernehmen. Ob nuhn wol gnediger geliebter Herr Vatter mir liebers nichts gewesen were alss ds ich meine forgenohmene raise in Schottlandt[2] wie auch die *resti[er]ende* in Frankhreich beywilligter massen noch vor meiner raise in di Niderlandt hette vor die hand nehmen mögen, die weil aber wegen meines zuegestendenen fluss und bakhengeschwulst sich mein dasein in Engellandt über mein Verhoffen verlengert, und Ich mich dero gnedigen *resolution* ds ich meine wüderkunft *maturiren* ~~solle~~ auch uf ds lengest über fünf monat nit aussbleiben, *item* ds ich zue der königlichen Mt. in frankhreich so lang sie sich in dem kriegswesen uffhalten, zue erhaltung der *neutralitet* mich nit verfüegen solle gehorsamlich erinnert, und weil ich fast Unmüglich zu sein erachtet in einer solchen zeit nach Schottlandt und Frankhreich neben den Ni / derlanden mit *Page 13* nuzen zu verichten, weil die gänzliche sag in Engellandt

---

[1] The Hague. [2] Scotland.

gangen ds ob wol der könig iezo sein beij lager zue *Lion*[1] halte sich also bald her nach wüder dem kriegswesen zue begeben werde, und ich also nit erachten mögen, weil ohne ds dem könige mein durchzug durch Frankhreich von den *Gubernator* von *Mez*[2] wie auch Ihr K. Mt. Schwester der *Madame* von Parr, zu wissen gemacht sein werde, wie es sich schikhen wolle also in I. K. Mt. land nochmaln weiter rummer zue zihen und dieselben nit anzusprechen, weil ich besorget, ds umb die selbe zeit wenn ich die Niderlande antretten wurde schon der früeling herbeij nahen und allerhandt *impresse* und kriegsrüstung von beijden theilen für die handt genomen, und dise raise also unsicherer und mit wenigerm ruh verrichtet werden müesste, so hab Ich neben den beij mir wesenden für rathsam und guet befunden die Reise in Schotten[3] weil uns ohne ds bedunkhet ds ettliche Engelländer solche raise nit gern sehen wöllen auch auf die selbe zuem wenigsten noch 7. monat gangen were einzustellen; die noch *restierende* aber in Frankhreich biss zue E. W. G. fernerer

Page 14 *resolution* zu verschiben ob villeucht / die raise nach dem Kaiserlichen hofe nit so eilends sein, der Kreig zwischen Frankhreich und *Savoyen* immittels gestillet werden, oder der König sich gar von dem Kriegswesen begeben, oderaber E. W. G. nach volbrachter Niderlandscher reise den könig auch in dem kriegswesen zuezuzihen und die noch *restierende* reise in Frankhreich (welches dann von Prüssel[4] aus von dennen uber 7. oder 8. [?mich Zeitverleng sei] nach *Paris* oder *Lyon* nit sein ?wider den füglich geschehen könte Da sich gleichwol mein hoffmeister zum höchsten entschuldiget, ds Ime solche fernere raise von Niderlandt aus wegen vilfeltiger eh[renh]afften mit zu

---

[1] Lyons.   [2] Metz.   [3] Scotland.   [4] Brussels.

thün unmüglich, Ich hab aber ihm doch so weit *persuadiret* ds er vollendts biss zue den *Ides Martij* beij mihr zuverharren versprochen) zu voln zihen bewilligen möchten. Wann aber in dem reise an den Kaiserlichen hoff ich nit wol lengern vorzug leiden könte oder es sonsten E. W. G. g[nedig] willen, denn ich mich in allem gern willig thue zue *accomodiren* [ ] were ds beij I. K. Mt. in Frankhreich (ich mich ieziger Zeit anmelden oder auch die fernere reise in Frankhreich zu volzihen soll so were meines und meines hoffmeisters einfeltig bedenkhen ds es nit schädlich sein könte [?wann] beij S. K. M.) ein entschuldigung meines nit beij derselben *presentirens*, (und vertröstung ds solches ins künftig geschehen solte) eingewendet wurde (besorgen auch auf den fall der keines geschehen solte ds S. K. Mt. ds ich beij ander und beij ihro mit angemeldet würklich *ostendiren* ?werden möchte) des vorsehens es würd E. W. G. diss unser vorhaben in einem und anderm nit zu imffallen gereichen, und sie darüber sich ehists möglich erkleren Auch dere gnedige *resolution* auf Prüssel sint emahl mit der hülf Gottes bald dorthin zue kommen verhoffen zu schikhen. Neben disem werden E. W. G. auch hiemit die von meinem hoffmeister ihr zugeschikht rechnung was in Engellandt und Seelandt ufgangen gnedig zuem versehen haben, und ob wohl die verehrungen uf ein Zimliches sich erstrekhen, so werden doch E. W. G. dagegen die grosse ehr die mir allerseits wüdersehen, gnedig *conside* / *riren*, und ds man dagegen *Page 15* weniger nit thun können, betrachten.

So vil die Pferd anlanget, so man als oben gemelt notwendig erkaufen müesen als sie auch wol auf ein zimliches anlaufen, so sein sie doch solche klepper ds E. W. G. da mir sie anders glükhlich ?vorausbringen des geldes nit gereuen soll, auch da sie deroselben nit alle annehmlich Ich sie wol wüder [ ] solches geld darausen hinzubringen verhoffe. Also ds Ich keinen Zweifel E. W. G. mit den noch biss daher aufgelaufenen ausgaben gantz gnedig und vatterlich *content* sein werden.

~~Sonsten bin Ich meine reise dermessen zu fürden willens ds ich bald durch Hollandt und nach Prüssel zue kommen verhoffe dahin E. W. G. dero *resolution* schikhen können~~

Welches E. W. G. vertröstermessen gehorsamlich zuwissen zumachen Ich nit underlassen sollen und thue dieselbige und was ambtlich in die gnedige *protection* des allmechtigen ihro aber zue Vatterlichen genaden mich iederzeit bestes fleis bevelchen. Datum zum Haag den 17. *Januarij* A.D. 1601.[1]

Hauptstaatsarchiv München, Bestand Pfalz-Neuburg, Fasz. Lit., Nr. 1151.

---

[1] For the visit to Woodstock, see Sir Henry Lee's letter to Sir Robert Cecil, *Cecil Papers*, 10. 427–8. Sir Edmund Chambers (*Sir Henry Lee*, p. 181) mistakenly says that Lee's visitor was the Duke of Bracciano, who however did not arrive in England until almost two weeks later. As for Wolfgang Wilhelm's report that he was 'magnificently treated to breakfast' at Christ Church, the Disbursement Book of that college records that the sum of £10 19s. 9d. was spent 'at the entertaynment of the Duke of Bavaria'. See W. G. Hiscock, *A Christ Church Miscellany* (1946), 178.

INDEX OF INTERPRETATIONS

INDEX OF INTERPRETATIONS

253

255